I Will Disentangle
Myself
…. and Leave

by
Bob Williston

Author's Photo by Portraits by Altenburg Studio

I Will Disentangle Myself .... and Leave

Library of Congress Control Number: 2018930644
ISBN-13:   Paperback: 978-1-64151-425-5
            PDF: 978-1-64151-426-2
            ePub: 978-1-64151-427-9
            Kindle: 978-1-64151-428-6
            Hardcover: 978-1-64151-424-8

Printed in the United States of America

LitFire
PUBLISHING

LitFire LLC
1-800-511-9787
www.litfirepublishing.com
order@litfirepublishing.com

Contents

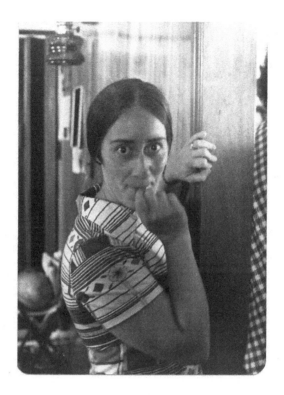

This book is dedicated to the memory of my wife,
Judy (Bugden) Williston,
who passed away on February 8, 2017.

She has been to me an example of the virtue of
being *strong in the strength of gentleness*, of which
we have often sung. Despite her fears and profound
timidity, she never wavered in her approval of any
decision I made throughout our lengthy struggle.

We came six months from celebrating fifty years together.

INTRODUCTION

As indicated by the title of this book, I have indeed left the church I write about. People leave churches every day and never write about it, but some such choices involve drama, and trauma. I've read numerous accounts of such *escapes*. I used to consider such accounts as contributions to the market for dramatic personal stories, but in retrospect I realize they can be as much a cry to be understood as they are a story to be told. It's for this reason that I write this book.

I needed to understand myself, my situation, and my reaction to it; and writing is the way I have always best done that. Writing articulately requires that I analyze the causes and effects that either confirm or deny the wisdom of my decision-making process – so this I have done in this memoir. As my experience became more intense and complicated, I began keeping notes. I realized I'd never keep everything in perspective if I didn't. This is how I managed to identify the various threads of this story. This account will both allow me to forget the issues that I have struggled to resolve, and help me remember what I learned about dealing with abuse. If reading this account is of any help to anyone else, then I'll consider it a bonus return on my efforts.

I didn't leave the fellowship primarily for doctrinal reasons. I left as a result of a decade of abuse to myself and my family by the hierarchy, so I wasn't searching for lessons on doctrine or theology, or sympathy from anyone, or advice on how to get along with people. I know who I am, what I believe, and importantly why I believe it. I just need to remember how it was that I became pawn for the abusers in the system so that won't ever happen again. Why am I so cautious? At the ripe old age of fifty-six I'd lost my faith, my health, my career, my whole social structure, everything but my family – and writing this book has helped me understand how that happened.

This is a true story. Unless some individual is identified in a quote from someone else, I know all the individuals of whom I write. I have also deemed it inappropriate to name many individuals who were involved in incidents I write about. The alternative names I use for these people are indicated by single quote marks (") at the first appearance of their name. For sure a few people would be uncomfortable that I have used their names in this book, but I felt I would be remiss if I failed to credit them personally for their good and righteous acts.

I know this book will be condemned by many within the group I left, and I will be cast in the most evil of light. This happens because the hierarchy has an *omertà* style protective shield around their *kingdom.* The problem is this: too many of their *subjects* are dispensable when the comforts of the hierarchy are threatened. When one has a problem, such as I had, the established advice is, "Don't talk about it." Even overseers who are sympathetic to one's plight normally forbid people to mention it. In my case, when I had a problem with someone I went directly to that person about it. The lesson learned from that was that those people had no difficulty telling others about it to garnish sympathy to themselves – such that preachers far away who did not know me were advising people against me. This is an important part of my story.

This is not a scholarly work, it's an account of my own experiences. Nevertheless, I make many assertions about the history and development of religions and denominations. For this reason I have included notes and a bibliography for readers who are interested in following up on many of my statements. Also included is a glossary of terms that have somewhat unusual meanings to those within the fellowship. Three terms need special mention. In this book there is a distinction to be made between "worker" and "Worker". The lower-case version signifies the standard dictionary use of the word, and the capitalized version is used for members of the fellowship's clergy, who are always referred to as Workers. Similarly, the word "friend" indicates the universal meaning of the word, and the capitalized version, "Friend", refers to a lay member of the fellowship, who universally refer to each other in this way. And the capitalized word "Truth" refers to the fellowship of the Friends and Workers, while the lower-case version indicates the usual dictionary meaning of the word.

This book deals with three main topics. The first, naturally, is a record of my own interactions with the ministry of this faith fellowship. I recognize the point at which our relationship began to disintegrate, and I understand why I had no conscientious option by which to repair it. Secondly, I relate the brief history of the fellowship, from its taboo origins through its frequent episodes of schismatic discord; and the abusive practices that stir them up. Finally, I relate my journey through the maze of religious belief to where I find my most peaceful resting place ... best described as a clear understanding of the elusive foundation of *religious truth*.

The number of people who have either intentionally or unintentionally contributed to this expression of my experience, is much too long to list. Suffice it to say that many very close friends have encouraged, even pressured, me to pursue this project. Three individuals I must recognize for their articulate communications with me: Nathan Lusher II, Alan VanDermyden, and Edgar Massey. Several have assisted me in clarifying details and proofing composition, most notably my daughter Karen and my friend Cherie Kropp. I recommend Ms. Kropp's website, http://www.tellingthetruth.info/home/index. php, as undoubtedly the most extensive and best moderated source of history on this religious group.

To those whose friendship with me has not faltered through this decade of upheaval in my life, please understand that you are precious gems in my portfolio of best memories.

The word of the Lord came to me: [2] *"Son of man, prophesy against the shepherds of Israel; prophesy and say to them: 'This is what the Sovereign Lord says: Woe to you shepherds of Israel who only take care of yourselves! Should not shepherds take care of the flock?* [3] *You eat the curds, clothe yourselves with the wool and slaughter the choice animals, but you do not take care of the flock.* [4] *You have not strengthened the weak or healed the sick or bound up the injured.*

You have not brought back the strays or searched for the lost. You have ruled them harshly and brutally. ⁵ *So they were scattered because there was no shepherd, and when they were scattered they became food for all the wild animals.* ⁶ *My sheep wandered over all the mountains and on every high hill. They were scattered over the whole earth, and no one searched or looked for them.*

⁷ *"'Therefore, you shepherds, hear the word of the Lord:* ⁸ *As surely as I live, declares the Sovereign Lord, because my flock lacks a shepherd and so has been plundered and has become food for all the wild animals, and because my shepherds did not search for my flock but cared for themselves rather than for my flock,* ⁹ *therefore, you shepherds, hear the word of the Lord:* ¹⁰ *This is what the Sovereign Lord says: I am against the shepherds and will hold them accountable for my flock. I will remove them from tending the flock so that the shepherds can no longer feed themselves. I will rescue my flock from their mouths, and it will no longer be food for them.*

¹¹ *"For this is what the Sovereign Lord says: I myself will search for my sheep and look after them.* ¹² *As a shepherd looks after his scattered flock when he is with them, so will I look after my sheep. I will rescue them from all the places where they were scattered on a day of clouds and darkness. ....* ¹⁶ *I will search for the lost and bring back the strays. I will bind up the injured and strengthen the weak, but the sleek and the strong I will destroy. I will shepherd the flock with justice.*

²⁰ *"'Therefore this is what the Sovereign Lord says to them: See, I myself will judge between the fat sheep and the lean sheep.* ²¹ *Because you shove with flank and shoulder, butting all the weak sheep with your horns until you have driven them away,* ²² *I will save my flock, and they will no longer be plundered. I will judge between one sheep and another.* ²³ *I will place over them one shepherd, my servant David, and he will tend them; he will tend them and be their shepherd.* ²⁴ *I the Lord will be their God, and my servant David will be prince among them. I the Lord have spoken.*

~~ Ezekiel 34 – New International Version

CHAPTER 1

The Fortieth Year

It was just by coincidence that, on my fortieth birthday, I symbolically crossed the Mississippi River. I was headed west on Interstate 80 with my wife Judy and my daughter Heidi, towing only our necessary and treasured property in a small trailer. I'd lived my first forty years in the Northeastern United States and Eastern Canada, and we were moving to Nevada. I remember that at the time I wondered out loud to Judy whether I would get to live forty more years on the other side of the continent.

Looking back, I realize what a significant turning point that day became for us. We had no way then of knowing that we were headed into circumstances that would uproot us from everything our lives had been before, and make it impossible for us ever to return. It's been an experience with religion that I certainly never believed I'd have to face. But I did. And today, nearly three decades later, I find myself more settled and at peace than at any other time in my life. Despite the scars that remain, the experience, in the end, was good for me.

Many months before, in Eastern Canada, I'd applied for a teacher exchange in the United States. When my assignment came, it was for a place called Minden, Nevada, and there were two things I needed to check before I accepted it. First I located Minden on a map. I knew what Nevada was like, and I didn't want to take my wife and daughter to some lonely, dusty, desert crossroads. But Minden was comfortably close to both Reno and Lake Tahoe, and within sight of Carson City. That made the prospect of living there exciting.

The second matter of concern was whether there were any Friends in that area. We referred to all our coreligionists as *Friends*, and we knew from having spent our whole lives in the group that, if there were any of them in the area, we'd be received by them like family and have a ready social network. That had been our experience several times in the past when we'd moved. And the information I needed was as easy to come by as finding Minden on the map.

Ministers in this religious group are itinerant homeless preachers called *Workers*. They are assigned in pairs to various areas yearly, and annual *Workers Lists* are compiled and distributed for each of the various states or other regional jurisdictions. These lists include all the Workers' names with their assigned *fields*, or territories of ministry, as well as their contact addresses and telephone numbers. On an old California Workers List I found a Reno telephone number, so I dialed it. A young lady answered, I identified myself as one of the Friends, and she referred me to a man in Carson City. In a short conversation with that man, he invited us to stay at his house when we arrived in Carson City. That next morning I made my acceptance known to the teacher exchange agency.

I'd always been interested in adventurous teaching assignments, teacher exchanges being most convenient. To me it really didn't matter where I got to go. Any adventure was worth some inconvenience. But this one was very much to my liking. Relatives of my family, including an uncle, had migrated to California years before and had visited back and forth ever since. I wanted to see that part of the world for myself. Of course, among the staff at my school in New Brunswick I got gently razzed about moving to the land of gambling and prostitution.

Judy, on the other hand, had dreamed of palm trees and warm winters for years, and the proximity of Minden to Sacramento's palm trees had her fully sold on the adventure. But she had something else to look forward to. During her upbringing in Massachusetts she'd been subject to all the strict dress and hair style codes related to our religious group, as well as the life style and entertainment restrictions. It had been widely rumored in the Northeast that all of these rules and restrictions were far less strictly applied, if not omitted altogether, on the West Coast. This discrepancy was so obvious that some people in the Northeast would even opine that not all the Friends in California were really saved. But we didn't mind the prospect of having any restrictions lifted, and I understood well how she felt about that. Being male, and perhaps because my upbringing had been less strict than hers, I still understood her craving for a less repressive environment.

Our 3,500 mile trek from Miramichi, New Brunswick to Carson City, Nevada became a three week vacation in itself. Then came our wonderful reception in Nevada. Within two weeks of our arrival we had in many meaningful ways become part of the local congregation, as well as comfortable in the larger community.

We arrived on a Saturday afternoon in August at the home of Merle Bunch, the Carson City man who'd invited us to stay at his house. By the time dinner was over that evening we'd done what Friends so frequently do when meeting new Friends – we established who all our mutual connections were. It turned out the Bunches knew most of my family's relatives in California. Merle also told us that one of them lived with her husband not far from Carson City, which surprised me. But how amazing it was to find that we already had a relative in the local *meeting*!

The next day being Sunday, and because the usual Sunday morning fellowship meeting was held at Merle's house, we got to meet all the Friends in the Carson City area. There were between 25 and 30 people in attendance. A few of them were teenagers who immediately made friends with Heidi. Everyone was pleased that we were in Carson City to live, and it was obvious that we'd joined a good group of people.

That afternoon the Bunches took us to a picnic in a park in Reno. The Friends in Northern Nevada were saying good-bye to a young couple of Friends who were moving away. We also met the family whose telephone number I called in my first inquiry about Reno. To this day the young lady I spoke to and her husband keep in contact with our older daughter, Karen.

If that were not enough for our first day, news came later in the afternoon that three young Workers had been in a head-on collision on a freeway in California – one was dead, and two others were very seriously injured. And one of the survivors was the son of a couple who were in the meeting with us that morning. So we were there to share that emotional time with our new Friends.

The next day, Monday, we went to San Francisco for an exchange teachers' conference on Tuesday and Wednesday. Then we went on to an annual convention of Friends and Workers in Gilroy on Thursday thru Sunday. Merle's plans were to be away from home when we returned to Carson City, so he presented us with a plan. I left our loaded trailer behind his house for safekeeping, and accepted a key to the house. He directed us to come back when the convention in Gilroy was over and stay for as long as we needed.

When we arrived at the convention in Gilroy, a sister Worker we'd never met made conversation with us. When she learned where we'd come from, she shared with us that a sister Worker we knew well in New Brunswick had passed away while we were traveling. We were saddened of course, but equally impressed that a Worker so far away had learned about her passing so quickly. It assured us that we were not entirely in strange company after all.

As expected, the Bunches were not home when we returned from our busy week. We let ourselves in and spent the night. A few days later the lady we were trading jobs and houses with let us move into her apartment, and we were comfortably settled in. We've always appreciated the way the Bunches received us when we came to Nevada.

Soon after we returned from the convention in Gilroy, one of the two survivors in the California freeway accident passed away. The other survivor, Alan Van Dermyden, was able to leave the hospital and came to Carson City to recuperate at his parents' home. Over the weeks that followed he and I discovered we had some intellectual interests in common, and became very good friends. To this day I consider him an exceptionally good friend, as well as his siblings and parents.

Just a few weeks later another couple of Friends moved from Oregon to Yerington, a small desert town probably 40 miles from Carson City. And they joined our Carson City meeting. They later told us we were their first friends locally – we'd invited them to lunch in a restaurant following their first Sunday meeting with us.

Then Alan Van Dermyden's brother moved to Carson City with his wife and children. Within a couple of months, the local meeting of Friends had grown considerably in number, and nearly half of them were newer to the area than we were.

I enjoyed my first day of work in Minden. It was a nice school, with a good staff; and since I was to be teaching French, I had a Spanish teacher assigned to care for me as I became familiar with the school. But by then it was the eighth school I'd taught in, in three different provinces of Canada and in two different languages, over seventeen years, so I had very few problems adapting. I did have to learn that it was a *notebook*, not a *scribbler*, and a *restroom*, not a *bathroom*. But the students were impressed that I did pronounce *Nevada* correctly. But I had a very hard time accepting that there really is such a thing as *extra credit* – I'd never heard of such a thing in Canada. And apparently my pink dress shirt was as amusing to them as their enormous cowboy buckles, boots, and hats were to me. Minden, after all, was in ranching territory. But I evolved gracefully.

Heidi was upset because they put her in a *bonehead* Math class, as she called it. The reason: She thought there were only ten inches in a foot, so had failed the placement test. When I told her there were twelve inches in a foot, she remarked, "Who ever heard of there being twelve of anything in something else?" Cups, pints, quarts, and gallons quite boggled her mind, and one hundred degrees on the thermometer sounded like science fiction to her. English class was another interesting situation for her. Until we moved to Nevada she'd never gone to school in English, but she was quickly moved into an advanced English class because, in her words, she "knew all the sophisticated English vocabulary because they were just normal French words."

After the teachers had gotten to know me, one of them confided to me that my exchange teacher had told them something about me before she left for Canada. She said that they need not worry about me finding my place in the community, because by the end of my first week in Nevada I'd located dozens of relatives and hundreds of friends. We had indeed dropped into an enviable social network.

CHAPTER 2

My Roots

When I was born not everyone expected me to live. One of my great grandmothers declared, "Pearl will never raise this child." Pearl was my mother, and I'd been born prematurely. I've also been told that I survived a fractured skull from being struck by a car at age two. I also grew slowly – at age ten someone asked me if I'd started school yet. I was just a bit insulted. But they all should see me now!

Memories of my childhood are all about my mother's kindness and the fun of going places with my father. I have four younger brothers, but remember the births of only the last two. I remember that I'd decided to be a teacher before I started grade one, but it certainly didn't help my parents on my first day of school. They had to hold my arms and legs together to get me through the school door. Fortunately, I recovered from that trauma within twenty-four hours.

Very importantly, I knew before I ever started school that we were Friends – that is, we went to meetings on Sunday mornings and Wednesday evenings. I also knew that the adults were all professing, because they took turns speaking in those meetings. What I found fascinating about what they said in meetings was all their talk about things, which I, in my child's mind, understood to mean toys and such. But I definitely understood enough from their discussion of the Bible that, when my grandfather died when I was seven, I asked when the Book of Roy would be added to the Bible. My grandfather's name was Roy. After all, weren't all the books in the Bible about dead professing people?

While I was growing up, my paternal grandparents lived about a quarter mile from us, and one of my greatest joys was to visit them when they had company. My grandfather and his friends would talk for what seemed like hours, recalling events in their lives that I found so interesting. They discussed everything from the first time they'd ever met a Worker, to the recent Holocaust in Germany. The Holocaust discussion was frightening – that night, as I walked home in the dark, I half expected some Nazi to jump out of a driveway and grab me.

Clear in my memory is the account of my grandfather being the first in our family to meet Workers. He saw two young men walking along the side of a road and offered them a ride. In conversation he learned that they were preachers who did not believe in a collection during their services because, as they claimed: "That would not be scriptural." He'd been raised Anglican, but from this chance encounter he and my grandmother, and all their family *professed. Profess* is also the word used for one's conversion to that faith. Common among Friends when meeting new Friends is the sharing of remarkable *testimonies*, stories of how they came to meet the Workers and subsequently profess. That tradition is almost gone these days, because the *Truth* (the insiders' word for this faith) became well established in North America in the early 1900's. The experience of the majority of professing people today is the same as mine – we were born to professing parents and had no experience with finding a new religion to convert to. So, I never had anything dramatic to tell for a testimony. The few times when I was asked for my testimony, I would tell the story about my grandparents' conversion.

Also clear in my memory is how frequently it was preached that the Truth has remained unchanged from the days of Jesus. Just as frequently, it was mentioned that all other faiths, unlike the Truth, were started by men. Of course, a ten-year-old has not lived long enough to see any changes happening in his own religion, so has no reason to question the wisdom of people who make his life safe and comfortable. I had to trust the implication that there was something wrong with the rest of the world, and that somehow, *we* had survived from the days of Jesus' mission in Palestine.

Aside from my parents, probably the most important figure in my younger life was my father's younger sister, who never married. She is reported to have doted on me because I was her first nephew. When I was first learning to talk she took me with her to the post office, and when the postal clerk asked me what I was going to do when I grew up, I replied, "I'm going preaching with Willie Martin." I don't remember anything about Willie, but he was a young and charismatic Worker in the area at that time. For sure I was tutored by her to give that response. In any case, as early as the age of six I began to prefer my parents' guidance over hers. She proved far too conservative and prudish for my liking, and I fear that over time I've disappointed her with more than a few of my life choices.

Most important in my upbringing, of course, were my parents. Some of our Friends would surely consider them liberal, maybe even slack, but I never thought of them as anything but diligent, reasonable, and honest. We kids were never lectured on religious doctrine – we were instructed in good morals and the consequences of bad behavior. We were never told to read the Bible or say our prayers, or sit for Bible studies each morning. But we knew perfectly well that our parents read their Bibles and prayed – we'd often find them reading their Bibles or praying in some quiet place. We were not restricted from playing on Sundays as some others were, and we were never restricted from having neighbor kids in the house or from visiting other kids' houses, as some of my cousins were. Most comforting of all, I cannot think of anything my parents ever lied to me about, or even misled me concerning – not Worker foibles, not even Santa Claus. I understood we didn't celebrate Christmas – that meaning that we didn't have a Christmas tree. But we still got presents and festive dinners just like everyone else. Never once did we think we were missing out on anything at Christmas time. The only ritual we were required to observe was the saying of grace at meal time. I was always glad I had the parents I did instead of many others I knew.

But all that didn't prevent me from knowing what was really expected of the Friends, because we were frequently reminded of it by the Workers. Much of it involved restrictions on women: no pants, no jewelry, no makeup, no short hair. My mother never complained, and I had no sisters, but when I got married I began to appreciate the weight of these restrictions on the women. It wasn't just the cost to them of suppressing a desire to be inconspicuous in public, but it entailed a variety of difficulties with hair care, swimming and sports attire, and appropriate winter wear. One infamous requirement that had disappeared where I lived before my time was that women were to wear black stockings. However, there were the occasional women around who never gave up their black stockings. Even when they were no longer available in local stores, the occasional Worker would advise that there was a company in Boston where they could be ordered by mail.

I was a good child – I didn't ignore good counsel. In grade one I had a crying spell in school because the teacher had us listen to a program on the radio – the Friends didn't believe in radios. I was relieved when my mother assured me that it was okay to listen if the teacher wanted us to. It seems like that was also the year of my education in dealing with the world outside the Truth. That year I woke up Christmas morning and found my parents had set up a small Christmas tree among our presents. When the celebration was over, we kids played with the tree for maybe a month. But when my influential aunt came to visit, she made a point to tell me that "We don't believe in Christmas trees." There was never a prohibition that she could restrain herself from educating me on. We really loved our aunt, but I remember wondering if she knew the difference between playing and pretending, and making something a serious traditional ritual. I now think that was an astute observation for a six-year-old.

As a kid growing up, *convention* was a highlight of the year. At that time, it was three days of sitting in meetings, but with lots of time to visit with other Friends' kids from all over. We were with kids who were growing up with similar restrictions, and we could expect more empathy from each other than we could from the kids we went to school with. I have a lifetime best friend from those childhood days.

One thing that always tickled me was any funny incident happening in a meeting. Among the Friends, meetings are very solemn occasions; and for many, anything out of the usual formality is an occasion of embarrassment or perplexity. For we kids, these incidents were occasions of sometimes painfully suppressed laughter. On one such occasion, my brother loudly passed gas during the quiet time before the meeting started. The sound echoed through the metal folding chair, which only caused him to laugh and pass more gas. Our mother was mortified.

My grandmother sometimes made homemade grape juice for the meeting at their house. One Sunday my brother and I both noticed that one lady happened to sip up the end of a stray grape skin, which dribbled down the front of her dress after she passed the cup on to the next person. Another time Albert, the meeting elder, moved to begin passing the cup and somehow upset it and spilled it on the floor. To a chorus of gasps, a couple of horrified ladies jumped to wipe the grape juice off the coffee table and floor, and the lady of the house ran to the kitchen to refill the cup. It was a major disruption, to be sure. Why is it that things are twice as funny when everyone is supposed to be so serious? I happen to feel the same way about wedding bloopers.

The funniest of all such liquid instances was the time my nine-month-old cousin tossed his nylon nursing bottle into the middle of the room, and the bottle spun around several times before it finally laid down. But the bottle was full of ginger ale, which sprayed out in a circle around the room, spraying an elderly man in the face while he was testifying. I had to duck myself, but when I looked up again there was ginger ale dripping down the wall behind the poor man. He just wiped his face and carried on with his testimony, which tickled me further.

There were some rough times too. Once when I was thirteen, Betty, the daughter of one of our Friends, and I walked from my grandparents' house to my house after Sunday meeting. When we arrived home Hugh Roberts, a Worker, was there. Betty was twelve at the time, and in front of my family he told her she was a "spot on the carpet" for walking on the street with me. There was nothing romantic about it – we were just two kids walking. He didn't say anything about it to me, which made me furious.

Sometimes I got bored in meetings, especially in gospel meetings when the preaching got boring. But I coped well. I'd developed a file in my mind of matters I needed to meditate on. It saved me on many occasions, I am sure. I could sit there with eyes wide open and my mind miles away, concentrating on some matter I had to settle in my mind.

Going to college proved far more difficult. In the summer before I started college, Bill, one of the Friends in another city, gave me a stern lecture about college. He said it was an evil place, and professing people had no need of a college education. I didn't believe him, but I wasn't shocked that he would say such a thing. When I was in high school, George Semple, the Worker Overseer for Atlantic Canada, had said in a Sunday meeting near where I lived that a high school education was bad for professing people. There were probably a dozen adolescents and teens in the meeting, and the parents were angered. And doubly angered when a number of them wanted to quit school. Education was widely regarded as suspect. But ironically, when Bill's own son graduated from high school he got a scholarship allowing him to go to university and become an engineer – and he used it, of course.

I had no intention of missing out on a college education. I started at the New Brunswick Teachers College, and graduated two years later with a teachers' license. Unfortunately, they were two traumatic years – not because of my studies, but because of the degrading treatment I experienced where I was living. My uncle had a six-bedroom house in walking distance of the college, and most of the professing college students in the city boarded there. So, it was just expected that I'd board there too. However, I did not appreciate my aunt's persistent prying, or the way she criticized other boarders when they were out of the house. She did our laundry, and made fun of the other guys' underwear – probably mine too when I wasn't around. There was a Sunday meeting in their house, and she criticized everything people wore to meeting. She was insulted if I wouldn't tell her which girl I had been out with the night before. She literally raged at me when I took a free week to go to Boston to see Judy – I told her ahead of time that I'd be gone, but I didn't tell her where I was going. I was naive enough to add to a conversation once that my father had worn a turtle neck sweater to a Sunday meeting. Her response was that the Workers wouldn't approve of him speaking in a meeting without a shirt and tie – I didn't appreciate that condemnation.

She always made me think of the expression, "more Catholic than the Pope." There seemed no way to avoid her disapproval. Long story short, it was a crash course in what never to tell anyone professing unless you wanted everyone else, and especially the Workers, to know all about it.

The final straw came the day my aunt was making fun of a Catholic priest who had supposedly advised his congregation to vote for a particular party in the upcoming election. I foolishly reminded her that George Semple had done exactly the same thing just a couple of weeks previously. I was never good at tolerating people's hypocrisy. I got the most degrading lecture of a lifetime from her and my uncle, with all the other college students around the dinner table. I was never asked to say grace for a meal again. The message was clear. I'd committed the ultimate taboo by intimating an impropriety on the part of a Worker, and I was unworthy of recognition as a professing person at their table. The stress of being there almost cost me my teachers' license. I had always been in the top classes in high school, but I almost didn't make it out of my second year in college. The consolation was that I got very high grades on my practice teaching both years.

I got married and worked for four years before I returned to the University of New Brunswick, on the same campus as the Teachers College. We lived in an apartment during those university years, so I didn't have to deal with the negativity and criticism of the first two years. I subsequently earned two degrees, and my self-esteem returned with my high-grade point average. But that still didn't mean I was beyond the reach of the gossip mill. Judy worked full time in one of the libraries in the university, and I worked weekends in the coffee shop and pizza bar on campus. Pizza and coffee shop service ended at 2:00 a.m., so with my studies and my share of housekeeping and child care, I had a very busy schedule. Luckily, and fortunately, I had no idea what was being said about me during those years.

But it came as quite a blow a few years later to learn that Fergus MacElrea (the Worker in the area at the time) had been telling the Friends that I wasn't working on Friday and Saturday nights at all. He told them I was out running around with Bobby Hicks, and apparently everyone believed him. I had no time to run around with anyone – I was living on sporadic three-hour episodes of sleep occasionally for weeks. Fergus was often suspected of making up stories, but I hesitate to believe Fergus made up that story himself. I recall that one evening when I was taking summer courses, I met a former classmate from Teachers College in the university library. We wanted to catch up on our lives and went to the bar in the city's largest hotel to catch up. I'm sure he had a beer, but I had a soft drink. It happened, while we were there, that the door to the hotel lobby opened, and Bobby Hicks appeared in the doorway with some woman not his wife. He saw me sitting there, and quickly closed the door. I never thought it necessary to tell even my wife about the incident, so I can only speculate on how Fergus came to have his version of the event.

Oddly enough, Fergus never approached me about any of this. It's definitely expected that a Worker who suspects someone of drinking with an unprofessing person would get a corrective visit from the Worker, but Fergus never did. Bobby Hicks was widely thought to be cheating on his wife, which would make him bad company. Also, alcohol was *de facto* forbidden among the Friends there, so appearing in a bar could be interpreted as inappropriate no matter what one was drinking. But since I'd told no one, Bobby would have had a vested interest in not sharing the precise circumstances of our encounter. I've often wondered if the reason Fergus never confronted me was because he suspected I actually was working to support my family.

But about then I'd figured out that Workers don't *always* confront people about their waywardness, as many suspect. I learned once that a Worker, Gordon Hazelwood, had told my father that, when he had come to visit us, we had turned off the music when he came to the door. So, I went to him to tell him the difference, because it was absolutely not the truth. I could think of no way that he could have even heard music when he came to our door. But he gave me the lecture on *singing and dancing* anyway: "We don't believe in dancing, and music made people dance." But no one minded that I'd taken piano lessons for eight years and could play the piano for their gospel meetings. I was a language teacher, and I had both tape players and a record player, and I told him I would be keeping them. The best he got from me was that I would keep them out of sight when visitors were around. But to further impress on me the extent of my waywardness, he took advantage of the occasion to deal with years of other offenses. One point was that Gladys Dickson, another Worker, had told him that I'd appeared in a Wednesday meeting wearing an offensive white shirt with blue paisley print. I was going to say *so much for Gladys' taste*, but decided to say nothing at all. And another point was that 'Cathy', a fellow college student, had reported to someone that I'd said it wasn't necessary for women to have skirts *that many inches below the knee*. Cathy, by the way, dressed like the infamous FLDS women. But on the other hand, she'd borrow an elderly Friend's car (without his knowledge) to spend the night with an unprofessing boyfriend (a taboo) a hundred kilometers away. She had a key to his car because she ran errands for him. I'd long since decided that the exceptionally long skirts some girls wore were hiding more than knees. I was more shocked with Gordon's response than anything else. I'll return to this incident later in Chapter 17.

Raising children among the Friends can involve special difficulties. I've often wondered how much intrusion my parents experienced from the Workers into their parenting style. I know they protected us from a lot of it, and it made our childhoods much more pleasant. Unlike my years growing up with four brothers, having two daughters and no sons may have made a difference. What angered me most was that sister Workers would approach my wife when I wasn't around, and lecture her about how she was dressing our daughters. One of them, Gladys Dickson, insisted that Judy get my mother to sew a strip of cloth around the bottom of our six-year-old daughter's skirts so that her knees wouldn't show. I forbade Judy to do such a thing. Gladys, and some other Workers I know, prefer the style of FLDS women, but I'd determined that neither my wife nor my daughters were going to dress like that. My sense of modesty is that what can't be bought in the stores in your community is not modest on the street. In any case, neither my wife nor my daughters ever appeared out of place among the Friends because of their dress.

When I was at Université Laval, we were living in Québec. Muriel Molina, a Worker there, took Judy to task for sending our seven-year-old daughter to school in pants. Muriel didn't like Judy's response − Judy said she felt it was necessary for Heidi to wear pants to school. In the winter she had to walk a block in frequently -15°C to wait for her school bus, and she had to play in the snow during recess time when she got to school. As parents, we were caught in a very difficult place. Parents were chastised for allowing their daughters to wear pants. But a class picture of our other daughter Karen, then in grade eight, where she was the only girl wearing a skirt, convinced me that there wasn't anything modest about that. She stood out like a sore thumb, and I regretted ever insisting she wear a skirt to school, no matter what the weather. The fact is, I only did it to appease Workers' criticism. I always felt that little girls in skirts at school received far too much inappropriate attention from little boys. We let our girls wear pants far more than a lot of professing parents did, but allowing them to go to meetings in pants was absolutely out of the question.

As a parent, I learned that the gossip (or should I call it the tattle-tale) system flourished even in my home town. My brother Armand, who was a Worker at the time, came to me once and told me that one of the Friends in another town had complained because we wouldn't let our daughter go and visit his foster daughter. We had our reasons for not letting her go there – I didn't know what their home life was like, but I was never impressed with either the man or his wife, and I didn't want my daughter alone in the environment of those people. I'd also learned that adults would pump other people's kids to learn things about their parents, and I had no interest in having my children used in such a way. I don't know how Armand felt about being asked to confront me, but he didn't pressure me to reconsider.

At the same time, there were comforts to be had in being part of this group. There were eight meetings in my home town, and I never knew of anyone who couldn't get along with everyone else. People visited back and forth, and young people had comfortable relationships with each other. It may seem like a contradiction in light of the difficulties that I've mentioned, but it isn't, really. Families had moved there from other places and been readily accepted as one of us. We had an extended family kind of support system, and we found it comfortable to socialize with others who, like ourselves, were not going to be drinking, smoking, cussing, or dancing.

I have to tell an interesting story about raising children in the Truth. For some reason, it is very common among the Friends' children to play *meeting*. One time, though, one of my brothers and I were babysitting our kids. We were visiting and the children, all pre-schoolers, decided to play meeting. When it came time to sing, the words turned out to be nothing more than "Suffer, suffer, suffer ....." That was amusing enough. But shortly a fight broke out, and my brother commented, "I think there's discord in that church."

I have to confess that I had a mind of my own from the very beginning. I never intentionally rocked the boat, but I learned more than a few lessons about how to preserve my reputation as a peaceful person. Still, I frequently put people on the spot unintentionally. One time, after a sermon where it was mentioned about Peter's wife, I asked why the Workers had to be single while Peter had a wife. Of course, no one had an answer. I once asked why they believed that women were to have long hair, when I'd read that Paul said *we have no such custom*.[1] My other awkward question about hair was why women were required to have their hair up, as in a bun or similar style, when the Bible said a woman's hair was for a covering. The aunt I once boarded with even criticized any woman who had her ears covered with hair.

I was probably eleven when a Worker took me to task for saying that a whale was not a fish. I knew perfectly well why a whale was not a fish – I'd learned it in school. But I wasn't about to explain to an elderly sister Worker how whales came to be classified as mammals. I was comforted when I checked the story of Jonah, and my Bible said he'd been swallowed by a *fish*, not a whale.[2]

That said, I'm confident that I was well respected by the other Friends in my home town. I played the piano, and over many years I was called upon to play the piano for the singing in gospel services. I've been told that some people considered me the best piano player available for such occasions. Being a teacher, I was frequently called early in the morning on days when it was snowing, to see if the schools were closed because of the snow. They all knew how it was that teachers learned such things – but no mention was ever made about the radio we had in the kitchen cupboards. Not long ago I was back home at the time of the Friends and Workers annual convention time. After twenty-five years of being away, I was so pleased that, of the hundreds of people in attendance, everyone including the Workers I'd known while I lived there, came to greet me. One doesn't leave such a closely-knit community without missing it.

CHAPTER 3

Culture Shock

The warm welcome we'd received on our arrival in Northern Nevada was genuine, and we made some wonderful and close long-time friends there. Our older daughter, Karen, joined us shortly after we arrived. Within a very short time both she and Judy found jobs at the large electronics company in town.

It came as a surprise when Harold Hilton, the Worker in the area at the time, asked to designate our apartment for a Wednesday Bible study meeting. We were pleased about that. My shock was that he even considered asking us. After all, there was, at that time, a television sitting in our living room. But he knew we were living in someone else's house, so he asked us to move the television to one of the bedrooms. I found that very reasonable of him, considering that Workers in California refuse to accept gifts of money from anyone who has a television anywhere in their home. The meetings at our house continued until my exchange year ended and we had to give the apartment back to the lady I exchanged jobs with.

We thoroughly enjoyed that first year in Nevada. We had wonderful relationships with all the Friends there, and we weren't that anxious to move on, except that my job had ended. I could have returned to my old job in New Brunswick, but we liked the area, the people, and climate too well. In fact, Judy and I a couple of times had shared that we'd each had the occasional dream about going back east, and they weren't pleasant dreams. I interviewed for teaching jobs in the Sacramento area and the Los Angeles area. But of the two job offers I got, one offered a salary that would not even cover rent in the area, and the other offer was to teach Spanish, a language that I didn't speak and had never studied.

Upon my return from the last of these interviews, all three of my family informed me that they didn't want to move to California. I'd actually that very day made the same decision myself as I came down from the Sierra Nevada into the Nevada desert on my way home. I saw the desert laid out before me as such an awesomely beautiful and tranquil place – quite unlike the dirty barren wilderness I first saw it as. I loved it.

We moved to a townhouse in Carson City, and I took odd jobs during the two months it took me to obtain a Nevada teacher's credential. I planned to do substitute teaching until I could get a contract somewhere. As it turned out, my first day of substituting was in the high school where I'd done my exchange teaching. By the end of that day I'd negotiated a plan with the principal there to establish a special program for non-English speaking students who needed high school credits to graduate. I was trained in French Immersion techniques in eastern Canada, so all I did was apply them in English with the students at that school. Aside from teaching them English, I also taught them American History, American Government, and Geography. At least one teacher complained because I was a non-American teacher teaching American subjects to non-American students in an American school. The principal's response was interesting: "He has a straight A grade point average in these subjects, and you guys don't know how to talk to these kids."

It was a very heavy teaching load, and when I got the chance I took a position teaching American History and Government to mainstream students. I remained in that school for thirteen years, and enjoyed my time immensely. Judy and both daughters in time were all hired in the state civil service. I even had the privilege of being an attaché in the Nevada State Senate in its 2001 legislative session, as secretary to the Senate Finance Committee. All four of us have now retired from public service. Nothing dissuaded us from wanting to stay here. And I'm over half way to my second forty-year residency – this time west of the Mississippi.

Concerning the expected differences in customs – they were for the most part exactly as expected. As customs go, there were none among the Friends here that were more onerous than there had been in the Northeast. I actually never expected anyone or anything to be perfect. I'd occasionally heard it said, "The way is perfect, but the people aren't." That always satisfied me, because there was nothing about the style of worship that I ever disagreed with. Furthermore, everything I ever disagreed with I attributed to some person's error, on some level – which I found I could always tolerably live around. Mostly it involved minding my own business and keeping others out of mine.

Among the innocuous differences was the custom of standing in meetings to *take part*. *Take part* is the expression used for giving one's testimony in a meeting. In the Northeast people normally remain seated when taking part, and stand only when it happens to be an especially large gathering. I didn't know it mattered whether one sat or stood, but I soon learned that some people think it does. One Sunday the elder of the meeting noted that in the East people sit to speak, and declared that it was a disrespectful way to speak in God's presence. I appreciated that at least individuals with handicaps aren't deprived of their speaking privilege.

Another such difference was that the wine for the *emblems* was passed in a glass, instead of a cup. *Emblems* is the usual term among the Friends and Workers for the Eucharist. Also, though it is called *wine*, in North America it is normally grape juice, not wine. I cannot speculate on how North America adopted this substitute, but for some reason alcohol became largely forbidden among Friends on this continent. Then one day after meeting an Irish visitor confided to me that he didn't think a glass for this ritual was appropriate. He criticized both the glass and grape juice being substituted for the cup and wine. It was a reasonable observation, considering that the California Overseer Worker had prepared detailed written instructions on all aspects of this sacrament, down to the style of table it sat on and the kind of napkin used to cover it. But the substitutes remain acceptable.

Certainly, most of the women in the meeting would have been noticeably out of place in the Northeast. In meetings there were white and colored shoes, sandals, and hair falling over shoulders. My wife also noticed that not all women wore panty hose – and the Northeast had only recently emerged from the black stocking mandate! But how could one blame them for wearing no nylons – it was 100°F in the shade! I certainly didn't disapprove of how any of them were dressed, but after forty years of conditioning it still called for a second look. After we'd been here for a couple of months I remarked to Judy that the Northeastern dress code had been violated in every meeting we'd been in since coming to Nevada.

But it turned out there were things about one's clothing that did draw people's attention in meetings. I frequently received comments on my ties – but no indication of liking, approval, or disapproval. Just, "Look at this tie!" I've never figured out the criteria for making a necktie noteworthy. In fact, I never did figure out the California dress code for women, except that pants are forbidden – even if some women wear them on occasion. But there has to be one. I've heard a few Workers mentioning that some woman looked "like she had a problem", a reference to either hair or clothing. It certainly had nothing to do with overly expensive clothing – one brother Worker I know routinely wore an obvious $400 attire. Who knows? Maybe they thought we looked like we had a problem too.

It was quite amusing one Sunday to hear someone say in meeting that he'd heard something on the radio. Where we came from, radios were taboo. In California and Nevada, the Friends have them in their homes. But one year my cousin from Maine had the radio antenna cut off her car during the night while at convention.

Wednesday Bible study meetings had a new twist as well. In the Northeast most meetings have some kind of input into what the Bible study topics will be. I remember when I was thirteen that I got my turn to choose a topic for the next Bible study. However, on the West Coast of the United States and in all of Western Canada, yearly lists of mandated weekly Bible study topics are distributed, and it seems to be inappropriate to even deal with any of them on the wrong dates. I never did find out where these study lists come from in the first place, and no one seemed to care.

But there were other things that concerned me from the very beginning – things that I couldn't interpret as difference in customs, but rather differences in belief. The first one that really bothered me was a sermon at our first convention in Gilroy. A Worker was speaking about his experiences in East Africa. It was all quite interesting, but he proceeded to explain that he'd discovered it was a waste of time to preach the gospel to the desperately poor – all they wanted was food. My immediate thought was, *but they still have souls.* The Workers pride themselves on a *homeless* and *penniless* ministry – I was aware that penniless was an exaggeration, of course. And I'd always believed that Workers who went to such places lived like the locals so they would *not ... know anything among* them *save Jesus Christ.*[1] I'd also frequently heard that the virtue of such a ministry was that their message of salvation would not be compromised by other interests. I understood that preacher's concern, but I thought he sounded incompetent to take the gospel he preached to the desperately poor. And I was shocked that he'd say such a thing to such a group of people. I was further shocked to hear the same thing mentioned in a Sunday meeting some time thereafter.

The second shock I got at that convention was when I made conversation with a man who had come from Pennsylvania. Somehow the name George Walker came up. George was, I believe, the first Worker to come from Ireland to the East Coast, and had been the Worker Overseer for most of North America east of the Rockies for much of the twentieth century. I made a favorable comment about George, and the man contradicted me. To him, George was *evil*, and he'd never return to Pennsylvania because of what George had done there. George, according to him, allowed people to divorce and remarry, and that was why he (the man from Pennsylvania) moved to the West Coast where such a thing was not permitted. I'd never heard of anything of the sort, so I didn't know what to say; but it provided me with my first inkling that there was a simmering schism between East and West.

I volunteered for night watch at that convention, so I was around when 'Don', the man in charge of breakfast preparation, arrived in the kitchen. In conversation with him, he shared that Doyle Copeland, a California Worker, had packed his bags and left the ministry in the Midwest because he disagreed with the divorce and remarriage policy there. He'd come to California, and subsequently been accepted as a Worker here. I assumed Don knew what he was talking about because he was an ex-Worker himself. It was a confirmation of what the man from Pennsylvania had already told me. But it quite conflicted with what I'd so often heard about Workers never worrying about inviting Workers from other places to come and visit. The reason given was that they knew such visitors never differed with them on doctrine. I learned later on that some Worker Overseers actually do confront their Worker visitors about preaching something contrary to local doctrine. One Overseer even shared with me personally that he'd done so with a visitor from Australia.

The incident at that first convention that really surprised me was the man, not a convention attendee, who parked his car on the county right of way through the convention property and hung signs on his car denigrating a number of individuals by name. I knew none of the people mentioned, but I learned he was a frequent protester against the Truth. He stayed there between the morning meeting and the beginning of the afternoon meeting, but the adults seemed to pay no attention to him. The children milled around his car, staring at him like a curiosity.

Then there came a visit from a journalist – something else I'd never seen before at a convention. She did look out of place, walking through the crowd and through the meeting tent with short hair and a camera, and wearing shorts. Her report of what she witnessed was favorably interesting, and it got widely circulated among the Friends when it appeared in the local newspaper. That was without a doubt a memorable convention.

Following the convention season, the Workers all dispersed to their various assigned fields, and Harold Hilton and Mark McGee came to Northern Nevada. I was impressed that the Friends in all the meetings in the area had a picnic to welcome them to the area. It was a good occasion for us to become more familiar with all the Friends in Northern Nevada. I was, by that time, quite impressed with the devotion of the Friends to the Workers. I noticed that they had a habit of referring to some older male Workers as *Uncle* – I didn't care much for that. All my life Workers were considered our brothers and sisters, not uncles. I understand some of the sister Workers are called *Aunt*. I know of a few places where children are instructed to call the Workers *Mr.* and *Miss.*

After the convention, several things that I heard stated in meetings concerned me greatly. The first one was: "The health of the kingdom depends on the authority of the Workers." *Kingdom*, of course, referred to the community of Friends and Workers. I accepted that Workers needed to have authority in spiritual matters. But I knew the difference between authority and power. That difference was best described by a legislator I once worked with. He explained that "Authority is given, and power is assumed." I had long suspected that some Workers interpreted their exercise of power over others as evidence of their authority. And it seemed to me that they often overstepped their *authority* in spates of cavalier judgment.

This comment on authority soon translated for me into a totally unacceptable doctrine. I was also told one Worker had made the claim that Workers are *God's word made flesh*. My gut response was that *the world has already had enough people who thought they were God*. I had two brothers and a number of close relatives who were Workers – no, they were not *God made flesh*, they were *flesh attempting to serve God*.

Where I grew up we often heard of the Workers telling people that they should only follow a Worker as long as the Worker was following Christ. We were told by Workers not to follow any Worker if he was wrong. The implication, I concluded, was that we had a responsibility to recognize when a Worker was wrong. So, I was predisposed to reject outright any such notion of *God made flesh*. I've since come to understand this new notion to be a major justification for any kind of abuse imaginable.

Another statement disturbed me. Mention was made in a Sunday meeting about the role of the Workers. Apparently Jack Carroll, a pioneering Worker on the West Coast of the U.S., had taught that the role of the Workers was not just to *invite people in*, but also to *keep the wrong people out*. My earliest understanding as a child was that there was no flood of people wanting into the fellowship, and those who were misbehaving didn't need to be told to leave – they'd normally leave on their own because they wouldn't feel like one of us.

As well, I didn't know of anyone in the New Testament who'd been denied access to salvation – which I understood to be the whole message of the gospels, and thus of the Workers. I also knew of only one person in the New Testament who had been denied temporarily of his place among other Christians – he'd been fornicating with his father's wife.[2] I'd actually known a Worker who refused to allow people to profess, for strictly arbitrary reasons, and it disturbed me because I thought it was wrong. And I also knew of Workers who put people out of fellowship for something as simple as speeding on their way to convention, which also disturbed me. But the speeding incident also amused me, in a sense. I once passed a police officer on the highway who was writing a speeding ticket for the Worker Overseer of Eastern Canada.

My parents taught us to respect the Workers, but they discussed them like they were human beings, with habits, preferences, and possibly faults. My grandfather had no problem criticizing Workers when he thought they were wrong – and not disrespectfully either. I'd always known about people who *worshiped Workers*, as the expression goes. And I'd also known of Workers who'd committed various serious offenses, ranging from denying accepted Worker teachings, to sexual indiscretions. I remember hearing my parents discuss one situation where a Worker had excommunicated someone for some trivial reason, and they agreed that the one who was excommunicated was better off than the one who excommunicated him. They made no pretense of Worker infallibility, any more than they pretended there was a Santa Claus. I considered them more honest with us than a lot of other parents were, and I learned that the approval of the Workers was not going to determine my eternal destiny.

What convinced me that the Workers in California were accepting of a place of worship occurred one Sunday morning about a month after conventions were over. It was announced after meeting that the annual photograph of the California Workers was available for purchase. There were two sizes, each with a different price. The elder of the meeting was to collect the money and send it to the photographer, who would then send him the pictures. It's a well-known fact that the Friends love pictures of Workers, and many people display them around their houses. But I was totally shocked that the Workers would permit merchandising of professional quality photographs of themselves at meeting time. It didn't leave much cause for one to consider them the humble ministry they claimed to be. The only time I'd ever known of money being passed openly after a meeting was when the meeting elder was charged with taking sealed envelopes of money to some very needy Friend.

And then there was the visiting sister Worker, Shirley Doolittle, who declared that "God had not instituted a ministry of poverty – He had instituted a ministry that accepted money in secret." I found that patently offensive – not the *giving in secret* part, but the acceptability of wealth. Her statement was further exacerbated by another Worker, the one who dresses in $400 finery, when he told us that he accepted money from a very poor man. He said the poor man knew it was a blessing to give to the Workers, and he "could not deprive the poor man of that blessing." I'd known Workers to refuse money from some of the Friends because they felt their children needed it more than the Workers did. I thought this new concept was a shameless flaunting of their belief in their own worthiness.

But I never felt any need to dispute these things with anyone. Individual Workers with rather weird ideas were nothing new to me. I knew a sister Worker who examined everyone's cookware because she refused to eat anything cooked in aluminum cookware. And there was a brother Worker who showered naked in an apple orchard in a thunder storm. A lot of these things don't really hurt anyone, and who are we to undertake to correct other people's idiosyncrasies?

Unless, of course, they do damage to others' lives.

CHAPTER 4

Naivete Lifting

Harold Hilton was the Worker responsible for Northern Nevada for two years. Then in 1989 Leo Stancliff came to the area. He was an elderly man, and a hell fire and brimstone kind of preacher. He impressed people with his apparent command of the Bible. Workers don't have hard copies of the sermons they're about to deliver, but Leo could pepper a half hour sermon with dozens of chapter and verse references.

The first year he was in Nevada he visited our home a few times. We found him comfortable enough to visit with. And his companion Worker during the first year was David Olson, a meek man of about forty, who was no thunderous preacher, especially compared to Leo. But he was a remarkably honorable man. When Leo returned for the 1990-1991 year, his companion was John van den Berg.

And the strangest thing happened. As soon as Leo returned to the area he called me just to talk. I didn't think we had such a close relationship that he would call me just to talk. Then I became suspicious. He told me there was a great need to *clean up* the area. I had no idea what he meant. Even so, if he had no problem with me, I wasn't interested in knowing anything about it, especially if it had nothing to do with me. As much as I respected him, I frankly didn't find him the kind of person I wanted to be confidant to.

A short while after this conversation I went to New Brunswick for a ten-day visit. About the third day I was there Judy called me and told me that Karen had met the son of one of the Friends in Reno, and they were now an item. The problem was that Leo had begun calling Judy almost every day to tell her what an unfit guy this boyfriend was, what a mistake Karen was making, and how terrible her life would be if she married him. Judy was beside herself with fear, most of all that Leo would show up at the house and want to talk to her.

She became more depressed with every phone call. I don't know what he thought she could do about anything, and I don't believe he ever spoke to Karen to warn her about anything.

I know what triggered Leo's actions. He made no pretense of having much respect for the boyfriend's mother. I don't know whether Leo considered her professing or not. She was married to her third husband and wasn't permitted to speak in meetings, though she was allowed to attend meetings. And the boyfriend was not professing at the time. Here on the West Coast marrying such a person isn't considered a reason to excommunicate someone. But Leo knew that on the East Coast anyone who married an outsider would have his part taken from him – at least temporarily. He once made a weak attempt to justify his actions on the grounds that Karen was from back east, but he knew no one would have supported that.

When I returned to Carson City, I got another phone call from Leo. His opening remark was: "We've got a problem. I've been told that Karen is sleeping with the young man she's been seeing." I don't know what I said to him, but I did remind him that Karen was over twenty-one, she had a responsible job in the head office of the Nevada Highway Patrol, and she was fully supporting herself. He seemed frustrated that I didn't have a ready plan to deal with it, but as I told him, she was past the age where it's appropriate to force her to do anything.

He left us alone for a while. Then one-day Karen came home with a diamond, and I did have a discussion with her and cautioned her on what she was getting herself into. But she was adamant that she was doing what she wanted to do, so I said nothing more to her. Then at about six o'clock on a Saturday morning Leo called me again. He knew where Karen was – as did I. She was at her now fiancé's house where he lived with his mother, stepfather, and sister. Leo asked me to go to Reno and we could go together to catch Karen in bed with the guy. I was offended that he even thought I'd do such a thing, and told him I couldn't go. If I'd known the man better at the time I'd have had a much different conversation with him, but I just ended the conversation.

A short while later the phone rang again. Leo was at her fiancé's house, and the fiancé's mother had let him use her phone. He wanted me to call back and ask to speak to Karen, so I did, and the mother answered. When I asked to speak to Karen, she said, "She's sleeping." And Leo demanded that someone wake her. Leo took Karen outside to talk, and according to her account of the event he told her that she was shameful and that she was to have no more part in meeting. A few days later I asked her if he'd told her why he was doing that, and she said she had no idea. She just thought he'd quite taken leave of his senses. I didn't ask her anything more, and she didn't volunteer anything more. But I already knew Leo's version of the encounter.

It was hardly twenty minutes after Leo's previous two calls that morning that he called again. First, he said he had some bad news. It was that he had taken Karen's part in meeting from her, and that he expected her to lie to me about what had transpired. Then he proceeded to tell me that one of his skills was in taking people's part from them. He told me that some of the sister Workers found it difficult to do that, and they would call on him to do it for them. He related how he'd been visiting in San Diego and was asked to put a young unmarried couple out of the Truth while he was there. In detail he explained how he followed their cars to one of their apartments following a gospel meeting, and watched them go inside. When no one came out after an hour, he knocked on the door and they let him in. At that point he told them they were no longer professing.

Then before Leo hung up, he told me he'd made a mistake – he'd forgotten to tell Karen that she was also not to appear in any meetings. I was aghast. No apology, no comfort – he just hung up. And never in my lifetime had I heard of someone being banned from attending meetings for such a thing. In fact, one Worker Overseer once told me that the only reason a person should not be allowed in a meeting is if he is drunk, or intent on being disruptive.

My daughter and her fiancé just went and got married, and to Leo's consternation both continued coming to meetings. But Leo refused to be wrong. He called me about a month later and reported that he'd gone to their apartment one night at 8:00 p.m. to see whether they had a television, but they wouldn't answer the door for him. After a few other similar "snooping" incidents I asked him and his companion, John van den Berg, to come for a talk. I was up-front with him about his cavalier approach to people's salvation, and I told him I thought he'd made a mistake, and I asked him whether he would consider changing his decision. He skirted the facts I presented him with, and gave the most skillful spiel of double-talk I've ever encountered in my lifetime. He reminded me of an expression my father used to use: "He's as crooked as a Philadelphia lawyer!" I was really shocked because I couldn't believe a Worker would talk to anyone the way he was carrying on. John began to cry and said we couldn't "accomplish anything today". He was right, so I dropped all attempts to discuss it further. They very quickly got up to leave, and Leo had the nerve to suggest, as he was leaving, that one day we would "look back at this and laugh". He was as graceful as a bull in a china shop.

About 6 months later the Friends had a gathering at Karen's mother in law's house, and Karen was playing volleyball. One of the young people asked her if she should be playing volleyball. She asked why not, and was told that pregnant women shouldn't play volleyball. She told them she wasn't pregnant, much to the surprise of a number of people present. I found it interesting that Karen's mother in law had assured people that Karen had done nothing wrong. Of course, that would be her word against Leo's.

In one gospel meeting my son in law went to the restroom while Leo was speaking, and after the meeting Leo told him he shouldn't do that too much or he'd not be allowed to go to gospel meetings. It was notable, because Leo had never confronted anyone else for going to the restroom during a meeting.

The following summer Karen and her husband moved to Las Vegas. They arrived there on a weekend, and on the following Thursday the Workers in the city (two women) extended their series of gospel meetings by one meeting so Karen and her husband could profess. I don't know how those Workers brought it off, because they had apparently talked at length to Leo about them. Incidentally, Leo did not call me to tell me the good news.

In August of that year we went to the new convention at Mountain Ranch, California. Karen and her husband flew to Sacramento, where we met them and took them to convention with us. Everything went fine until Saturday at noon. Her husband had gone out to the restroom during hymn singing about mid-way through the morning meeting. When the meeting was over Doyle Copeland, a Worker, called him aside and gave him a lecture, telling him he shouldn't go to the restroom during meetings. I was suspicious of Doyle's motives for speaking to him, because there was a large number of others who had left during that meeting as well. Furthermore, none of us had even met Doyle before this time.

I went to Doyle and told him my son in law had never been to a convention before, and I wanted to know why he had done such a thing. He gave me a condescending lecture about twenty-five year olds who couldn't sit for two hours without going to the restroom. I should have asked him if Leo had pointed us out to him.

Later that same day we were standing in front of the meeting shed talking to some friends, and Leo approached us and took Karen and her husband aside to talk to them. I watched, and it wasn't long before the conversation got heated. In a couple of minutes Karen threw her hands in the air and walked away. I asked her what was going on, and she said Leo was demanding that she and her husband apologize to me for lying to me. I asked her what Leo thought they had lied about, and she said she didn't know.

I followed Leo around the side of the building and asked him what the problem was. He said they had lied to me about their fornication and they had to apologize to me or they couldn't be saved. I reminded him that it was he who told me she would lie, and for that reason I'd never discussed their offenses with either of them. My motto is: if someone is a liar, why ask him questions? And I asked Leo again what indication he had that they'd been fornicating, and he said they were sleeping together. I reminded him that he had not actually found them in bed together, and he acknowledged that he hadn't. But he explained that our son in law's aunt (who did not live with him) had told Leo that he and Karen had been sitting on the couch one night and Karen laid her head on his knee, and they were discovered sleeping that way. So I asked him if he thought that constituted fornication. He said the Bible doesn't say anything about having sex – it speaks about the sin of lying with a woman. And since Karen had been lying down, that was grounds for him to put her out of the Truth. To emphasize the appropriateness of his decision he said that he'd discussed Karen and her husband with his companion, and his companion had agreed with his decision. I decided the man really was crazy. I thought to ask him if the passage he quoted also applied to a woman sitting with a man lying down, but I wasn't in the mood for humor. You remember, I'd already determined he was a slippery talker.

The next day at lunch I went to John van den Berg, who'd been his companion at the time. I told him I was really concerned because Leo was still harassing Karen, now almost a year later. John told me that he'd told Leo that once in an area where he'd been preaching it had been discovered that a young couple were living together, so the Workers talked to them. The couple said they were very much in love, so they got married and everything continued as before. And it wasn't long before the Workers put a meeting in their house.

So – John had not agreed with Leo after all. At that point I realized I had a problem of my own – I'd been so conditioned against uttering a Worker's name in the same sentence as the word lying that I couldn't even say someone was lying. It didn't matter to me which one may have lied – just faced with the undeniable fact that one of them had misrepresented their conversation to me was jarring. I had just been conditioned to assign some other verb to conflicting statements by Workers. I was forty-four years old and that was the first time I'd ever attempted to verify a Worker's word to me, and that's what I found. I now credit it with changing my life. The rest of this book will explain why.

What really happened was that Karen's husband's aunt didn't want Karen to have anything to do with her nephew. It was reported to us that she told Leo they'd been sleeping together in an effort to separate them. I never bothered to question anyone about that report. There was obviously a rumor mill in Nevada too, and I wanted nothing to do with it. Instead, I wrote Leo a stern letter, and have included some excerpts here.

You told me ... [Karen] would be a good example for other young people who fornicate. You told enough to enough people that everyone would know exactly what you wanted them to know. People began asking us why she "wasn't going to meeting any more" even before the next meeting came around. Where do you think people got the idea she was pregnant? You scandalized my daughter as thoroughly as a worker possibly can.

....

You told our relatives how concerned you were about us – that's all I heard of what you told them. They weren't gossiping – it was a slip.

....

I don't want you to talk to Karen and [her husband] about it again unless you feel you have an apology to make. I've told them to tell me if you ever do.

Of course, I'd long since decided that Leo had an ego that wouldn't quit. Not satisfied with his share of sermon time at conventions, he recruited people for his own private talks between meetings. Several times he bragged about all the comments he'd received over the years about his outstanding preaching. When he was in Nevada he had more than gospel meetings. One other such meeting he called was to tell us about his experiences in the Philippines as a prisoner of war during World War II. We were to invite any of our outside friends and acquaintances as well. One of the things he told us was that he was more fit than most of the other prisoners, and thus survived. The rest of the narrative I learned in high school. On another occasion he called us to a talk on the history of the Catholic church, basically since the third century CE. Maybe everyone else thought he was an expert. I understood clearly that he'd read one book of the Protestant version of the history. Of course, he carefully explained how the Workers' ministry survived unaffected by the changes and developments in the rest of Christianity through the centuries. We were soon to learn that most of what he knew about that matter was a deception he should never have indulged in.

One of the things that Workers pride themselves in is having a fresh word for their gospel meetings, the result of their continuing study of the scriptures. Or a word in season, the result of the Lord's moving them to answer the needs of people that they were not even aware of. I believe most Workers actually operate that way. Leo, on the other hand, frequently had more than one sermon to give, and before he began to speak he would ask us to vote on the options he presented. I was highly amused the time he settled on the losing option. I've since learned how he managed this. He confided to a Worker cousin of mine that he kept a recipe type box of cards containing notes for sermons he could use. Apparently, he thought it was cool, but my cousin wasn't at all impressed.

He also had more to say about a topic than the time he was allotted. A few times he decided to go long over the scheduled time, but on the hour would tell us that the time was up and anyone who didn't want to hear the rest of his sermon was free to go. Of course, no one left. The most uncomfortable time of all was when we sang a hymn, his companion prayed, and then Leo announced that his companion had graciously agreed to let him speak for the whole hour because he had a long topic that he wanted to speak about. His companion was visibly embarrassed. One of the tenets of the Friends and Workers religion is that preachers preach in pairs. Of course, he never hid the fact that he thought his companion, poor David, was not that great a preacher anyway.

For my own satisfaction, I decided to check the chapters and verses he used to pepper his sermons with. He may have had the right chapter and verse two thirds of the time, but who was taking notes. That wasn't so bad – he was an old man and I don't remember chapters and verses myself. What I did find fault with was how he preached that the Bible was our book of rules. Leo preached that it was all rules, but it was only rules about things that applied to Bible times. Now that we live in an age when there are so many other matters to deal with, it is the duty of the Workers to make rules about those matters. I didn't know how he got off with that, because I'd never heard of such a thing. Workers are more apt to say that the Bible is complete and sufficient for all time. Furthermore, all the Workers I'd known would invariably say, even insist, that we have no rules – and explain that the Friends decide with their own conscience what to refrain from. Most people know better, of course, but they'd never want the Workers to hear they'd verbalized it.

Leo was all law, crime, and punishment. On one occasion the wife of Mike Colson, a man who'd recently converted from Catholicism, had professed in one of Leo's gospel meetings. A few days later he went to her house to visit her and told her he'd come to explain the rules to her, now that she was professing. I don't know how many rules he had on his list, but among the ones she mentioned were: no cutting of hair, no makeup, no jewelry, no pants, no shorts, no television – the usual list. She panicked, and called an elderly lady in Reno and asked if it was true. She put the woman in a terrible bind, really. I wish I knew what she told the young lady to put her at ease.

Leo had some concept of grace apparently, but I never did find out what it was. I was curious, because I didn't know there were different concepts of grace. I always wanted to hear his version, but I never had the opportunity. It obviously differed from that of another elder Worker on the West Coast, because he's recorded as declaring that "there is no such thing as saved by faith, and no such thing as being saved by grace." I didn't believe that was scriptural either, but I expected Leo's version was a skilled construction that allowed for Worker mandated behaviors.

A few years after Leo left Northern Nevada, there was a reunion of professing World War II veterans in Reno, and some Workers who were involved in some way with that war were going to speak at a meeting that would be held for both the reunion attendees and the local meeting Friends. Leo was one of them. He told an elderly friend of mine in Reno that he'd decided he would speak about grace at that meeting. He explained that the people in the East had a very different, and very mistaken, concept of grace, and he wanted to take the opportunity to explain grace for their benefit. My friend advised him not to do that, he could cause big problems by doing so – so Leo changed his sermon.

I relate the incidents in this chapter not primarily to criticize Leo Stancliff, but because I discovered his behaviors were quite acceptable to the Overseer Worker, whose only response to his behaviors was that he would not concern himself with them. That attitude makes such behavior de facto acceptable. I hoped other Workers who came to the area were not like him, but I feared that there were more like him because of the Overseer's attitude. Sad as it sounds, it was my experience with Leo that convinced me I shouldn't trust the souls of my children to the Workers just because they're Workers. Today I cannot change my mind. Not only was Leo highly revered among the Friends, but I later learned that some Workers used him as mentor on how to deal with the Friends. Only one person was openly sympathetic to our situation, an elderly lady named Bea Rabe, who lived in Carson City and at whose home we went for Wednesday Bible studies. We loved her dearly.

About this time, I also witnessed how duplicitous Workers can be. A young professing man came to the area to work, and it wasn't long before his girlfriend came from California to visit him for the weekend. She spent the whole weekend with him at his apartment. I had no interest whatsoever in what they did, and I fully expect that they did nothing they cared to hide. But the fact remained that they seemed to feel no need to worry about repercussions for sharing the weekend alone in his apartment. My daughter Karen did not miss how different their treatment was from hers.

Another young couple later moved to northern Nevada. They'd conceived a baby before they were married, and were not permitted to speak in meetings. But by some logic they were permitted to reprofess before the baby was born. And I hasten to stress that I do not think they were unduly well treated.

It was a very difficult time for us, and we were glad when our lives returned to normal. One thing had become clear to me – I didn't know the Who's Who of the Friends in California, so I had no way of predicting what would happen to whom as a result of what behaviors. There is always a Who's Who!

A grandchild did eventually arrive in our family, but long after some folks expected it.

CHAPTER 5

1997-1998

Life in northern Nevada became quite pleasant again. Karen returned to Carson City with her son, but by 1997 she and her husband had separated, and we were content to leave the circumstances of their marriage in the past. Our Workers at that time were Linda Passage and Phyllis Munn. We'd first met Linda when we were visiting Karen in Las Vegas, and I'd met Phyllis when I was perhaps fifteen and she was visiting New Brunswick. She was there to visit a very elderly Worker named Helen Harrison. Phyllis actually had a special place in my life, though I'd only met her that one time before she came to Northern Nevada.

Helen, by the early 1960s, was the oldest Worker in the world – she lived to be several years over the age of one hundred. But since she was no longer able to preach, she came to be cared for by my grandparents. Young people loved her, and teenagers occasionally got together to go visit her. One day, on my way home from school, I dropped in to see her and she handed me a letter she'd received and told me I should answer it. It was from Hinh, a teenager in Viet Nam, who wrote that he'd heard Phyllis preaching in Viet Nam and had professed. Then he wanted to know how Phyllis had come to know about the Friends and Workers. Phyllis must have told him about Helen preaching years before on Prince Edward Island, where Phyllis' ancestors once owned the convention property. The letter was his way of establishing his connections among the Friends and Workers.

I answered his letter, and found we had a lot of interests in common. Not long after Helen received that letter Phyllis, her sister Jeannette, and her parents went to New Brunswick to visit with Helen, and that was when I met Phyllis. She was a pleasant lady who appreciated that I'd begun corresponding with Hinh, and fascinated me with her stories of Viet Nam. Since that time, Hinh and I have both graduated from high school and college, become second language teachers, gotten married, had two children each, and eventually both migrated to the United States – and now have grandchildren. The pen pal days gave way to Internet communications, of course, and our wives and children have had numerous visits back and forth over the years. It has been an enriching friendship for me.

By 1997, Merle Bunch had passed away, but our Sunday meetings continued to be at the Bunch home. Ernie Rabe, at whose home we had Wednesday Bible studies, became the Sunday elder as well, and I'd been designated as his alternate elder. More Friends had moved to the Carson City area, and besides the Sunday meeting at the Bunch's home in Carson City, there was a new Sunday meeting established in nearby Gardnerville – at the home of Ken Forbes. Besides the Forbes family, two other new families had come to the Gardnerville meeting as well – the 'Norman Dunn' family with four school aged children and the 'Andy Dunn' family with two high school aged children.

Norman's oldest daughter, 'Alice', and Andy's daughter, 'Bernice', were both of high school age. One day, a single man, an engineer who was a recent graduate from a university in California, moved to the area to work. His name was 'Bill Frost'. Both girls descended upon him the first time he appeared in their meeting.

In Carson City one of the new families was 'Jane Marklee' and her two daughters. In such a small and tightly knit community, Jane's daughters formed a lively friendship with the Dunn girls. Speculation immediately arose as to who would succeed in winning Bill's favor, Alice or Bernice. It soon became evident that Alice had won out. In fact, it was rumored with great excitement among the women that they had plans to marry, though no one expected it would happen before Alice finished high school. What drew a lot of people's attention was Alice's aggressive displays of affection. Being a high school teacher, I didn't notice anything particularly unusual about it – except that it was a bit flagrant by Truth standards.

Bernice meanwhile had found a love of her own – Souza, a fellow who lived a couple of houses down the street from her. He had no connection to the Friends, but the two young couples would spend time together. They included the Marklee sisters from Carson City and one or two young, single guys from Reno. At some point during this period, Souza had begun attending meetings along with the others.

An unusual situation had developed in the Carson City meetings. Jane Marklee did not speak in meetings. It was an indication that she'd been excommunicated, though we certainly never knew why. A retired couple, Ken and Mary Hornady, had come to town and they didn't speak in meeting either. We assumed, rightly, that one or both of them had a prior spouse who was still alive. And then there was the young married couple who moved to town. The wife was clearly well into a pregnancy and they didn't speak in meetings either. It was obvious that the baby had been conceived before their marriage. It was awkward enough in Wednesday Bible studies when seven people got to participate and five adults and two adolescents did not. It was even more awkward the evening a couple of visitors came in and a couple of regulars were missing – six people got to speak and nine people did not. It gave me an uneasy sense that things were quite out of balance for a meeting of the Friends.

Then, at the beginning of the school year that August, a strange thing happened. Bernice was registered in one of my classes at the local high school, but she was shown to have withdrawn before the second day of classes. No one at the school knew why she'd left, but I learned from the Marklee sisters that her parents had sent her to live with her grandparents 800 miles away, in Arizona. The explanation was that she couldn't control herself around Souza, and her parents thought she'd be better off in Arizona. I didn't ask any more questions, but I couldn't imagine what was so drastic that she had to be sent so far away. After all, they were, from all appearances, a very normal, stable, well-adjusted family. Word soon circulated that Souza had begun seeing some other girl in town. Some people thought that would discourage Souza from continuing to come to meetings, but he continued to come to meetings anyway.

Suddenly, in the spring of 1998, Bill and Souza were reassigned from the Gardnerville meeting to our meeting in Carson City. We thought it only slightly unusual, because Friends are frequently reassigned by the Workers for any number of reasons. I didn't know what had transpired in the Forbes' meeting, but it was rumored that Alice's and Bernice's parents had asked the Workers to move Bill and Souza out of the Forbes meeting. We did appreciate them being in our meeting. Souza, of course, was not professing and did not speak, but Bill was a helpful part of the meeting.

Then one Sunday morning we had a surprising incident. Alice appeared in our meeting, not with her family, but with one of the Marklee sisters. When she came into the room she made a mad dash for the empty seat next to Bill, and did a great lot of tittering with the Marklee girl, who had taken the seat on the other side of her from Bill. Bill was visibly upset about what they'd done. I was certain it was because he found himself sitting between Alice and Phyllis Munn, the Worker, who'd so recently had asked him to come to our meeting – to avoid being around Alice. Phyllis visibly gulped and took a second look. Her eyes were about popping out on her cheeks with shock. Then, when Alice discovered that Phyllis was also in the meeting, she stopped laughing and behaved herself. When the meeting was over she and the Marklee girl quickly slipped outside.

Soon after that we went to meeting one Sunday morning and found the Workers sitting in their car at the entrance to the Bunches' driveway. No one sits in their car waiting to go into meeting, much less the Workers. And they stayed in the car until exactly one minute before time for the meeting to begin. When the meeting was over, someone whispered to us that Bill had been arrested – and it was serious. He'd sexually assaulted a minor.

We were told by a young lady who worked for Alice's father, Norman, that it was Alice that Bill had assaulted. At another time, Phyllis whispered to Judy that what Bill had been doing was totally disgusting, which I interpreted to mean something way-out perverted. Otherwise, why would Phyllis have known the intimate details? After all, even elderly and celibate female Workers know that premarital sexual intercourse is neither that unusual nor that disgusting. What puzzled me most was that, if it had been so dreadfully disgusting, why had Alice clambered so badly to be in meeting with him just days previously. Most puzzling of all was that her parents had let their assaulted minor daughter spend the weekend with her friend who would be going to the meeting Bill attended.

I was still reserving my opinion on the whole matter when we heard that Linda Passage had told Norman Dunn to call the police on Bill – that Norman had wanted to avoid the police, but Linda had prevailed upon him to report. At that point I accepted that there must have been some compelling reason to have Bill arrested, or a Worker would never have come to the family and insisted on his arrest. We also learned that Linda had sent letters to all the meeting elders in Northern Nevada advising them to call the police if Bill attempted to go to meeting in their houses. The letter stated that Bill was a great danger to the children, and was a repeat offender. This really shocked me – first of all because I knew the ministry did not even believe in reporting fellow Workers who were molesting children; and more often than not such offending Workers were not even removed from the ministry. And secondly, for Workers who had been put out of the ministry for this reason, the consequence was normally nothing more than being assigned to a meeting where there were none of his victims. As a teacher, I understood why no child predator should go unreported. But this situation shocked me for its apparent unprecedented break with the tradition of Workers not involving themselves in the Friends' legal problems.

So, it really disturbed me that Linda wouldn't even allow Bill to attend a meeting – anywhere. But it did remind me of what I'd previously heard about *keeping the wrong people out*, and this presented me with a glaring contradiction. In a group that believes there is no soul salvation aside from the Workers' approbation, such a prohibition as Linda's amounted to eternal damnation – and this situation allowed for no saving intervention on God's part. It was simply a conclusion of my own logic, but I expected that people who believed in a personal relationship with God needed some refuge from humans who would deny them salvation. I often recalled that in the Bible the only person to be ejected from Christian fellowship was a man who'd been shamelessly sleeping with his father's wife, at best that being his own stepmother.[1] My problem was that I couldn't relate that Biblical account to Bill and Alice's situation, so I reasoned that he must have raped her – but I really couldn't believe that. So, I decided I was never going to find out what happened.

By April we began to notice other upsetting things. Maybe we'd just been shocked out of complacency, but it occurred to me that Linda had never spoken to Judy and I at any meetings. Judy brought this to my attention, and we found that invariably, after a meeting, Linda would work her way around the room so that we never happened to cross her path or shake her hand. It became a conspicuous avoidance.

One Sunday morning Bea Rabe, the elder's wife, asked us for lunch. The Workers were going there after meeting and had asked Bea to invite our daughter Karen and grandson to eat with them. Karen had already made other plans for lunch, so Bea asked Judy and I to join them. It had been almost a year since the two Workers had come to our area and we'd not had a visit with them, so we accepted gladly.

We were not long at the house before we determined that Linda was offended by our being there. I had no idea why, but it was obvious. She never once looked at us while we were at the table. During the conversation she changed the topic every time I contributed a comment. After the main course she declined to have dessert, excused herself from the table, and went off to a bedroom and never came out again while we were there. I didn't take it very seriously – I just figured she was perhaps a bit strange. But Judy was quite affected – her perception was that for some reason Linda disapproved of us.

In another Sunday meeting that month Bea was the first person to speak. She was totally in tears. She said she'd been told she really wasn't part of the Truth at all, but she said she'd been professing for over 40 years and she believed what she was doing was right, and she just hoped we'd accept her to continue among us. I was disturbed – after all, she was eighty years of age, and the meeting elder's wife. After the meeting Bea's daughter told us that Linda Passage had told Bea about her unworthiness at breakfast that morning. The reason, apparently, was that Ernie was Bea's second husband. But Bea's first husband had abandoned her more than fifty years earlier, and had long since died – Bea had a copy of his death certificate. Among the Workers, there are variations on the treatment of divorced and remarried people from jurisdiction to jurisdiction, but to my knowledge there is not and never has been a prohibition against being married to a second spouse when the first one is dead.

At that time Linda and Phyllis were having Gospel meetings in Reno on Sunday afternoons. One Sunday Linda made a call for professions – or as it's called among the Friends and Workers, she tested the meeting. I suspect the word test originated because the effectiveness of the gospel preaching was being tested. In any case, one of the people to profess was Souza. The young couple who were expecting a baby also professed, even though the baby had not yet been born. Some places they would be required to wait until after the baby was born, but I was quite pleased that they were restored when they were. It was like finding an unexpected leniency in Linda's judgment.

The fourth person to profess that day was Jane Marklee – remember, she'd not been having a part in our meetings. What shocked us was that after the meeting was over Linda explained to her that she (Linda) had no authority to allow Jane to profess. We knew Jane had recently been separated from her husband for some justifiable reason, and had gone through some very difficult and troubling experiences in the aftermath. But she'd admirably made a new and stable home life for herself and her kids. There was no impediment in Jane's life that I could see that would preclude her from being allowed to profess. It turned out that Linda apparently didn't know why Jane wasn't allowed to profess either – she'd just been told by someone above her in the hierarchy not to let Jane profess. There I was at fifty years of age, the alternate elder of the meeting, and more thoroughly confused about what was going on than at any other time in my life.

Just about that time, Ken and Mary Hornady were moved from our meeting to the Forbes' meeting. Despite the fact that Ken had an ex-wife somewhere, they'd been attending meetings faithfully for about thirty years, and no one had an uncomplimentary word to say about them. But when they went to the Forbes meeting, the elder's wife immediately began giving them the cold shoulder. She'd turn her back on them after meeting so she'd never need to shake their hands. And then it became obvious that when Ken and Mary were sitting directly across the room from her in meeting she would turn sideways in her chair so she would not be looking at them.

Then it got even stranger. It was a Sunday meeting, and 'Jay Clark' was the first person to speak. This is a very close summary of what he said: "I've observed that there's an abomination being practiced among people in this church and I'm fed up with it and I'm not going to tolerate it any more. It's the matter of wives not submitting to their husbands. The Bible teaches that this is required or they'll all go to hell. And I see that the husbands are equally at fault because they're not seeing to it that their wives do submit to them. The old women are just as bad because they're not being an example of submission to the young women, and the old men are equally as bad because they haven't taught the young men to demand obedience from their wives. The mothers are damning their daughters to hell by not teaching them to submit, and the fathers are equally at fault because they're not teaching their sons to expect obedience in their wives. And despite the fact that Linda is in this meeting, I have to say that the Workers are as responsible as anyone else for this abomination because they're doing nothing to assure that wives learn obedience to their husbands."

I was relieved that I was not the sole individual involved in the abomination–I was quite curious, though, about who would follow such a testimony, and what he would say. But we didn't have to wait long to find out.

'Deana', a lady who was visiting from out of town, immediately stood up. A short version of her testimony went something like this: "I can't say how much I appreciated what Jay just said. People in this religion have lost all respect for the laws of God. I was divorced (I think she said something like 20 years ago) and I've respected the rule of not remarrying ever since. I've learned that in 37 states people who are divorced and remarried are allowed to be professing, but I am so glad that our Workers have forbidden that.

There was an unusually long pause before someone else spoke, and the meeting proceeded as civilly as usual. As shocking as this all was, and as concerned as I was about where all this aggression was coming from, I felt very much like an observer. We always thought we had a very good relationship with everyone in our meeting, and our socializing was well-rounded, if somewhat limited by our busy lifestyle.

By late May, Ken and Mary stopped coming to meetings altogether. We were told they'd taken offense at something and had never come back to meetings. By that point Judy and I, and our daughter Karen, were the only ones in the meeting who hadn't been involved in some untenable encounter in the previous six months, and I realized that Linda Passage's fingerprint was found in every one of them. So, I decided to do something I'd never done before – I would investigate something a Worker had said. I knew perfectly well it was taboo in the Truth to question anything a Worker said or did, but at the time I had no intention of doing anything other than finding out exactly what had happened with Ken and Mary. We liked them a lot, and I wasn't willing to let them leave without knowing that we'd still be their good friends.

We invited Ken and Mary to dinner, and I asked if someone had offended them. Ken said he wasn't actually offended, but he'd been given conditions for continuing to go to meeting that he wasn't prepared to accept. The Workers had gone to his house and Linda had told them they should be divorced if they wanted to continue attending meetings. Apparently, the rules in effect for several previous decades were not acceptable any more, at least to Linda. In any case, Ken and Mary were both in their seventies, had been married for about forty years, and divorce would be nothing less than trauma for both of them.

A few things Ken shared about his visit with the Workers I found quite interesting. During the course of the conversation Ken told Linda that the people in the Forbes meeting were shunning them, and Linda enthusiastically added that they (the Workers) would be part of the shunning too. Ken reminded Linda that on the eastern side of the state (which is in another Overseer's jurisdiction) people in Ken and Mary's position could be invited to participate fully in fellowship. Linda acknowledged that is true, but confirmed that in this jurisdiction their marriage was not acceptable. Ironically, while Linda was arguing for them to be divorced, Phyllis observed that their marriage was both "legal and moral"

That was when I began keeping notes.

During this time we began hearing rumors about Bill's evil powers over young girls. Alice was reported to be still in the grip of his controlling mysterious power over her, even controlling her thoughts from jail. I presumed this was an explanation for Alice's having reported to a number of friends that "they made [her] lie to get Bill arrested." No one ever specified who they were who made her lie, though. However, it doesn't quite explain the volumes of messages she left on Bill's answering machines both at home and at work, even after Bill was arrested. But it was the mention of evil and controlling forces that Bill was supposed to be exercising from his jail cell that actually made me wonder who in their right mind was going to buy that foolishness. It was obvious to everyone with any sense – Alice was not going to leave him alone.

More disturbing were efforts to recruit witnesses against Bill, mostly by her father, Norman Dunn. Bill had been ordered to have no contact with anyone under eighteen years of age, and apparently Norman had heard that Bill had called the Marklee house intending to talk to Jane, but one of her daughters had answered and turned the phone over to Jane. Norman then told Jane she had to report to the police that Bill had been talking to her minor daughter (when she answered the telephone). Jane told him she wouldn't call the police or testify against Bill, because she wasn't a witness to anything criminal that Bill might have done. Norman was upset, and Jane told me she finally hung up on him when he began screaming at her.

Soon after that the district attorney called Jane and wanted to talk to her daughters. Jane told them he couldn't talk to her daughters. He became quite demanding of her, threatening warrants, etc. But Jane held her ground and told him he was wasting his time because she was "not going to lie to the court in support of the Dunns." The district attorney must have determined that there was nothing to be gained by pursuing the Marklees, because they were not called to court.

Souza was coming to meetings and having a small part in the few weeks since he'd professed. Everything seemed to be quite in order with him – until one Sunday morning as the meeting ended. Andy Dunn, Bernice's father, went quite literally berserk right in the meeting room. (Recall: Bernice had been sent to Arizona nine months earlier.) As people were getting up to shake hands, Andy began yelling at Souza and threatening him with prison. It alarmed everyone, because he was loud and shook his fist and pointed his finger. Andy and his wife left without greeting anyone, and Souza followed them to their car to try to talk to them. But Andy spun dirt and shook his fist at Souza while he drove away.

But no one seemed inclined to even acknowledge what was happening, and no mention was made of doing anything about it. I talked to Ernie, our elder, and he said he "wouldn't talk to any Worker about anything" because he'd learned over the years that "whoever takes things like this to the Workers ends up in big trouble himself." Nevertheless, I considered such behaviors to be patently unacceptable, and being the alternate elder of the meeting I felt a responsibility to get some help for the situation. But before I did, I evaluated my own position, because I also believed Ernie was right. I had long perceived that if anyone wanted some help from a Worker, he had better known ahead of time that the Worker had nothing to confront him about – otherwise he'd indeed be in trouble himself. I could think of nothing the Workers could accuse me of. Furthermore, I felt confident that a Worker would trust me because it had been leaked to me that I was in line to become the next elder of the meeting – Ernie being quite elderly and not that enthusiastic about continuing as elder.

Since I never got to talk to Linda, I called her. I explained what had happened, and how alarming it was. And I talked to her briefly about Souza's good attitude. I recall telling her that Souza had told my daughter of some changes he'd made because he'd professed. Abruptly Linda said, "Someone is lying." She informed me that Souza had been "participating with Bill", and she would look into the situation. She promised she'd get back to me.

I felt somewhat relieved that I'd handed this problem over to the Workers. I thought I'd get at least some reassurance that we weren't going to be left to the mercy of these people who had become so aggressive with each other. But I was really alarmed to learn that Souza had "participated with Bill". I imagined some kind of wild orgy going on with Alice Dunn, something even more bizarre than anything I'd previously imagined.

The next Sunday Linda appeared in our meeting. I should say, we found her sitting in her car at the entrance to the yard. She came into the meeting at one minute before time to start. At the end of the meeting she announced that Souza would no longer be coming to our meeting. She said he had a very serious psychological problem, and it was dangerous to have him among us. She went on to explain that he'd been told not to contact the Friends. She added that she wouldn't "advise anyone to treat him badly, but ...." The implication was clear – she really wasn't advising us to treat him well. In the Forbes' meeting that day it was announced after the meeting that Souza was not to associate with us anymore.

I wasn't about to disturb the "peace" of the meeting by asking questions about Souza's serious psychological problem, so I decided I'd get my opportunity to ask when Linda got back to me. But Linda never did get back to me, and I was about to learn that Linda and I weren't going to have any mature discussion about anything.

CHAPTER 6

What Really Happened

In July of 1998, Linda left the area to go to Idaho for convention. She was only gone a day or so when Phyllis called and asked if she could come for a visit. We were really glad to have her. We'd looked forward to having her visit us, but the year had passed and the Workers hadn't come to our house. We'd even bought a wok because we were told that Linda wanted her vegetables stir fried. My wife remarked that it was interesting that Phyllis had come to visit us as soon as Linda left town.

We had a very good visit with Phyllis – three or four days. We shared lots of memories, pictures, and thoroughly enjoyed each other's company. One evening while she was with us, Bill called and asked to speak to Phyllis. What he wanted was an opportunity to meet with people in the meeting to offer an apology for what he'd done. Phyllis didn't want to give him an answer. She was actually the more elder of the two Workers, but because of her age she no longer took the *responsible* role for the area where she was preaching. That made Linda the *responsible Worker*, as one would say. So, she said she'd talk to Linda and get back to him.

After Bill finished talking to Phyllis, I talked to him. I asked him if his case had concluded, and he said that it would be later in July that he'd know what was going to happen to him. I got him to promise that he'd let me know where he was, should he be locked up, and he agreed. I felt uneasy asking him some things in our conversation, but we'd not been given any information about what was going on with him. All we'd heard was repeated mention that we weren't to associate with him. I don't know what Phyllis thought of my side of the conversation.

Phyllis then called Linda at the convention property in Idaho, and Linda said she'd have to pray about it and would get back to her. And she did get back about an hour later. Her message was that it would not be appropriate for him to apologize to the church. She said it would be nothing more than a ploy to get the sympathy of the people in the meeting. Phyllis was clearly uncomfortable calling Bill and giving him that message. I was aghast. I'd never heard of a Worker talking like that about someone's attempts to apologize.

A while after the telephone conversation Phyllis began to talk about Bill. I didn't ask any questions – she just volunteered the information. She said, "You know, Bill has not lied to anyone about anything." That startled me in its implication. She proceeded to say that if Bill were not restricted by the law he'd be free to go to some other state and fully participate in meeting again. She was clearly uncomfortable with the fact that Bill was isolated from everyone else. What I understood from the conversation was that we, and probably most others, really didn't know what had happened – and Phyllis was not at liberty to counter anything Linda had led everyone to believe.

Why would Phyllis tell us that Bill had not lied to anyone about anything? Well, there's somewhat of a taboo among *people of Truth* about accusing any of the others of actually *lying*. So the best Phyllis could do was tell us that Bill, the only one accused of a crime, had told the truth – and as it turned out, we'd been forbidden to communicate with him. Phyllis obviously had no problem with me talking to him, or she could have said something to that effect.

The case I had let rest in my mind abruptly became active again. And more than that, I got a sneaking suspicion that I was on dangerous ground – that is, I knew something I wasn't supposed to mention.

About this time I got a phone call from Andy Dunn. Linda had asked him to call me and tell me that she'd sent a letter to Souza. Andy had a copy of it, so I concluded this was Linda's way of getting back to me. Andy volunteered to read the letter to me, and it went something like this:

I have concluded, after talking to Bob Williston, that you should not be allowed in the company of the Friends any more. You have very serious moral problems, and we do not want you contaminating our young people. We are demanding that you not appear in any fellowship meeting, Bible study meeting, gospel meeting, special meetings, convention, or any social gathering of the friends. Before you are allowed to associate with our Friends again in any way you must get psychological counseling and sign a waiver allowing the counselor to discuss the contents of your treatment sessions with the Workers.

There was not a mention of anything he had actually done. I was so completely shocked that I couldn't respond.

Then Andy volunteered to tell me more about Bill's *problem*. According to him, there had been a big wild party at Norman Dunn's house and Norman and his wife had come home unexpectedly in the middle of it and called the police on Bill and two other guys. This was quite a new twist to the story. But I couldn't quite figure out where the assault came in if it was a party – surely there were other witnesses at the scene who could testify against Bill if that were the case. And it didn't make sense that Alice's parents just by chance arrived home to be able to catch the assault in progress.

Andy went on to explain that Bill had a history of molesting young girls, and he named a girl in California who was supposed to be his victim as well. He commented that it was too bad he had not been arrested in California – it would have gotten him off the streets before he came to Nevada. As luck would have it, I knew the parents of the girl in California. I'll take a brief skip forward here and mention that sometime later at a convention I got to ask the mother of the girl if they'd ever met Bill Frost, and she looked bewildered and said she'd never heard of such a person.

I was so distraught about Linda's using my name the way she did that I went to the store where Souza worked. I told him Andy had read Linda's letter to me, and I asked him how the letter had been delivered to him. He said Linda and Phyllis had just come into the store, walked up to him, handed it to him, and immediately turned and left. I assured him in no uncertain terms that I had not given Linda reason to do what she'd done, and he said he knew the minute he read the letter that I hadn't said anything negative about him.

I mentioned to Bea and Ernie how upset I was that Linda had used my name the way she did. Bea was upset too, and said they'd not been given any reason for his banishment either. She did tell me that she'd also gone to the store to tell Souza she was sorry for what had happened. But like she said, "What can we do?"

It was following this incident that I began waking at night and wondering what this was all about. I couldn't deal with the fact that Linda had *used* me to kick someone out. I was beginning to feel walled in because there wasn't anyone who would respond to any comment or question about either Bill or Souza. It was like they'd all frozen up and were making sure there'd be no communication about these matters that could be traced back to them.

Meanwhile, the occasional tidbit of a rumor would come along. I don't ask many questions – I learn more by just being alert. One mention was that the police had recovered pornographic pictures of Alice from Bill's apartment, as well as his diary. The diary was reported to be a sick discourse of religious and sexual ranting. I don't know where this originated, but it was repeated by the Workers.

I didn't know the *Who's Who* of the West Coast Friends, but I'd become good friends with 'George', an elderly Friend who lived in Reno. He'd lived in the California jurisdiction all his life and knew most Workers and prominent Friends very well. Several times he'd explained the *who's who* behind some baffling incidents for me, so I decided to discuss this ongoing situation with him. He became as troubled as I was. To this day he remains the one person in the area to assure me of my integrity in dealing with the situation. In fact, he was the only person who even had the backbone to describe what was going on, and he called it *disgusting*.

In September 'Norma Frost', Bill's mother, called me from 'Michigan'. She'd been trying to find me for quite some time because Bill had asked her to let me know where he was. It turned out he was in the Minden Jail, almost within sight of the school where I worked.

I told her I was concerned about a lot that was happening in Northern Nevada. She said she was most discouraged because of the treatment she'd received from our Workers. Linda had berated her for providing bail for Bill when he was first arrested – Linda thought he should have been left in jail. Linda told her Bill's final sentence was a *mere pittance* compared with what he should have received. Norma said the most humiliating experience of her life was to be in court and see *all the buns* (the most common hairstyle of women among the Friends) on the other side of the courtroom demanding more punishment for her son than even the prosecutor had recommended.

Norma volunteered to send me a copy of Linda's letter to her. To call it shocking is an understatement. First of all she told Norma that Bill had never approached her about making things right, and I knew that to be a lie, as I have already mentioned. She described Bill as ...

> *what his thinking and egotism have driven him to do. [She told Norma she should] search [her] own heart to see if [she] contributed to his feeling that he is somehow superior to others, immune to laws that apply to others, worthy to receive but not required to give if it isn't convenient or comfortable, exempt from the consequences that others must suffer for wrongdoing.*[1]

Linda acknowledged that Norma had called and left her a message, but she said she hadn't called back because it seemed worthless to do so unless Norma came to agree with her that ...

> *a normal foundation for social interaction with others appears to be missing in Bill's thinking. [She claimed that Bill's] deliberate dishonesty destroys confidence and discredits much or all of what [the workers] say.*[2]

I arranged to visit Bill in jail, and walked over one day after class. We talked through a glass window by telephone. He was completely broken up, and obviously quite confused about what was going on among the Friends regarding him. I had a good visit with him, and promised to go back. This I was able to do many times while he was there. But we could write letters to each other through the mail.

A day or two after my first visit with Bill, my daughter Karen came to me quite distressed. She was working as a parole and probation caseworker and had just been assigned to supervise Bill when he was released from jail. She couldn't let me read any of her documents, but she told me I'd better investigate Bill's case because she was shocked at what she'd read about him. Her summary statement was, "He's been shafted and we've all been lied to."

So, with Bill's consent I investigated the court records, and I also was shocked. It described in detail everything that had taken place, and it amounted to making out – petting, if that's the term in present day usage. Interestingly, it stated that both parties were still virgins. The report emphatically stated that (a) no force was used, and that (b) there had been no sexual intercourse. As a father of two daughters, I could not even imagine by what perverse means such activities were even discovered, much less reported to the police – especially considering that Alice had been allowed to travel unchaperoned out of state with Bill.

The court had even received a complaint that Bill had gotten Mexicans to harass the Dunn children on their way to school. That was patently ridiculous. The Dunn children didn't even go to school, and Alice managed the household while her mother worked. Fascinating was the fact that the judge had asked why the family wanted him (the judge) to exceed the punishment recommended by the prosecutor. The explanation given was that people in the church were not comfortable with him being out on the streets. To my knowledge the church was never consulted.

You will recall that we were told that Bill was a repeat offender. Ironically, the judge is on record as noting that Bill had never offended before. The court also recognized that Bill had been a coach for a number of years for juvenile girls' volleyball teams. The judge asked what the family made of the fact that he had received many letters from these teams and the girls' parents recommending Bill very highly for his propriety. The family had no response for that.

The prosecutor actually asked that Bill be given a period of probation. However, the judge in that court is an elected public official, and they have to recognize that the clergy in such conservative communities deliver votes – thus my suspicion. Instead of probation. the judge sentenced him to 6 months in jail and 5 years' probation. Without any doubt, what influenced the judge was the fact that the Workers were present and (Linda for sure) wanted him locked up.

Word quickly got around that I'd been visiting Bill in jail. For a while there'd been no verbal violence in our meetings, but I did sense there was still some tension. Then late in the month I was informed by a couple of people that I should be careful because I was being preached at continuously in meetings – Nancy (wife of Jay Clark, of the fiery Sunday testimony about unsubmissive wives) was speaking every meeting about the need to obey the Workers in all things. I guess it was obvious to others that I was the one in the meeting who was disobeying the Workers. I'd never been told personally not to associate with Bill, but I probably would have visited him anyway – I once visited a murderer in prison because of the positive relationship he and I had. But I did begin to notice that disobedience was Nancy's constant theme, with a variety of barbed asides for anyone who wanted to accept them.

At this point I was still trying to attribute the whole situation to a miscalculation on Linda's part, for lack of a better term. I figured she had a problem, but I didn't know exactly what it was. My friend George had the same suspicions. He gave me a copy of a letter she'd sent to all the young people in the area. It was about fornication, and in her introduction she wrote that professing parents were not giving their children proper instruction about sex. She stressed that with respect to fornication the male has to be more responsible than the female – no reason given. I found it quite disturbing that she would emphasize that the most important thing to teach young people is that *there is no forgiveness for fornication*. I did not believe that, and I didn't think the Workers, in general, believed that either. As a parent, I found it offensive that a Worker would presume to offer sex education to juveniles without their parents' approval. It occurred to me that, to be a Worker, she really wasn't any more qualified to teach sex education than the child predator Worker who'd previously been in the area.

There came another report that I decided to follow up on. It was that a meeting had been held with Bill, the Workers, the Dunn family, the elder and alternate elder, and brother Workers from California. Reportedly, Bill was warned at this meeting to "stop what he was doing". But that meeting did not take place, or I would have been there myself. I asked the elder of our meeting if he'd heard of such a meeting, and he said he'd never heard of it.

Probably the most interesting piece of information I received was that, while they were booking Bill at the time of his arrest, he told the policeman that he should call Alice's parents and they would assure him that he (Bill) had not "raped" their daughter. The policeman laughed and said, "They're the ones who reported you."

In October the annual Special Meeting Day came about – a full day of meetings for the whole area with a full slate of visiting Worker speakers. During the week of Special Meeting Sunday it is normal practice for every household in the area to receive a visit from one or more Workers, be it for a meal or for an overnight stay. In Northern Nevada it was also normal for all the Friends in the area to get together for a pot luck dinner one evening during the week. That year, however, my family didn't get a copy of such a schedule, and neither had we received any notice about where and when the potluck was to be held. At the Sunday meeting before the Special Meetings someone made mention of the potluck. So I asked about it, and someone pulled out his copy of the week's visitations and gave me an extra copy that he had. He also reminded me that we'd need our own copy so we could plan on our visit from the Workers.

When I got home I checked the schedule – we weren't even listed on the schedule. Since it was undoubtedly Linda who'd made the schedule, my wife accepted it as a snub and suggested we weren't invited to the potluck either. But we went anyway. I convinced her that we were automatically invited.

On the day of Special Meetings we had a visiting Worker from Oregon who had a wonderful message for us. It was all about how to treat a brother that had been overcome in a fault. His whole sermon was completely contrary to what we'd been told to do concerning Bill. I watched people's faces, and the two people who were the most openly supportive of Bill's banishment were enthusiastically nodding their heads in agreement through the whole sermon. It kind of sickened me – this Worker was abundantly explicit in his description of how not to treat a brother. On the way out of the meetings that day I asked one of these men if any of that applied to Bill, and the answer was a terse: "Bill is not a brother – he's a heathen."

A couple of times that day I came into a position to meet Linda, but both times she changed her direction and we never did meet. While we were having lunch we were chatting with 'Helen', an 80 year old lady who had one of the Reno meetings in her home. She began crying – she said she'd been professing for 35 years and she'd never been overlooked for a Special Meeting visit. We tried to comfort her because we were in the same situation. But she continued and told us that Linda had been to her house for meeting many times, and she'd avoided shaking Helen's hand every time following the meeting. As it turned out, there was another elderly lady in the area who was also receiving mean treatment by Linda, much to her distress also.

Following Special Meetings I decided that something needed to be done. Not only did we have a serious problem among us, but no one was going to do anything about it. Since I was the alternate elder in our meeting in Carson City, I felt I had a responsibility to do something. Other than the couple of very close friends that I'd discussed this with, I hadn't really mentioned it to anyone. I decided I should first of all discuss it with Linda. I was still hoping that she'd consider my concerns valid.

On October 16, I wrote her a letter. I explained that I was shocked at the difference between what we'd been told about Bill and what actually went on in court. I wrote:

I read the court record and I became deeply disturbed. I learned that Bill Frost did NO THING that I myself have not done. I anticipate the response will be that such things should not be mentioned among us. I agree. But the fact remains that (and you will have to pardon my frankness) all the things he did, without exception, are things that lovers do. ... What I read in the court record sounds like an invasion of privacy, and I shudder to think of the devious means by which such information should have originally been brought to light. These things are not perverted they are private. The disgusting part was that they were made public. Incidently, these two people are both still virgins they did NOT have sexual intercourse.

I probably should not have used the word "lovers", because I have no idea what Linda considers lovers to be. I realize some people don't consider couples to be "lovers" until they do have sexual intercourse, but at the time I was mostly concerned that she'd treated it like some violent perversion perpetrated upon an unwilling victim.

I also told her that I was offended that she would use my name to put Souza out of fellowship. I told her I was afraid to go to meeting any more because I didn't know when I would be the next person to get yelled at. I begged her to help us deal with the horrible situation we had come to. Following Special Meetings she was gone for a couple of weeks for Special Meetings in other places, but I knew she had her mail forwarded to her while she was on her tour. I felt relieved at having taken this to her because I thought it was something a Worker would be concerned about. But before I got an answer from her, another shocking incident occurred.

About 3:00 a.m. one Monday morning the telephone rang, and I got a computer message advising me that I was about to get a collect call from the Minden Jail. That was where Bill was being held, and it crossed my mind that he could be in some kind of predicament. I'd told him he could call me whenever he wanted. But the phone call was from Jay Clark. By this time I was sitting bolt upright on the side of the bed. The conversation went something like this:

ME: Hello,
JAY: Hi. I guess you know who's calling and where I am.
ME: What side of the window are you on?
JAY: I'm on the inside. I've been arrested for domestic violence.
ME: Oh.
JAY: What do you think of me now?

ME: You're a brother, and brothers make mistakes. I think you're the same person I had fellowship with yesterday morning.

I went on to explain to him that in the position he was in there would be lots of people who would want to punish him, but it was not a brother's place to punish. I assured him that until everything was restored to order again, I'd stand beside him for whatever help he would need. He sighed, and said, "It's been a long hard lot of years." I felt sorry for him, and I was glad to have the opportunity to assure him right from the beginning how I'd treat him.

The next day, from my school, I called the jail to see if it was possible to visit him, and I was told that his brother had raised his bail and Jay had gone home. But when I called his house his wife Nancy answered, and she told me he was at his mother's house. Naive me, I asked her if she would ask him to call me when he came back in; and she told me that he couldn't come back – he had to stay over there for a week. And it dawned on me that he was on his cooling down restriction.

I assumed that, since he'd called me, it was safe enough to mention his predicament to Nancy. I told her that I was very sorry about their situation and I wanted to assure her I would do what I could for either one of them. To which she sharply replied: "How did you learn about this?" I told her Jay had called me from jail, and she didn't seem to appreciate that. But she did go on to tell me she'd called "911" because her girlfriend had made her promise that the next time he *did it* she'd call the police. So, she dialed the number to satisfy the promise, but hung up before the police could answer. Thus, she learned that when a "911" caller hangs up a police car is immediately dispatched to the location of the caller. She also told me that what worried her most was that he would lose his well-paying government job because of this. How typical the predicament.

Then I called Jay and we talked briefly. He was appreciative, and I left things as they were. But what surprised us greatly following this incident was that Nancy from that day to this has not spoken a word to either Judy or Karen. Perhaps she knew that Judy kept criminal records for the state, and Karen was a parole and probation officer for the state corrections, and it embarrassed her. After meetings she would turn her back on them and avoid them at all cost. This was difficult for Judy and Karen to deal with because not only did we meet with them every Sunday, we also went to *union meetings* in their house. *Union meeting* is the term used for a combined meeting of two regular meeting groups on the first Sunday of each month.

Then to top off this eventful month, there was going to be a birthday party picnic in a county park between Carson City and Reno. It was to be held on Hallowe'en, which was a public holiday in Nevada. It was also Karen's birthday as well as Ben Hull's, a young man who lived in Reno. Ben had recently returned from Peru where he'd been living for some time. He'd been married down there, and he'd just returned in September with his wife, who at that time was pregnant. A couple of nights before the picnic Ben's grandfather, in whose house they were living, rolled over in his sleep and hit the "911" button on his telephone. But as with Nancy Clark, because the police did not get an answer when they called back, two policemen were dispatched to the house.

To the police officers it aroused suspicion of a burglary in progress. Not seeing any life in the house, they tried a door and it opened, so they walked in. Ben's wife heard them coming in and she woke Ben and told him there was someone in the house. He got out of bed and went to the living room, and reached for a fireplace poker as he entered the living room. The policeman then turned his light on Ben and, when he saw the poker lifted, shot him dead. This was a most tragic time for everyone in the area.

And we were still waiting for Linda to return to the area and calm our uneasiness.

CHAPTER 7

How The Game Is Played

On the first Sunday of November it was time again for union meeting at Jay Clark's house. We wondered what would happen after Jay was arrested – considering what Bill's non-violent offense had cost him. A rumor had quietly circulated that Linda Passage suspected a divorce was in the offing, which I dismissed as nonsense. Hearing no alternate instructions, we went to Jay's house as usual. He was seated between Linda and Nancy, everyone else arrived, Linda began the meeting on time, and Jay officiated as normal. When a Worker is present, his role involves only passing the emblems.

After the meeting, as I helped put chairs away, Linda approached me and said: "Bob, I received your letter. About your concerns, the brother Workers in California decided what was to be done. And I have to add that my companion and I are very disappointed and disapprove of the lifestyle you and your wife have chosen." Three sentences. I know I stared at her with my mouth open. I said nothing.

I didn't actually believe what she'd told me – or I should say, I didn't believe what she *wanted me to understand* from it. She didn't outright lie, of course. But neither had she said that her *Overseer* had decided what was to be done, and neither had she said that *Phyllis* had actually told her she disapproved of our lifestyle. By then so many contradictions had come from the local rumor mill that I was really suspicious. We'd heard that both Linda and Norman Dunn had on occasion claimed to be responsible for Bill's arrest. Interestingly, we'd also heard that they'd both blamed the other for his arrest. I concluded that the Overseer needed to know what was going on.

On November 4 I wrote to Dick Middleton, who was relatively new as Worker Overseer for the California jurisdiction. So he'd know I wasn't misrepresenting my communications with Linda, I included a copy of my letter to her. I was almost frozen with fear when I dropped the letter in the mailbox because of everything I'd ever heard about reporting a Worker to his/her Overseer. But my conscience reminded me of what I might be responsible for myself if I didn't voice my objection to what I believed was seriously wrong doctrine, say nothing of ruining lives. The whole idea of shunning and banishment was totally foreign to me, and I found it loathsome.

The following is an excerpt from my letter to Dick:

> *This past Sunday morning Linda did acknowledge receipt of my letter ... It amounted to a summary dismissal of my concern. I was told Bill's punishment was recommended by brother workers in California. She also took advantage of the occasion to tell me that she was "sorry my wife and I have chosen such a lifestyle, but she and her companion disapproved." I know what she meant. In the context of our dialog she as much as told me that my wife and I have a sexually perverted lifestyle. I thought that as a concerned brother, a respected husband, father, and grandfather, and a successfully and happily married person, and one who has endeavored from an early age to live righteously, that I could offer her the assurance that there are normal things about love relationships that she is not familiar with. I am not personally offended, but I have never heard of a worker making such a demeaning comment about a respectfully married professing grandmother. It also concerns me that others have gotten such cutting remarks when they have approached her about matters of serious concern to them.*

I remember deciding, when I took my problem to the Workers, that I'd be meticulous in everything I wrote. I'd tell them nothing about anyone without knowing exactly who told me, and that he/she had witnessed it personally. Fortunately, I'd previously begun keeping a record of troubling incidents; and I occasionally asked questions of unsuspecting people, checking to see if they could refute something I'd been told. It was the wisest move I made, because over time it became obvious that I'd have fared far worse had I reported anything incorrectly.

On the first Saturday of December I visited Bill in jail, and learned that Jay Clark was in there with him. He was serving a 2-day sentence for the domestic battery he'd called me about in the middle of the night. While locked up together, Jay told Bill that he really shouldn't be speaking to him because Linda Passage had told him that Bill was evil, but he talked anyway. One of Jay's concerns was that he be let out by his scheduled 6:00 a.m. Sunday morning release time. That Sunday was another union meeting day, and he had to be home early enough to get the house ready for meeting and the pot luck planned for afterwards.

Jay was indeed home when we went there on Sunday morning. It's possible no one but we and Jay's family knew he'd been in jail overnight, so the meeting proceeded as uneventfully as the meeting following his arrest – this time Phyllis was there instead of Linda. We didn't stay for the pot luck; not because we had a problem with Jay, but because Judy and Karen were uncomfortable with the way Nancy was snubbing them. The meeting went smoothly, but Nancy called Jane Marklee the next day and berated her for gossiping about her (Nancy). Jane understood that Nancy was upset by something Bill had told Jay in jail, but Nancy wouldn't tell her what it was. Then a few days later Nancy called Jane back and explained that she wasn't blaming her for what Bill had told Jay, because Bill could have heard it from anyone.

About that time I began weighing in my mind some of the Workers' duplicitous adjudications. It appeared that if Linda were properly representative of the California ministry, then spousal battery could be excused, but *making out* was cause for banishment. One of the justifications for Bill's treatment was that he was far too much older than Alice for them to be a couple – I'm estimating their difference in age was at the very most eight years, but with her parents consent she could have been married. Ironically, there was a newlywed ex-Worker in the meeting whose wife was thirteen years younger than him, but that seemed not to be a problem despite the fact that they were a teen-and-thirties couple instead of a teen-and-twenties couple. The greatest inconsistency of all about Bill's case was that there was the other newlywed couple in the meeting that had actually conceived a child out of wedlock and were never prevented from coming to meetings, and were even permitted to re-profess before the baby was born – and nothing Bill and Alice did could possibly have produced a baby.

The other puzzling duplicity was that Linda had advised Ken and Mary Hornady, the elderly divorced and remarried couple, that they shouldn't return to meetings until they divorced. Yet there was a lady in a Reno meeting who was on her fourth husband and still came to meetings. She even got to take part in meetings in the period between her third and fourth marriage. I do believe there must be consequences for certain offenses – after all, no organization can permit individuals to openly defy their tenets. But if the consequences for the same offense are not equal for all individuals, it speaks loudly of favoritism. For me, even when I feel the consequences are more severe than necessary, such variations in the consequences only speak more loudly of abuse and favoritism. Duplicity of treatment is not acceptable in any case for a variety of reasons. Furthermore, I believe it's simply not acceptable for anyone who purports to be a minister of truth to lie or mislead anyone on any matter – no matter what expedience it affords. After all, the Workers refer to their ministry as "the Truth".

I received no answer from Dick Middleton through December. It was rumored, though, that Linda and Phyllis had received a letter from him in which he asked whether they'd been to jail to visit Bill. They hadn't, of course, but Linda didn't go anyway. Phyllis did go to see him, but Bill wasn't much encouraged by her visit. She explained to him that he was there because of what he'd done, as though he didn't know that. Concerning his permission to return to meetings, she advised him that it would involve a very long time of proving himself. He confided to her that he'd once thought he might volunteer to go into the ministry, and she suggested he was having *visions of grandeur*. Of course, what else could she say to him, having to account to Linda for any hope she'd give him. I presume she still remembered what she'd told me about the possibility that he could be fully participating in meetings if only he could move to some other state. Interestingly, by the time Phyllis visited Bill, his release date was less than a week away, and the visit left him really depressed.

It was telling, and strangely amusing, that Velma Bunch speculated out loud that it would now be okay for people to speak to Bill – since Dick Middleton had suggested the sister Workers visit him. I mention this because it was such unquestionable evidence that people were actually forbidden to even speak to Bill.

Bill was let out of jail a couple of days before Christmas, and his mother and father came from Michigan to spend Christmas with him at our place. On the morning he was released, there was a small number of us there to greet him – Bill's parents, the Hornadys, a friend of Bill's from where he used to work, and Judy, Karen, my grandson and me. It was a Saturday morning, and there was no one else in sight, anywhere. We just waited near the door, then suddenly the door opened, Bill stepped out, and the door closed. All he had with him was a clear plastic trash bag with his belongings in it.

The contents of Bill's clear plastic bag turned out to amaze me. For no other reason than to see if they'd returned all his belongings, he examined the contents of the bag. He was talking to me, so I felt no need to give him privacy, and to my surprise he drew out the *disgusting* items that were supposed to have been confiscated at the time of his arrest as evidence against him. If it had been evidence, neither he nor the jailer would have had it. I knew how that court operated – I routinely took my government students there, where they not only witnessed court procedure, but got to have discussions with both judges and attorneys.

Bill offered to let me read the *disgusting diary*, and I was just a bit worried about what I'd read. But I had no need to worry – it turned out to be not dissimilar to the contents of my day planner, a record of appointments and notes about concerns. And the *pornographic picture* of Alice turned out to be a picture of her in a yellow two piece swim suit – not in any aspect more revealing than swim wear I'd seen on married professing women in public pools. There was nothing in the bag that even remotely resembled the sex toys Bill's brother was rumored to have sent him from a state on the east coast. I've never mentioned anything to Bill about such reports about him. But after having seen the full range of physical evidence against him, I felt that I'd be proud of any twenty year old son of mine who had the police scour his apartment and find nothing more than they'd found in Bill's apartment.

Bill also offered to let me read a note Linda had sent him while in jail. It was scribbled on a scrap of paper, and in fewer than a hundred words she berated him for assuming that he could communicate with her, and advised him that he needed to accept that he wasn't worthy of fellowship with the rest of us. It was terse and nasty.

We felt rather nervous going to meeting the next morning. People knew we had Bill at our house, and Bill's mother went to meeting with us that morning. Bill stayed home with his father. Bill's mother apparently didn't fully grasp the bitterness of some in the meeting against Bill, and she did something that made me hold my breath. She mentioned how much kindness Bill had received from various Friends and Workers while he was locked up. The reaction around the room was priceless. Some people looked at her like she was nuts! I dared not even smile, but it was the most innocently delivered slap in the face one could imagine.

One of the stipulations of Bill's probation was that he couldn't be around any person under eighteen years of age. People who wanted to permit Bill to visit them with their children present had to write letters of agreement to the Parole and Probation office that they'd at no time allow their children to be alone with Bill. Judy and I also wrote letters for our two grand-children, to cover times when we were caring for them. The Marklees, who'd also visited Bill while he was in jail, also provided a letter so Bill could go to their house.

Our daughter Karen had other restrictions placed on her because she worked as a parole and probation case Worker. She wasn't allowed to have social contact with any convicted person or his family without the prior permission of her boss. This she had to do for each occasion that she visited with Bill or his parents. That restriction remained in effect for as long as she worked in that government department.

In January of 1999, after Bill's parents had gone back home, and it was obvious no official permission was going to be granted for us to associate with him, the few Friends who'd stayed close to him got together with him on weekend evenings for perhaps a couple of months. Making it a Bible study was suggested, but that never materialized. Meanwhile, most Friends who had children gladly wrote letters to Bill's probation officer allowing him to be around their children. It was only a short time until all but four families in Northern Nevada had done so. One couple even wrote a second letter because they'd had a new baby after they'd written their first letter.

When I finally heard from Dick Middleton he asked for a copy of the records available from Bill's case, so I faxed them to him. Then on a twenty-four-hour notice Dick wanted to see Bill and me in the Bay Area at 9:00 a.m. For us it involved staying overnight in a motel so we could be there for that hour. It turned out we were also meeting with Eldon Tenniswood, the previous Overseer who'd left his duties to Dick. It was curious to me that we were meeting them in the Bay Area, because that year they were both located in southern California. I later realized they were just passing through the Bay Area on their way back from a very troubling situation in Alberta – which was not entirely unlike the problem we were having in Northern Nevada. I relate more about that situation in Chapter 23. But at the time the most egregious problem for them, whether they realized it or not, was a California Worker who was a child sexual predator, which I write about in Chapter 15. The coincidence of that case erupting at the same time as Bill's case just exacerbated a troubling aspect in Friend-Worker relationships.

When we arrived at our appointment, Dick and Eldon saw Bill first, in another room with the door closed. I spent the morning visiting with the man of the house. At noon, the lady of the house provided us all with a lunch, and then I got to talk to Dick and Eldon. Looking back, I suspect it was quite on purpose that Bill and I weren't allowed to be together when our concerns were being discussed.

Despite all I'd written to both Linda and Dick, Dick asked me to tell him what I was concerned about. I told him I was there to support Bill in his efforts to be allowed to attend meetings. I didn't offer much.

Furthermore, it was he who called the meeting, and I figured he should have been telling me his concerns, not the other way around. So for some time I mostly waited and made him ask questions.

Finally I got a question that allowed me to tell him I was concerned that Linda had led me to believe he'd approved of everything she'd done. That shocked him, and he blurted, "I didn't tell her to do that." Then he caught himself and regained his composure.

Before long, I figured out why I was there – I was having my integrity scrutinized so I could be put on the defensive, and they'd never have to address my concerns. I knew exactly what was going on – I'd taken college courses on how to deal with students who were shrewd enough to use those tactics on teachers and make their lives miserable. Dick asked me about things I'd written, clearly attempting to find me in some kind of error on each point. He made a few of attempts to show that Bill had contradicted what I'd said, and I pointed out that he was actually misquoting what I'd written. I offered nothing more, and just sat and waited for him to think of something else to ask.

After one such pause he reached into a briefcase and pulled out a couple of papers. I immediately recognized the one he began reading to himself. It was a copy of the nasty letter Linda had written to Bill's mother, and I marveled that Linda had even provided him with it. I'd expect a Worker to be ashamed of having written such a letter to anyone. Dick was letting his finger slide down the page as he read, so I waited until he came to the precise paragraph where Linda had told Bill's mother that Bill had never asked to return to meeting. When he got there, I spoke up and said, "The paragraph you're pointing at now – that's not true. Before Linda wrote that letter I personally delivered a message about that from Bill to Linda, and I know Linda answered because I listened to Phyllis delivering Linda's answer. She said it would not be appropriate for him to meet with us and apologize." That ended any discussion of Linda's letter.

Dick then made an attempt to cast aspersions on Bill's family. He suggested that Bill wouldn't necessarily understand good family morals anyway because his parents were separated. That surprised me, but he was equally surprised when I told him that was not true, Bill's parents did indeed live together and had visited us together in Nevada.

It would be interesting to know where he got that idea, but I didn't want to put him on the defensive by asking.

When Dick first broached the matter of Bill and Alice's behavior he told me that he understood lust, as though to dispense with any discussion of mitigating circumstances. Then he added that he believed most of the professing young people in California could be trusted to behave themselves. He'd never have said such a thing if he'd known how many daughters of meeting elders were taken to the doctor for birth control pills at the time of their first monthly period. I was not about to let him believe that Bill and Alice were a rare exception in California.

He attempted to make the point that Bill had raped Alice, which surprised me because I assumed he'd read the documents I'd sent him. I reminded him that the police report stated clearly that it was not a rape. I also pointed out that, while some of the charges against Bill were dropped – undoubtedly because Bill never protested any of the justifiable charges against him – none of them were for rape either, not even for statutory rape, which in Nevada allows little defense because of the hard and fast rule involving the 18 to 21 age gap. In any case, Alice was legally of age to consent to sexual intercourse without her parents' permission – her only restriction was that she was limited by law to only having sex with people under the age of twenty-one. However, that restriction wouldn't apply if she had parental permission to marry.

But Dick persisted. His apparent definition of rape included everything except the consensual non-manually assisted penile penetration of one's wife. He explained that he'd read in the newspaper that a married man had been convicted of rape because he'd digitally penetrated his wife. It was obvious he couldn't imagine the circumstances of such a rape. I felt like laughing ... but it was disconcerting for two reasons, first that he was so incredibly naive, and then to realize that from his perspective and position he got to pass such judgments for which there was no appeal process.

But I'd gone all that distance and spent all that time and money to oblige him with the discussion, so I gave him a brief lesson on what constituted *normal* sexual behavior – undoubtedly outside his moral code, but perfectly normal according to the definition of *normal* – even for normal *professing* people. I never imagined in my whole lifetime that I'd ever have occasion to discuss such intimacies with a Worker, but I found myself much more comfortable with it than he did.

So I asked Dick about the young married couple in our meeting who'd conceived a baby out of wedlock. Eldon, who was sitting with us and appeared to be nodding off occasionally, abruptly opened his eyes. Eldon was the Worker who'd told the couple not to speak in meetings, but had never banished them. I noted that they'd apparently done a lot more than Bill and Alice, yet they were given vastly different treatment. Neither made a comment. I further reminded him that I knew of Workers who'd done far worse than any of these young people, and they (the offending Workers) were not even told to stop speaking in meetings. Dick admitted: "We have sheltered others from prosecution."

Then I brought up the treatment Ken and Mary Hornady had received, compared to the other divorced and remarried people in our area. I knew Ken and Mary had professed as a married couple in Dick Middleton's meetings, and he'd even advised Mary that she could speak in meetings because she hadn't been aware of the Workers' rules on marriage before she'd married Ken.

At that point Dick apparently decided to deliver the blow. He said, "You know, you're really far out on a limb with this." I asked how so. He said, "You wrote that Bill did no thing that you have not done." I said that was true. And he asked, "Have you committed a crime?"

I decided not to answer. This restrained tug of war had already gone on for two hours, and I'd not gone there to discuss my own failings, or Bill's either for that matter. So I said, "We didn't come here to have anything excused. It's now over two years since this incident occurred, and Bill has completed his time in jail. Now we have a prodigal beating on the door and we have Workers locking the door and wanting him banished. What, if anything, can you do for us?" He was quite stunned at that. He obviously hadn't intended to deal with that. He stood up and walked around the room, and said something about hoping he wouldn't get shingles again.

He said to me, "I've been told that the Friends in your area don't want Bill in their meetings." And I replied, "It doesn't surprise me that you were told that. But I'm here to tell you that all but four parents in the field have already signed agreements with the police to allow Bill to be in meetings with their children present." Then he said, "I don't like to interfere with Workers in their fields." And his final comment was that I was "promoting immorality among our young people." I decided not to dignify the comment with an answer. However, the one thing I have to say for Dick Middleton is that he never lied to me or attempted to deceive me in any way.

As I was leaving I got the most comic insight into Dick's naivete. For some reason he told Eldon about one of the Friends who'd gotten to shake hands with President Clinton. And Dick added, "I asked him if he washed his hand afterward." And they chuckled. I gave him the benefit of the doubt and took it to be a political joke rather than a risque reference to an incident in a White House closet.

Later in February Dick wanted to see me at my house on a certain day at 3:00 p.m. So I took the afternoon off work to meet with him and Harold Hilton. Dick began by asking me to relate my concerns to Harold. I was exasperated – they'd apparently bought airline tickets to come to Nevada to ask me again what my concerns were! So I just asked Harold if he'd read the letter I'd sent to Dick. He looked rather sheepishly at Dick, who didn't respond, and then said he'd been given an idea of what it was about. There was nothing new to tell them, so I told them I was concerned that there was so much strife in the meetings, and I was worried I'd be the next person to get booted around in some manner. I intentionally didn't say much, and they said practically nothing. Dick casually repeated his opinion that I was "promoting immorality among our young people." That I did not care to hear at all, especially from him – so I said nothing more. My only inclination at that moment was to tell him he wasn't doing all that well at promoting morality among his Workers, but I refrained. After an awkward period of quiet, one of them looked at his watch and noted that it was time for them to move on to their next visit. They'd scheduled fifteen minutes with me, and they left on schedule. They flew back to California and no one had a clue what they were doing, looking for, or intending to do about anything. It never crossed my mind to give them anything.

Linda and Phyllis were holding gospel meetings in Reno at that time. Probably the most memorable thing Linda said in that series of meetings was that she knew "which of the Friends like [her] and which ones don't". Bill, of course, didn't attend those meetings. But most times as we left the meeting Alice Dunn was standing there beside Linda – with her hands around Linda's neck and sliding her body against Linda's. Perhaps Linda thought Alice was still a little child, but she looked quite mature and stood as tall as Linda. It was the most unusual behavior I'd ever seen at a gospel meeting, and I often wondered what an outsider attending the meeting might think of it.

Because of all that was happening behind the scenes at that time, attending those gospel meetings became a seriously stressful way to spend three and a half hours every Sunday afternoon, so we eventually stopped attending. I was beginning to wonder who was better off – Bill, who was not allowed to go to those meetings, or we, who were expected to be there and endure whatever abuse was meted out.

But Bill still had no idea what was expected of him, so in March he wrote to Harold Hilton and asked what would be expected of him to return to meetings. Harold's answer was that he didn't know. So Bill wrote to Dick, and his answer was that an elder would have to report that Bill had showed appropriate signs of repentance. That made sense, except that none of the elders had permission to associate with Bill. By then most of the elderly people didn't mind saying that Bill should be allowed to go to meeting, but ironically none of them were elders in the sense of directing meetings.

Since there was obviously nothing to be done, I decided to do what Bill couldn't do ... ask the last four people for letters for Bill. I should explain that this letter of agreement wasn't to give any great freedom to Bill. The ground rules were that Bill was not permitted to be in any place where there was any person under the age of 18 years. The only exception was for children whose parents signed a letter of agreement with the police to never allow their children to be out of their sight in his presence. They also had to acknowledge that they were fully aware of Bill's offenses, which by then only posed a problem for the ones committed to obeying Linda at all cost. Even with all the local parents signing such agreements, Bill would still have to leave a meeting if a minor came in without his/her parents, or if visitors showed up with children. If Sunday fellowship meetings were held in a church building, there'd have been no question about Bill being allowed to attend, except if the Dunn family were there. But the Friends have meetings in private residences and the owners had been ordered not to allow Bill on their property.

The first person I approached was Dave van den Berg. Dave was the elder of the Minden meeting at the Forbes house. As it happened, Ken Forbes, Dave, and Dave's wife Jean were all engineers at the same company Bill worked for before he was incarcerated. I approached Dave first because he and Jean had visited Bill a couple of times when he was first incarcerated. I was aware that they'd stopped visiting after their first couple of times – undoubtedly they'd been pressured to stop. Dave's only question was if the Workers wanted people to write such letters. I told him Linda certainly didn't, but Dick Middleton had indicated a way for Bill to return to meeting, and it involved providing such letters. He said he'd consult with Jean, and I never heard from him again on that matter.

But what Dave did next was almost bizarre. He invited Bill in an email to go to his house for a visit, or maybe go out to lunch sometime. Appropriately, Bill wrote back and told him he could only go to lunch with them if they left their kids at home because they hadn't signed a letter for him. And he also said that he couldn't go to their house for a visit because they lived over the border in California, and Bill was not allowed to leave the state except with written permission from his probation officer.

Dave was offended at Bill's response, and he told him so in November of that year – but Bill had no other options. My personal opinion was that Bill should have been offended that Dave expected him to violate his probation requirements just to make Dave look good.

The second person I approached was Ken Forbes, by e-mail. He fired back that he wouldn't sign any letter because the Workers didn't approve. And he gave me a lengthy lecture about "subverting the will of the Workers". Also, he said he wasn't going to do anything to offend the Dunns. He confirmed that he approved of the treatment Ken and

Mary had received at meeting in his house. He explained emphatically that they wouldn't be welcome back in meeting any more unless they got a divorce. It was interesting that a fellow in his 20s had such authority as to lecture the elderly on who could and who could not attend meetings. I'd been professing twice as long as he'd been alive. He finally emailed Bill and me to inform us that the Workers had told him to no longer communicate with either Bill or me.

In April I approached Mike Colson for a letter. Mike was in his 40s, and had been a devout Catholic until he'd met the Workers about 7 or 8 years earlier. He'd professed at that time, and by 1999 he'd been made elder of one of the meetings in Reno, and was assigned to our Carson City Bible study meeting on Wednesday nights. I thought at the time that he and I were on good terms – he'd frequently come to me after meetings to ask my opinion on things. So I asked him one Wednesday night if he'd consider writing a letter for Bill. He immediately said he didn't think the Workers wanted him to do that. Then, at home that evening, I realized that if Mike supported Bill, it would open enough meetings for Bill to attend regularly. So I e-mailed Mike and told him how critically important *his* consent would be for Bill.

The following Wednesday evening he told me he was going to call me about his thoughts concerning my e-mail. He did call, at 4:30 p.m. the next afternoon, and he talked nonstop for a full ninety minutes. I said practically nothing. Judy came home from work at 5:00 p.m., got herself some dinner, and went out shopping all while Mike was talking to me. At one point, after Judy realized I'd still not said anything, she asked, "Is someone talking to you or are you on hold?" I whispered to her that I was talking to Mike Colson, and she had a good idea what was happening.

It was quite amazing. Mike was actually screaming more than talking. I've never endured a more immature and abusive tirade from anyone in my life. He began by telling me that I have a very good word in meetings. He said that: "When Bob Williston begins to speak it's time for [me] to perk up and listen carefully." Then he started screaming – he was disturbed by my request. He told me he'd spent the whole previous day on the telephone calling people, who knows whom, and asking them what to do. He told me I ought to be ashamed of myself for not obeying the Workers. He quoted scripture like you wouldn't believe that supported shunning and banishment. He told me he'd spent a weekend in Oregon asking people about how to deal with what was going on in Nevada, and they'd told him it was right to get rid of people who behaved like Bill. And Workers were to be obeyed, he told me, "no matter what". He not only obeyed them, he claimed, he supported them as much as he possibly could and I should too. He'd even gone to the Bay Area so he could spend Christmas with Eldon Tenniswood, who was visiting with a friend of his for Christmas.

As his monologue progressed, he got tremendously excited and began gasping for breath. At one point I said: "Mike, calm down. You sound like you're about to have a heart attack." His reply was that he wasn't going to have a heart attack at all – he just felt his responsibility to tell me how evil and immoral I was behaving and how damaging my actions were to the church. When it came 6:00 p.m. he was almost choking for breath. He said he had more to say, but he had to go to a business meeting. He finished by telling me he couldn't have fellowship with me any more, and slammed down the phone.

Needless to say, I was quite stunned. I alternated between laughing at him and pitying him. Fortunately I'd started making notes during the conversation because it lasted so long I'd have forgotten much of it. The following Wednesday evening when I saw him at meeting I just never let on we'd had that conversation, and after the meeting he enthusiastically shook my hand and loudly proclaimed that what I had shared in the meeting was very helpful. I was somewhat sick to my stomach at his twofaced approach to me.

About that time it was announced that there would be a baptism, and then it was abruptly cancelled with no explanation. We later learned that the husband of the young couple who'd conceived a child out of wedlock was supposed to be baptized. But between the time he asked to be baptized and the scheduled baptism date, he'd grown a goatee. He was to be the best man at his sister in law's wedding, and the wedding theme was "Old West". When Linda learned about his goatee, she went to him and thoroughly raked him over the coals. He later told me she was so vicious with them that he almost didn't come back to meeting again. Ironically, the number of men in our area who wore facial hair, including full beards, frequently outnumbered those who were clean shaven. All four meetings in the area had had elders who wore facial hair. So it was quite a puzzle that Linda canceled the baptism for that reason.

Shortly after that puzzling event, Linda and Phyllis went to visit with Bill – their last week in the area before they left for preparations for that year's conventions, and then to move on to new assignments for the next year. Linda assured Bill that she cared for his soul, but she had no authority to allow him to go to meeting. I was becoming increasingly puzzled about what authority she did have, other than that of prosecuting attorney. But I was able to give Bill one reason why Linda would not approve of him – he'd grown a full beard.

About a week after Linda left, Harold Hilton called from Mountain Ranch, California, where he and Linda were both preparing for conventions. He wanted to spend Sunday night with us, so I said he was welcome. Judy's immediate reaction was, "Now you're in serious trouble." I asked her why, and her answer was, "You annoyed Linda." But considering all I could be accused of, I was really wondering what kind of case he would present me with. So he came for dinner Sunday evening, and later while we were visiting he asked: "What is this business about you writing letters?" I acknowledged that I'd written letters to both Linda and Dick, and reminded him that he'd read them. "So what about these letters circulating about Bill?" I said I'd written a letter to Mike Colson, and I'd sent an email to Ken Forbes – and no one else, except Dick and Linda. I was being difficult, but so was he. Finally he said, "What about these letters for Bill?" So we were making progress. I told him I couldn't write letters for Bill – everyone had written their own, and none of them did it for me. I reminded him that I'd explained that to him and Dick months before. Other than that – there were no letters.

Then he told me that we'd been missing meetings. I told him we hadn't missed a single Sunday morning meeting or a Wednesday evening meeting in at least a year – the only meetings we'd missed were Linda's gospel meetings. He told me I should be supportive of her in her efforts. I remember my precise answer quite well, "Linda told me herself that she didn't approve of our lifestyle. I figured whatever good she was going to accomplish with her gospel meetings was not going to be helped by my presence in the meeting." He said I should be understanding of Linda because there'd been a lot happen in this area in the last year that she had to deal with. I suggested that Linda herself had provoked much of what happened. I suggested he should maybe consider all *we* had been confronted with in the past year.

He was upset with that. He told me he didn't know what all happened in Carson City, he didn't want to know what happened, and he didn't want me to tell him what happened. All he wanted was for everyone to keep quiet. He told me I had to drop *this thing with Bill* to keep peace. I told him I wouldn't abandon Bill under any circumstance – I was the only one of the Friends left who had not been intimidated into shunning Bill. I told him what I thought he should do is encourage the Friends to deal kindly with Bill, as good Christians. I told him I'd discovered that "the Friends would do anything a Worker told them – right or wrong – and [he] should take advantage of that to help make peace." That he did not like at all, but that was the end of that conversation.

The next morning after Judy'd gone to work he told me he wanted me to cancel a picnic I'd planned. I explained that it was a goodbye picnic for Jane Marklee and her daughters, who were moving out of state. I explained that she'd stood by Bill with us through everything, and I wanted Bill to be able to go to the picnic. Harold objected because the Dunns wouldn't be able to attend if Bill were there. So I told him that the Dunns had given Jane enough grief over the past year that I wasn't sure she'd enjoy having them at the picnic. He said he didn't approve of gatherings that all the Friends could not attend together. So I reminded him that we have three meetings a week that Bill cannot attend, and no one had given any indication that was ever going to change. I told him there was no reason why I should not have a picnic for the convenience of Jane and Bill and let others come if it was legal.

In exasperation he said, "You know, I am personally going to see to it that Bill is allowed to return to meetings." I told him I was glad to hear that, but it would even be better if Bill knew that. Not surprisingly, he did not comment. I'd given him a rough time, so I decided I'd strike a deal with him. I told him that, considering he was going to straighten things out for Bill, I'd cancel the picnic – one concession to compliment his one concession. As it turned out, that was not the last picnic I organized that Harold wanted cancelled.

When he left I felt sorry for him. He didn't get anything he'd come for. I knew the only purpose for his visit was to make sure I didn't talk about the situation, and the only reason he'd go to such an extent to keep me quiet had to be to protect Linda. I realized full well that neither Harold nor Dick nor Eldon was going to admit to me that anything out of order had occurred in Northern Nevada – their prime concern was clearly controlling damage to the reputation of the ministry. Despite the fact that Harold had made a booming acknowledgment of my being his *friend* in the meeting that weekend, I understood perfectly well that I was his prime candidate for scapegoat if things got embarrassing for the Workers. It was exactly like I'd been warned.

Following Harold's visit, a special event among the Friends and Workers was held in the Reno area. All professing World War II veterans were invited to a Professing Veterans' Convention, and the four local meetings were invited to join the veterans for a special meeting that Wednesday evening. Veterans from all over the United States were present, and we met some of the Friends we knew when we lived in Massachusetts. I was personally grieved that Ken Hornady, even though he was a veteran and lived in the area, couldn't be there because he'd recently been excommunicated – or should I say *banished*.

It was only days later that I got a frantic phone call from Bill. His probation officer had asked him about his presence at the Veteran's Convention in Reno the previous Wednesday night. She'd received a complaint from Norman Dunn that Bill had been in the meeting – with the Dunns in attendance. Bill was asking me to go with him for the meeting he'd been summoned to with the probation officer.

I explained to the officer privately that Bill hadn't been at the meeting. In fact, I'd gone to the meeting early to see if the Dunns were going to be there. When I saw them arrive, I stayed near the door of the hotel to watch for Bill, and when he drove up I told him the Dunns were there, so he didn't go in. It wasn't even a serious attempt on Bill's part to *crush* the meeting. His father was a veteran, and he and his mother had come from Michigan for the event and were staying at Helen's house for the duration of the convention ... Helen being the elderly lady who'd been crying to Judy at Special Meetings. Bill had driven all three of them to the hotel, and he returned when the meeting was over and met them in the parking lot.

Then the probation officer told me she was having difficulty with Norman Dunn's phone calls and complaints about things Bill was supposed to be doing. She wanted to know what my connection was to Norman, and I told her that except for being a coreligionist, I had nothing to do with him except when we both attended a gospel meeting or some other special event. She said she was curious, because Norman had also complained to her about me. Norman wanted her to do something about Bill's control over me, because it was causing me to conduct a campaign to turn the church against him (Norman). Norman had also called her supervisor and complained about her because she hadn't had Bill arrested for violating his probation. But she said she couldn't arrest Bill because he was meticulous in complying with every requirement placed on him.

I did find it amusing that the complaint about me was presented as *Bill's control over Bob Williston*. It was so reminiscent of claims that Bill had even been controlling Alice from his jail cell. I did get to make a few jokes about that claim – to the few people I dared tell them to.

Bill and I weren't the only ones who got fallout from the Veteran's Convention. When the convention was over Helen got a phone call from Nancy Clark, who proceeded to berate her for having Bill's parents in her house. She told Helen they were evil people, and she wasn't supposed to have anything to do with them. If she'd presented her concerns to Helen as her own personal opinion, Helen probably could have easily dismissed them as the product of rumor, but what disturbed Helen was that Nancy's complaint was laced with legal implications for everyone involved. The whole discussion left Helen unsure that she herself would not be arrested.

This probably will turn out to be the longest chapter in this book. However, it covers only the six-month period from November, 1998 thru April 1999. I assure readers that this is not an account of my own busy bodying. In fact, I behaved as the exceptionally good listener one of my principals described me as. Furthermore, I only followed up on things other people had also heard. And I told no one anything about anyone until I'd asked the accused about it first. I suspect the Workers believed that, if I had the audacity to take such problems to them, that I was also broadcasting it among the Friends – but that certainly was not so. I'd been warned in no uncertain terms by both the elder of our meeting and my own father about the consequences of taking any such matter to the Workers. Furthermore, I knew of an absolute certainty that saying anything negative about any Worker is virtually taboo among the Friends. I have to this day not even told Bill much of what I witnessed in that period of time. And I certainly didn't discuss the Workers' failings with the Friends.

Writing my letter of complaint to Dick Middleton occurred when my voice of conscience became louder than the profound fear of bringing the wrath of the whole ministry down on me. The only comfort I had in doing what I did came from the idealistic notion that truth would trump deception. But acting on my integrity really didn't remove the fear. Still, to this day, not a single person has suggested to me that I've lied or even misled anyone about anything. Furthermore, I'd promised myself that no matter what the consequences were, I would not betray the trust anyone had placed in me, and I would not damage my integrity by denying for any reason anything I'd witnessed.

Over the years I have several times said that my understanding of the power of prayer is in the memory that I'd prayed for the strength to maintain my own integrity. I believe I've thoroughly tested that maxim.

CHAPTER 8

The New Playing Field

May of 1999 proved to be a turning point in our experience. When I approached people about allowing Bill to attend meetings, I'd done exactly what the Workers feared most of all – I was talking to people about Bill. I knew what I was doing, of course, and fully expected that someone would tell the Workers – but that was part of the plan. They would tell the Workers things the Workers would not listen to from me.

After Harold's visit, it seemed like those who'd agreed with Bill's banishment had decided they'd won the battle and were going to put the rest of us in our proper place. Ken Forbes again informed me that the Workers didn't want him to write a letter for Bill, and he put Bill on notice that he wasn't to communicate with him any more.

Despite the prohibition of contact between families, Alice's mother did call Helen's house to talk to Mrs. Frost, but Mrs. Frost was too afraid to talk to her. One would assume that Mrs. Dunn knew the restrictions that had been placed on Bill – the Dunns certainly complained a lot about how they thought Bill was breaking the rules. I actually believe Mrs. Dunn had a charitable purpose in mind, but after the matter was given to the courts it was out of everyone's control.

We went to Mountain Ranch for convention that spring, and it was a very stressful experience. I wasn't offended that Norman Dunn approached me and shook my hand. I was disappointed that Linda Passage met me in an aisle in the meeting venue, and never even made eye contact with me. But I frequently saw Linda and Alice fawning over each other and deep in conversation during the convention. At one-point Harold came by while we were in conversation with another couple, and he put his hand on my shoulder and said nothing for about five minutes, and then left – and I didn't say anything to him. I suspect he was trying to mean well, but I wasn't comfortable speaking first.

On May 11, I sent an e-mail to Harold, expressing some of my thoughts and concerns:

- *I have risked my reputation among the friends for the cause of "truth", and I don't want to be discredited by people who do not know me.*
- *Unfortunately, the "timing" of my being brought to your attention confirms much of what I have suspected all along, and I am sorry about that because I will be terribly disappointed if this outpouring to you will change anything between you and me.*
- *None of these concerns are for myself personally .... The only real concern I have for myself that I will share with you is that, because of my straightforwardness, I may in some way be "made an example of ".*
- *Canceling the picnic is not the first concession we have made to prevent friction among us. We have associated almost secretively for nearly a year now, and it is most disappointing that our first attempt to be above board has been met with this set back. We did nothing to precipitate this state of affairs among us, and we were not consulted before the law was summoned to tell us how we are to have fellowship together. Still, we have been ready to comply with every requirement that our fellowship can be restored. It is not fitting that such loving, forgiving, and spiritualminded people as these should ever be accused of creating division. Yet such accusations appear to be increasing in frequency and "volume"....*

I got no answer. But the one positive thing that happened that month was that Dick Middleton wrote to Leslie White, the Overseer Worker for Colorado and Utah and got permission for Bill to go to Utah for convention. And the probation people gave him permission to leave the state for that purpose.

In the midst of all this turmoil yet another matter was thrust on me. It was the matter of the Workers hiding the origin of this fellowship. I'd always found it difficult to believe that this ministry existed continuously from the time of Jesus, even though I'd heard many people make that claim. It was constantly being preached that this way was the only religion that had not been started by any man. In truth, they were making a fraudulent claim to the legitimacy of their ministry. Sadly, for the younger Workers who were kept ignorant of the real origins, any claim they could make to the group's origins were still not legitimate.

I remember a few times when I was quite small that people told stories about the Workers organizing to go out from Ireland to North America and other parts of the world. It was always common enough to hear a Worker mention something about the *early days*, but it was never anything that happened before their lifetime. Otherwise, the only thing I'd ever heard from anyone about the history was that there was nothing ever recorded prior to about the time of the first World War.

When I learned that the fellowship was a mere one hundred years old, my first reaction was anger, and not simply because I'd been lied to. When I was in university I wrote a paper on non-standard English usage among members of the Truth, which subsequently was published in a professional journal. In the process I gave the usual explanation of the history not being known, and it embarrassed me to learn that at the time of my writing the paper there were living Workers that I knew personally who were involved in the group's founding events. I was embarrassed that I'd had my professional integrity betrayed by the trust I had in the Workers' legend of the group's beginnings.

I do remember that a young woman in New Brunswick had been extremely distraught when someone told her that the Truth was started by George Walker and a couple of other men. I wish now I'd paid more attention to what they told her to appease her, because she later was in the ministry herself for a short while.

When I was about twelve I asked Helen Harrison where the Truth came from before it was in the British Isles, and she told me Germany. I wish I'd known enough at the time to ask her more questions, because she was forty years old when her name appeared on the first Workers List. I believe she'd have had a wealth of information. On the other hand, I doubt she was perfectly straightforward with me. I've since learned that there was a concerted effort made to cover up the origins of the fellowship while she was in the ministry.

Judy was the one who discovered this history on the Internet, and was quite troubled. Karen was devastated – I expect because she'd never had occasion to hear stories about the *early days* as I had. Also, she'd not professed until we moved to the West Coast, and in the late twentieth century it wasn't at all unusual in this part of the world to have a Worker preach that the Truth has survived unchanged from the days of Jesus.

This discovery brought back memories Judy had from her childhood in Massachusetts. John West, a man in her meeting who'd immigrated from Ireland, had written a book about the history of the Truth. She'd seen only one copy in the home of one of the Friends. But there arose an immediate controversy around the book, and the Workers demanded that all copies of it be destroyed. They apparently succeeded in warning enough people not to have a copy, or destroy the one they had, because no one I've spoken to knows anything about such a book today.

Nancy Clark also addressed this matter several times in her testimonies. She berated the Internet, but like most other Friends and Workers had an email address of her own. On one occasion she told us that Harold Hilton had warned that anyone who read a certain book about the Truth would not be professing anymore. I don't know what book she was talking about, but I took it as a warning not to discuss the Internet with any of them.

Actually, having to review this history was helpful for me, considering the atmosphere in Nevada at the time. As is true for the faith worldwide, virtually all the Friends in Nevada believe that salvation is limited to the realm of Worker approval. This explained why some would believe that I should set aside everything, including honesty, in the pursuit of Worker validation. But I was very much of the opinion that a ministry that invented itself just a century earlier was not deserving of my unquestioning obedience ahead of my conscience. I also believe that *truth* is worthy of scrutiny, and when a report cannot withstand scrutiny it's a lie.

On the other hand, I've always remembered what my mother once told a preacher who'd knocked on our door. "If [she] found something better than what [she had], [she'd] accept it." I was never convinced she thought she'd ever find anything better, but I did understand that she never considered the church to be composed of anything more than fallible human beings.

Following conventions that year, Harold came to the area with Dan Nejely. It was a couple of months before they came to our place for a visit. When they did, Harold reported that he *did not believe* Norman Dunn would call the police on me anymore, but admitted that he *could not guarantee* that. I'd like to know what conversation he'd had with Norman on that matter.

But there came amusing incidents anyway. In July there was a Wednesday evening that I could never forget. It turned out that precisely on the first anniversary of Bill's sentencing, our assigned Bible Study was I Corinthians, chapter 6 – the chapter warning brother not to take his brother to the law. Mike Colson was going to be there, so I wondered what I'd feel comfortable sharing from the chapter, considering he'd be in the meeting. But that turned out to be the lesser of my difficulties with the study. When we arrived at the Rabes' house, we learned that the Minden meeting had been canceled for that evening, and the Dunns would be coming to our meeting. I decided I'd just not risk speaking – there were enough others to speak in the meeting anyway.

It turned out that the Dunns were not alone – they had a van load of visitors with them. It was family from Washington with a number of teenage children and an elderly grandmother. As it turned out not a single person during the meeting mentioned the part of the chapter about taking your brother to the law – that is, until this 90year old lady stood to speak. She carefully read the verse: *Dare any of you, having a matter against another, go to law before the unjust, and not before the saints?* And then she said, "I don't know why this is in the Bible. I just can't imagine one of God's children taking another to the law. But I guess it could happen or Paul wouldn't have seen fit to write this." I thought it was hilarious, considering it was the Dunns who'd brought her to the meeting!

During the year 1999 I made my way into a couple of chat rooms on the Internet, and made connections with a couple of professing people. Being profoundly fearful that I'd be recognized and reported, I created an Internet identity. Everyone I chatted with was so shocked when I told them what was going on, and they encouraged me to join an e-mail group. So I reverted to my legal name and joined them. They were professing people, from three continents, and the first thing that amazed me was that they'd speak their mind. It was like escaping from some kind of prison to find people who would express such thoughts. The most sympathetic reaction we'd gotten from anyone in our area was a muted comment of agreement. For the most part we were just being increasingly isolated from people because there wasn't anything about our lives that we could discuss with anyone. What amazed me even more was the discovery that what was happening where I lived was very much a carbon copy of what had occurred in many other places.

By Special Meeting time that fall Bill was quite depressed because he'd had no encouraging signs about being invited back to meetings. But in November, after Special Meetings, Harold did make a move. One week he told Bill he could call two couples to meet with him – couples who'd not signed letters for him.

So Bill called Ken Forbes and his wife. Harold and Dan were present, but said nothing. Bill ask them for letters to allow him to go to meeting. Ken said he was just going to do whatever the Workers said – but Harold still said nothing, so they agreed to write the letter. The second couple that week was Jay and Nancy, and when they arrived Jay announced that he was going to sign a letter, "even if it costs [him his] marriage."

The next week Bill invited the other two couples. Dave van den Berg also agreed to sign a letter, but not before he aired his displeasure that Bill had turned down his proposal for getting together illegally months earlier. One would think that a person of his intelligence and level of education would realize that Bill had no other option.

The second couple that week, and the last of the four, was Mike Colson and his wife. Mike, as usual, made the most vocal presentation. He was out of his seat and pointing his finger at Bill, and had much to say about both Bill and Bob Williston. I was a bit surprised that Mike even signed a letter – but at that point he was the only parent left in the whole field who had not signed. He was beginning to take notice that these four couples and the Dunns were not getting any support from the rest of the Friends in the field. However, it was not until February, 2002 that Mike told me why he agreed to let Bill go to meeting.

Then Bill had no more communication with Harold for nearly a month. Bill told me he was beginning to regret putting himself through the confrontation with the four couples because there was still no indication that he could go to meeting.

But in December he got an email from Harold inviting him to come to a gospel meeting at one of the Friends' houses. That was all it said – no elaboration. Bill called me and asked what that was all about. I told him it had been announced that there'd be two restricted gospel meetings at that house, and nothing more had been said. I said I suspected it was planned to be the formality of having him re-profess. He wasn't impressed. He said, as he'd often said, "I never stopped professing." I agreed with him. He decided he wasn't going to go to the meetings – he said he'd been begging and jumping through hoops too long, and he didn't want to play the guessing game any longer. He said he didn't trust them.

Later that evening I composed an email to him. I told him that I'd never asked anything of him, and I'd never ask anything more of him – but for my standing by him, would he just do one thing for me, just go to the first gospel meeting and see how he felt. He replied that he'd do that for me.

Later he called me to tell me about it. He said that after the meeting he'd gotten up to leave quickly, but when he got outside a couple of other young men came out after him and wanted to make him feel welcome. It was the first time he'd seen them since his arrest twenty-one months earlier. I was glad they'd done that, because I'd been sure all along that most of the Friends were not opposed to his going to meetings.

The next week at the gospel meeting Harold tested the meeting. It was Bill's opportunity to *stand up*, which he did. From that point on Bill was allowed to go to the Sunday morning meeting at Helen's house – ironically where Mike Colson was the elder.

It undoubtedly will appear to most people that Bill had gone far out of his way in his effort to be allowed to return to meetings. But the reality is that for anyone who has been put out of fellowship, even if he/she is still permitted to attend meetings, is never approached by any Worker with an invitation to return. I know a few occasions where people who have been excommunicated and have attempted to be reinstated have even been turned down – for whatever reason. For someone in Bill's position, he either had to make himself heard or he'd never have heard from anyone that he was welcome to come back.

Bill was also assigned to a Wednesday night meeting, but he still couldn't go to gospel meetings, special meetings, convention, and most gettogethers of the Friends. He was actually permitted by the probation people to go to any church service – it was just the fact that we had meetings in private homes that made the written permissions necessary. The reason he was going to be restricted from other meetings and gatherings was because he was required by the court to stay a certain distance away from everyone in the Dunn family, and the Dunns had never been asked to make any concessions.

Bill asked Harold what he should do if he were invited to a social gathering at someone's house. Harold was opposed to making any arrangements for him to be told ahead of time whether or not the Dunns would be at a gathering. Instead, he told Bill he could just wait in his car in the vicinity of the gathering and watch to see if the Dunns showed up. To my knowledge Bill never did such a thing. He was sure that if the Dunns showed up and saw his car parked in the vicinity they'd surely call the police. It was a wise move on his part, because nothing would look more like stalking than that.

After Christmas that winter Harold asked to come for a visit. Judy was extremely nervous, as was I, but I couldn't think of anything we'd done that might have called for a *corrective* visit. It turned out that we didn't get any correction at that time, but Harold was not his gregarious self, and there wasn't much in the way of conversation. When he left, Judy and I shared our thought that maybe we were getting off the *blacklist* after all. We'd recovered reasonably well from our fiasco with Leo Stancliff – why should we not expect the same this time.

When convention time came around that year, Bill asked the probation people for permission to go again to convention in Utah. He expected Alice would be going to one of the six California conventions, but the probation officer told him the Dunns had let them know that Alice would be going to Utah for convention. So Bill asked if he could go to one of the California conventions, and learned that it had been reported that the Dunns would also be going to several conventions there – so he couldn't go anywhere. Then I was told by a relative of the Dunn family in California that Bill had no restrictions on him with respect to convention, and the only reason he'd not gone to convention was because he'd decided to stay home and work instead. How easy it is to scandalize someone in a group where everyone is assumed to be telling the truth. I won't express my thoughts about this situation, but among the Friends and Workers everyone is expected to attend at least one convention each year. It sounded very suspicious because the Friends are also advised to plan to attend one full convention to avoid overcrowding at other conventions.

Following convention Harold returned to the area, this time with John van den Berg.

By the end of June that year I was beginning to feel the effects of the sustained stress we'd been under. Combined with the stress among the Friends, we got a *novice* supervisor at the high school where I was teaching. I determined early on that he and I weren't communicating well, and my students began complaining that he was harassing me. By the end of the year I decided I didn't have the mental stamina to tackle another year of teaching, so I resigned – as did fifteen others of the eighty teachers on staff. I'd been a high school teacher for thirty years and enjoyed every year of it. It wasn't the first time I'd resigned from a teaching position, but thinking it may be the end of my career, and having no idea what I'd move on to, made it a very sad day. I wasn't afraid I wouldn't get a job, but I didn't like the idea that I might not have enough income to help my two daughters who were by then both single mothers.

In September I began substitute teaching in Carson City, and it was much easier than contract teaching because it didn't involve long term planning and evaluation. Before long I had three one-day assignments guaranteed every week, which with the various assignments on the other two days made it a full-time job. I enjoyed that.

Then in midNovember Judy developed a back pain that didn't respond to her usual chiropractic adjustments. It developed into a full body tremble that persisted uncontrollably twenty-four hours a day. Our family doctor was able to give her medication that allowed her to sleep, but her life became a veritable nightmare. In all she missed seven complete weeks at work, then she went to work for half days until she was able to handle full days. We attributed her breakdown to the stress we'd been living under, and the snubbing she was experiencing at meetings. She didn't go to meetings for about three months while she was recovering. Eventually she got well enough that she could sit in a normal chair in meetings.

In the meantime, I was hired as an attaché in the Nevada Senate, as Secretary to the Senate Finance Committee. The Nevada legislature meets every second year, so the job lasted from December 2000, to October 2001. As well as being a tremendously exciting job, the Legislature was only two blocks from our house, which allowed me to run home during breaks to check on Judy.

After June that year our Sunday meeting had been greatly reduced in size. We used to have as many as thirty-five people in our meeting, and by June, 2001 we were down to about a dozen. Other than Nancy's snubbing, everyone seemed intent on getting along with each other. But our daughter Karen had to forgo Wednesday Bible Studies because she was a single parent with a full-time job. Further, she had an autistic son in the second grade who needed medication to get through each day, and needed to be in bed by 8:30 p.m. to be able to handle the next day. She had from 5:30 p.m. to 8:30 p.m. to get him dinner, help him with his homework, and do whatever housework she needed to do.

Nevertheless, I was frequently called upon to explain why Karen couldn't be at Wednesday meetings. When Judy got sick they also began telling me that she should be at meeting. A number of times after meeting Harold would say, "Where is Karen?" or "Where is Judy?" I would say, "At home." And he would say, "But meeting's here." It wasn't like they hadn't been told about Karen and Judy – I got tired of explaining. A number of times, in front of the whole meeting, the Workers told me Karen would have to do something about her schedule so she wouldn't miss Wednesday meeting. I got quite exasperated with their suggestions because I interpreted their persistence to mean Judy's and Karen's bests were not good enough.

It was during this time that Harold came to one of our Sunday morning meetings and Jay Clark offended him greatly with his testimony. Jay read and spoke about a chapter [Ezekiel 34:2-6] concerning shepherds who would not feed the flock but made themselves fat. I remember distinctly that he did not say the Workers today were doing as the shepherds of Israel were doing in that passage. He simply posed the question: "How could God's children trust Workers who pampered themselves and neglected the Friends as described in that chapter?" I thought it was a worthwhile question to pose, and I detected nothing of an accusation in what he said about the chapter.

The reason I paid such close attention to Jay's question was because he'd raised the precise question being addressed among the Friends and Workers in Alberta at that time. For me, the Alberta situation presented a disconcerting problem for my family, which I'll mention later in this chapter. Harold obviously took Jay's question personally, and Mike Colson later confided to me that Jay "took his correction well and promised not to speak like that about Workers again." Ironically, before Harold had a chance to give Jay a scolding for it, I had privately told Jay that, whether he knew it or not, he'd touched on a serious problem.

There were two things that bothered me about this incident. The first was that Harold had found Jay's question so offensive. Remember, I was still grappling with the newfound infallible status the Workers had assigned to themselves. The other thing that disturbed me was that Harold didn't recognize that Jay had made no accusation at all, but in fact had spoken so that any Worker could logically be complimented for not being counted among such offending Workers, if there were any. Looking back now, I realize there's a common problem among many Workers – they're simply not articulate enough themselves to accurately understand well-articulated statements from others. They take their interpretation of what was said and run with it. That was neither the first nor the last encounter I've had with that problem.

In the spring of 2001 Harold and John had a series of five gospel meetings in Andy Dunn's house in Carson City. Judy wasn't well enough to attend the first two, but she did go to the rest. Consequently she missed the humorous incident during the first meeting. Earlier that day John van den Berg called and said a lady who lived on our block would like a ride to the meeting, and asked me to pick her up. So I did. She wasn't exactly a sophisticated type, and when she and I went into the house together we got a lot of curious looks. Then in the quiet before the meeting started there was a loud noise outside like something had been banged against the wall. The lady, in her gruff voice, said out loud: "That sounds like my neighbor beating the shit out of his wife." I had a very difficult time keeping my face straight.

After the meeting John handed out printed invitations to the gospel meetings for us to give to our friends. I took one, but I seriously wondered who I could give it to. To begin with, the meetings were in the home of the man who wanted Souza put in prison, and who with Linda Passage had somehow implicated me in Souza's excommunication. Except for one other couple in the meeting, the rest of the Friends present either orchestrated Bill's arrest or were supportive of his banishment. Furthermore, Ken and Mary Hornady lived only a couple of houses away. I wasn't about to ask either my good friends or strangers to meet *the new family* indicated on the invitation.

Possibly in the first meeting Judy attended there, John delivered a sermon that shocked me. He was talking about people submitting to fit into the will of God. He elaborated with an account of his and his companion's visit with a married couple of Friends about putting a Sunday meeting in their home. He explained that they were extremely rich, the house was enormous and lavish, and there were very expensive cars in the yard. When they told the couple what they were there for, the couple were pleased to have been chosen for that duty.

But then John's companion said to the couple, "But there's something I have to tell you. Uncle Eldon [Tenniswood] knows that you (the wife) wear a wedding ring with diamonds in it, and he feels that a plain gold band is more appropriate." Whereupon the wife got down on her knees and prostrated herself before the Workers on the floor, made a loud moaning noise, removed the ring from her finger, and said: "You will never see this ring again." She got up and left the room. The husband protested: "That's my wife!" And John's companion explained that for the wife to be wearing such a ring might make women of modest means feel out of place coming to their house for meeting. John praised them, and said the woman has since then always been wearing a plain gold wedding band.

Aside from what I thought was ridiculous behavior, I found it interesting that the wife's ring was the offending indication of wealth – no mention was made of the lavish house and cars. Furthermore, I know that not all elders' wives in California wear plain gold wedding bands, and among married women it's common enough to see the wedding ring accompanied by a diamond ring. In any case, no wife of mine would ever prostrate herself on the floor before anyone. I was frankly embarrassed for John to be telling such a thing.

About that time Ernie Rabe decided to resign as elder of our meeting. I was actually dreading that, because Bea had told me once that she expected I'd be the next elder – she'd obviously discussed that with someone. In connection with that matter, I wasn't at all impressed to learn from John's sermon that the lady had only been asked to get rid of her offending ring *after* they'd agreed to host a meeting. The couple was obviously considered worthy of the honor prior to the Workers' proposal, so the real lesson from the anecdote was not really that a diamond ring had tarnished her testimony. Neither was the lesson that flaunting one's wealth was frowned upon. Considering that the theme of the sermon was submission, the real lesson was that *unquestioning obedience* to a Worker is *the* virtue – no mention made of the lady and her husband having any convictions of their own.

This incident is an example of a coercive tactic that I'll discuss in a later chapter. The ring incident may indeed sound like a petty matter, but considering what the Workers had been expecting of me over the previous few years, I was cautious. I had a ready list of requests I expected the Workers would be anxious to make of me, none of which I intended to comply with. I, of course, had no control over whether I'd be approached to be elder, and despite my efforts to be cooperative I was quite sure I really wasn't the kind of person they wanted for an elder anyway. So following that sermon I settled in my mind that if I were ever asked, I'd just decline to accept. If they asked why I declined, I'd tell them honestly and deal with the consequences.

I need not have worried. Harold and John came to the house later on and as expected they announced that Ernie Rabe was not going to be the elder any more. They informed us that Mike Colson would be coming to the Sunday meeting in Carson City to be the elder. They then announced that they'd like me to be the alternate elder. That was surprising – I already was the alternate elder, so appointed years before by Harold himself. But later on, when I got in much deeper trouble with Harold, he emphasized his disappointment with me by reminding me that he had appointed me alternate elder – in other words, you own me.

I was relieved not to have been asked, but a couple of people expressed their surprise to me. Mike was the novice of the meeting, and the *elder* – all the other men in the meeting had been professing at least twenty-five years longer than him. Mike had already been elder of a meeting in Reno for a while and his *immaturity* showed, but he was open to tutoring.

It's normal in Friends' meetings to pass the emblems from one to another around the room, and those who are not supposed to partake of them will simply pass them on to the next person. Apparently, in

Mike's Reno meeting, rather than let the ineligible attendee touch the emblems, he would take them from one person and pass them to the next eligible partaker. He may have been asked not to continue that practice, because he no longer walked around the room with them when he came to Carson City. However, it happened that there was an unprofessing lady who frequently came to meetings with Bea and Ernie, and when the emblems were passed, she partook of them too. Mike's reaction upon first seeing that was priceless. He was quite upset about it. When the meeting was over he asked me what rule I'd learned about handing the emblems to nonprofessing people. I told him the only thing I knew about it was that Jesus had offered the bread and wine to Judas. It was hard for him to swallow, I could tell, but he acknowledged that was true.

Perhaps I shouldn't be like this, but it helps me keep my sense of humor. I used to find Mike very amusing when he gave his testimony. Normally people just stand and hold their Bibles, and make eye contact while they testify in meetings. Mike, however, would stand up, put his Bible on his chair, clasp his hands in front of him, put his head back, close his eyes – and then speak. It was a most dramatic presentation. For fun I used to imagine how funny it would be for him to be dizzy when he finally opened his eyes, but that never seemed to happen to him.

Early in the year 2001 the people in my email group decided they'd like to have a gettogether. I volunteered to make arrangements for them to meet in Northern Nevada. The plans were to meet for a weekend in June. I reserved a gazebo in a park in Carson City for that Friday, and another gazebo in Reno for Saturday. It was planned that all of the local Friends would be invited to the Saturday get-together for a potluck picnic. I printed invitations and had them distributed to all the Friends in the area.

Then I became aware that our get-together was being discussed on the Internet, and apparently someone was reporting that it was to be a gathering of exes, which was of course not the case. As well, there came complaints from some folks that the gathering wasn't a come one come all event. I made it clear to people that, unlike a convention, it was a private vacation get-together by a group of friends who just happened to also be Friends, and the local people were invited to join us in a pot luck – nothing more. I thought most people would understand that.

I was also baffled to learn that I'd somehow *neglected* to get Worker permission for such a get-together. I'd never heard that groups of Friends needed permission to vacation together, even with some of their nonprofessing relatives tagging along. But one Wednesday evening after Bible Study, John van den Berg called me aside for a private talk. He said he'd heard a rumor that I was organizing a gathering for people who'd been put out of fellowship. I assured him I was organizing a vacation for a group of my *professing* Friends in an email group. He wasn't listening very well – he said he was concerned that I was hanging out with unprofessing people. So I corrected him, stressing that they were not unprofessing people. I told him I'd already spoken to Jay Clark about having a large number of guests in our Sunday meeting at that time, and I'd invited all the local Friends to spend the Saturday with them. Then he said he didn't want me bringing people here who would disturb the local Friends with their beliefs. I finally told him I didn't know where he got his information, but he'd just have to trust me to be telling him the truth. He obviously didn't believe me – he wasn't stupid enough to *misunderstand* what I told him.

Then he got on the topic of Karen and her son. He said he worried about them because they weren't getting to Wednesday night meetings. I told him they couldn't make it on Wednesday nights – but he already knew her situation. He went on to tell me he was concerned for their souls because they were missing Bible Studies, and before long he began sniffling about it. He made no mention of the fact that Karen and Jacob *never* missed Sunday morning meeting. I was quite exasperated with him, because I wasn't sure what he could have wanted me to do about anything he was talking about, despite the fact that he was so upset about it. He was upset and I was confused.

Shortly after that talk we heard from our friends in Houston, Texas who were coming to the gettogether. They'd had a visit from their local Worker, Diane Knob, and she'd told them she "was worried about [them] going to Reno because [they]'d be subjecting themselves to an evil influence." She informed them that it was going to be an *unconvention* for people who'd been put out of fellowship. Needless to say our friends were quite upset, and I had to assure them that the arrangements I'd made for everyone were exactly as we had all as a group agreed on. To this day I'm curious to know how exactly Diane Knob was prompted to approach them with that nonsense. I've never been to meetings in Texas, I've never met the lady, and I'd never even heard of her prior to that time.

Right about this time I also got an interesting email from someone who called himself *Floyd*. Here is what he wrote:

April 14, 2001: My understanding is you may have information about a get together some where out West. I think I have seen your name on a board as an ex, correct. It has been 10 yrs since I have been to mgt or conv. then another 10 before that. Have no intentions of ever returning although I knew a lot of people I appreciated and would like to see again, and meet new ones. Can you give me the information of where and when. Do you have an estimate of how many will be ex's? Just curious, because that is why I would come. I would appreciate any information you can forward. Thanks!

I have no idea who the man was, but I began to wonder if our quiet vacation get-together might turn out to be something we'd never planned on. I remain suspicious to this day that the email was sent by someone as an investigative tactic to confirm that I really was having a convention for exes. So when I answered I worded it carefully so that Floyd could pass the word along to all the appropriate *others* who were wanting to know about our *unconvention*. Here is what I wrote:

Thank you for your note. I am actually making arrangements for a get together in the Reno area in June, but it is not a meeting of exprofessing people. It is actually a vacation together for a group of professing people who want to meet some of their mutual friends from other places. To my knowledge none of them are exes, though I would not be surprised if someone may bring a relative who is not professing. I believe a couple of people who are planning to be here do not get to meetings regularly because of where they are located.

I personally attend meetings regularly, and have been professing for over 40 years. My name has been widely mentioned in the circles of exes, and I have a number of good friends among them, so it does not surprise me that someone would report that I am an ex because we seem to have come to a time when associating with exes is grounds for being put out of fellowship, at least in some places. It's a bit amusing to me that I have actually heard many times from my close friends that I am on the verge of being "excommunicated" because of the people I associate with, but that has not happened.

The troubling news I'd received from Alberta early that year was that my cousin, who had Sunday meeting in his home, had turned some people away from his meeting. They were a professing couple from British Columbia who were visiting parents in Alberta. Their problem was that they'd been to a meeting at the home of the wife's father, Dale Jordan. Dale and his wife Marlene had been excommunicated, and the Friends in Alberta were told not to have anything to do with anyone who went to their house for meeting. So when their daughter and her husband attended a meeting there, instructions obviously circulated that they also were banished from fellowship in Alberta – and it was my cousin who turned them away. To be sure I knew what my status was in Alberta, I asked Willis Propp, the Alberta Worker Overseer, if I could visit a couple of our friends in Edmonton who had been excommunicated and still go to my cousin's house, and I received no answer. I was deeply disturbed by that.

In early May, shortly before convention, Harold Hilton again wanted to have a visit with us at 1:00 p.m. the next day, so I agreed. I again wondered what was wrong this time. He brought John van den Berg with him, and it took them five hours to drive the 110 miles from the convention grounds in California because there was a big snow storm up in the mountains. But they arrived at our place right on time. So we went to the dining room table and got right to the business at hand.

Harold asked whether we were going to be at Mountain Ranch convention. I told him we couldn't, because I was working in the

Legislature and I was on call 24hours 7days a week until the session ended. I told him we expected to go somewhere else for convention after the session closed – I had lots of relatives in western Canada, and we'd been there for convention twice before. Harold promptly offered that he'd enjoyed being in Alberta for Special Meetings in 1987, and added that he'd not heard anything about Alberta since. I didn't believe that – in fact, I was sure he was well aware of what was happening in Alberta. So I decided that if he wasn't going to be above board with me, I'd try a little reality exposure on him. They didn't have anything on me, and I was sick of his efforts to intimidate me.

So I said, "They're having very serious problems in Alberta." John, who undoubtedly had been kept in the dark about it all, said, "Oh really?" And I said, "Yes, they've been excommunicating people for the most trivial of reasons." And John wanted to know what the reasons were, so I told him it was mostly because people wouldn't shun excommunicated people as the Workers had asked them. John expressed great shock at that – as though he had no clue that the same thing had happened right in his own field in Carson City.

Harold was becoming visibly nervous. So I went on to tell them that a number of meeting elders had been excommunicated and meetings disrupted. I told them some of these people just continued to have meeting anyway without the Workers' approval. And I told them that some people who hadn't been excommunicated were deciding to go to the unsanctioned meetings because they couldn't deal with the tension in the approved meetings. I added that one of the Workers from Saskatchewan had been put out of the ministry because she'd visited some of those people when she was passing through Alberta.

John couldn't contain his shock – all he could say was: "Oh my goodness!" Harold interjected some comment about the problems that occur "when the Friends can't get along with each other." So I reminded him that it wasn't a problem among Friends – it was the Workers who were abusing the Friends. At that Harold changed the topic.

He asked about the *convention* I was organizing. I told him I wasn't organizing a convention. "Well this gathering," he said, "whatever it is." I explained it again. He told me he didn't like to see that because these people would bring strange doctrines that would disturb the local Friends – as though he knew who we were expecting. I asked him what strange doctrines he meant, and he said such doctrines as the Ingram and Oyler doctrines. I assured him that I knew nothing about either Ingram or Oyler, and I knew for sure that none of my friends knew either. I admit I was curious about them, because they were reputed to be desperately evil, but Harold didn't even bother to tell me what to beware of.

John launched into an explanation of what his mother does when she invites her artsy neighbors in for an evening of music. She prepares a program for the evening, and when people arrive she gives them copies so they'll know when one person will play a violin number, and someone else will play an accordion, etc. He said people are more comfortable when there's a program. I couldn't imagine what he was telling me all that for. And then it hit me – he was fishing for a schedule for the unconvention. So I told him, "It's a picnic." And that topic didn't go anywhere. I didn't want to be sarcastic by mentioning it, but I thought how much fun it would be to prepare a schedule indicating who would first dish out the chili, then who would scoop out the potato salad – so people would feel comfortable!

For good measure, I told them that one of the people we were hoping could come was a lady who had multiple sclerosis, and we were going to get a wheel chair for her so she could get around with the rest of us. They discussed how difficult it is for people with MS to attend convention. And then I told them more about this lady. I told them she had about seven children, but she'd lost all but one of them. The last two she lost were within the last year and both were killed in car accidents. And I told them she didn't get to meeting any more in her home town because her husband had put her out and the elder of the meeting had a restraining order to keep her off the property. I added that at the funeral of the last daughter who died the elder of the meeting had almost caused a riot because he punched her in the face at the reception after the funeral. And for anyone who doesn't believe this, I will gladly put him in contact with a professing eyewitness. I figured since Harold and John didn't believe me anyway, I might as well give them a really good taste of *truth*.

John was aghast. But at that point Harold got up and announced that they had to be going, and they left. I've never seen Workers take off so fast.

Considering that Harold had of his own volition told me that he'd heard nothing about Alberta since 1987, I found it quite a coincidence that a few days later someone shared with me an email he'd received from Harold – the message, in very forceful language, being that Harold did not want to hear anything more about what was happening in Alberta.

I actually wanted to laugh at the haste with which Harold managed to get John out of the house that day, but I didn't dare, because I'd just decided that this was never going to end. Bea Rabe had told me one time that she'd come under scrutiny in some controversy years ago, and had accepted to take the blame for the sake of peace. But she added that she'd never do it again, because they'd been bringing it up to her ever since.

Then we waited to see which Workers would be coming to Nevada for the next year.

CHAPTER 9

The Picnic

June 2001

The widely publicized picnic scheduled for the first weekend in June actually came off mostly as planned. And despite our fears, no one crashed it. Some of our visitors arrived as early as Wednesday, so six of them went to Wednesday Bible study with us that evening, and except for a spouse who wasn't professing, all the others took part, including the teenagers. All of the regulars in the meeting made them feel welcome, and as we were leaving the meeting I heard the visitors inviting the others to our picnic on Saturday. Things were going smoothly.

Northern Nevada isn't lacking in tourist attractions, so there were things to do and things to see. One family went horseback riding. A number went to Virginia City for an experience with the Old West. The little kids played with each other, and the teenagers found a tennis court to play in. Everyone appeared to be having a wonderful time – except that a few were mindful of the fact that they were in earthquake territory. The one person who was unable to make it as planned was the lady who had MS.

On Friday I gave them all a tour of the Legislature building, showed them to my office, and had a few of them sit in the seat of the Speaker of the Assembly, beneath the portrait of President Lincoln that boasts several bullet holes. That evening we had dinner in a little restaurant across the street from the Legislature – where Judy and I routinely had lunch through the week. The restaurant closed every day at 3:00 p.m., but they open after hours for private catering. We had Bill come for dinner with us there so we wouldn't have to tell someone to leave if the Dunn family showed up. It felt just somewhat like a legal coup to have him there, because he never got to go to any other gatherings of Friends.

On Saturday we made our way to the park in Reno and set up for the picnic. We had a very convenient gazebo, and a large deserted parking lot to one side. Shortly after we arrived there, a van full of people pulled in, but parked at the far end of the parking lot – too far away for me to tell who it could be. Some of our out-of-state visitors arrived later and drove past the parked van, and recognized them as looking like professing people. But none of them ever came to our side of the parking lot.

After we'd been there for more than half an hour, Bea and Ernie showed up, and also Harry Spencer, a widower in our meeting. Then a professing lady from Reno arrived. As it turned out, those four were the only local people who showed up to meet our visitors. The people in the van just stayed there and watched us. Some small kids got out and ran around a bit – little girls in dresses and little boys with short haircuts. After a while the kids all got back in the van and they drove away.

I thought to go over and invite them to join us, but I decided not to run the risk of making the situation any more embarrassing than it already was. I never expected all our local Friends to attend anyway, but only four out of about one hundred definitely sent a message. But it was a pleasant afternoon of food and visiting after all.

Later that evening I talked to Ken Hornady. I'd invited him to the picnic, but he didn't go because he said it would be awkward for him to be among all the local professing people after he'd so recently been kicked out. I told him that only four local people had come to the picnic, and he told me he knew why. He'd gone out after lunch that day to get his mail – his mail box was beside Andy Dunn's house – and when he got there he found all the Friends in the area having a barbecue in the Dunn's yard. So it was obvious that an alternative get together had been arranged to boycott our visitors.

I supposed we could still have been welcome at Sunday morning meeting that weekend, but by that time no one of the visitors was really anxious to try it. No one had crashed our picnic – why run the risk of crashing their meeting? We'd reserved a meeting room with the guest rooms in the hotel where our visitors were staying anyway, so those of us who were still in town on Sunday morning had a meeting of our own there.

I was curious to know whether the Workers had actually told people to boycott our picnic, so I called a close friend of ours in Reno and asked her if Harold Hilton had said anything about our picnic to them. She said he had – he'd told them that it was a gathering of people who'd been put out of meetings, and the strong hint was for them not to attend. I felt betrayed, not by our Friends in Reno, but by Harold. It confirmed what I'd suspected all along – he didn't believe me and he didn't have the guts to tell me so.

After the picnic incident I figured I had nothing to lose. Ironically, it wasn't me who lied about anything, from the day Bill was arrested. The whole ongoing problem I'd been having with the Workers was all because I'd been telling the truth, ironically to no one but the Workers in the beginning – and it had by then evolved into a situation where the Workers were actively encouraging the Friends to snub me because I was *deceiving everyone* by plotting to expose them to strange doctrine. That has to be the high cost of telling the truth – and the right to look at myself in the mirror without a guilty conscience.

At the Bible Study meeting following our weekend get together someone told Andy Dunn's wife she was going to be missed when she moved to 'Montana'. Mrs. Dunn replied, "I don't know where people got the idea we're moving to Montana. We don't even have jobs to go to." So I said, "You have people telling stories about you too?" So she asked me what they'd been saying about me.

I had the audience, so I told her the Workers had been telling people I was having a convention for people who'd been put out of meeting, so none of the local Friends came to meet them at the picnic I'd arranged. Bea spoke up and said, "I know, the poor people didn't get much of a reception in Reno. And they were nice people too. Some of them were here last week for Bible Study." I added that not only did no one show up; a van load of people parked on the other side of the parking lot and just watched us. It was an opportune time to make the statement, because there were two visiting ex Workers and their wives in the meeting, and they really gawked as the discussion progressed.

Mrs. Dunn should probably not have said anything more, but she added, "We knew about that. We're sorry we missed it, but we had a last-minute invitation to a neighbor's graduation party and we felt we had to go to that instead." I was totally amused by that, because there were a few other people in the meeting who'd apparently also been to the "neighbor's graduation party" in Mrs. Dunn's yard – and not one of them corrected her!

Another Wednesday evening following convention we had three or four Workers in the Bible Study meeting. They were having a bit of a vacation before they went to their new fields, apparently. One of them was Lily Kirshvink. I knew she'd been in Sweden, so I thought I'd check her for attitude. After the meeting I asked her if she'd ever met Edgar Massey. I knew she had – he was an ex-Worker in Sweden who'd recently been excommunicated. She was startled, and asked me how I knew Edgar. I told her we were fellow Canadians, and she visibly relaxed. I told her I thought a lot of Edgar, and she told me briefly how busy he keeps himself. And then she moved on.

I found these incidents more saddening than amusing. I've been described by a former principal as a soft-spoken cooperative individual, but I nonetheless have gotten myself in trouble many times for pointing out an *inconvenient truth*, and more often than not for defending someone who was falsely accused. That appears to be the string that really pulls my chain. The first time I got chastised for it was in grade six when I complained to the teacher that she'd given the most beggarly looking kid in the class a poorer grade than me, despite the fact that we both had the same answers – and she still refused to increase his grade. I never liked her after that. So it wasn't really out of character for me to protest an injustice.

I also heard a rumor that Dick Middleton, the California Overseer, had discussed our gathering with Jim Price, the New Mexico Overseer who was visiting conventions in California. A Worker in another state volunteered some information to me about this. He asked Jim about his discussion with Dick, and Jim told him Dick had asked Jim what he'd heard about the gathering that was being held in Reno. Jim said he told Dick that he knew nothing about it. Of course, the person who started the rumor knew that we weren't expecting anyone from New Mexico, so the workers in New Mexico didn't need to be warned. We only received twenty visitors from Texas, Illinois, Wisconsin, Manitoba, Saskatchewan, Alberta, and British Columbia.

I understand there were supposed to have been two other Overseer consultations concerning our picnic, but I learned nothing further about them. I just couldn't believe that by then Overseers in two countries had been consulting each other on a picnic. One other rumor that circulated was that everyone who attended the get together was to be excommunicated. I thought that threat was quite ridiculous, but judging from the spate of excommunications that had taken place in some other places for trivial reasons, it made me wonder who of my friends would be in trouble once they went back home. Fortunately none were chastised for attending.

The weekend over, we anticipated getting back to our normal lives, going to work, enjoying our family, and just going to meetings without any hostility. But it wasn't all that easy – about one week after our friends had all gone home, I came down with a seriously painful case of shingles. The doctor asked if I'd been under any unusual stress recently. I told him "yes" – and he opined that it was undoubtedly from working in the Senate.

CHAPTER 10

The Tribunal

A stupid man's report of what a clever man says can never be accurate, because he unconsciously translates what he hears into something he can understand.

~ Bertrand Russell

Following conventions in 2001, Lois Austin came to our field, and her companion was Marilyn Denio. We'd never met Lois, but we did know Marilyn's family. Her parents and a sister had lived in Carson City for a while.

I was initially apprehensive about Lois. One of our friends had raised some red flags. Our friend didn't know Lois either, but she'd once been visiting someone in Lois' field somewhere in California and hadn't been to meeting for some reason while she was there. When Lois heard about it she wrote a stern letter to our friend, reprimanding her for missing that meeting. It reminded me of a scolding I'd gotten from a Worker in Québec. I'd been in Ottawa on business and had taken my family with me. On Sunday morning, with Québec being a five-hour drive from there in fine weather, I decided to miss meeting so I could get my family safely home before a huge approaching snow storm trapped us there. It annoyed me to be taken to task about it in person by the Worker in our field. Our friend in Nevada received her chastening by letter from a Worker she didn't know.

We attended a couple of Lois' Sunday afternoon gospel meetings that summer, though it was stressful. The meetings were held in Mike Colson's house, and it was close quarters to share with two dozen individuals who were vacillating between hyperfriendly after meeting and snubbing and critical at other times. But then Lois left on a convention tour in the South through August and September, and was away on Special Meeting tour in California through October. She told me before she left that our house was *top priority* for a visit when she returned to the field – but she never did come for that visit.

Through that summer it became obvious that more than one person was directing correction at me personally in their testimonies. Dave van den Berg was pointed about it one night in Bible Study. The topic that night was "Priscilla and Aquila". I quoted the passage where Paul had referred to them as *co-workers in Christ Jesus*.[1] In that writing they were obviously in Rome, but they'd elsewhere been recorded as being in what is now northern Turkey. When I spoke I noted that they were "fellow workers", and speculated that was the reason they'd been in such widely separated places. Dave got up immediately after me and made the point that it was *Paul* who was the Worker. And he said no less than seven times that Priscilla and Aquila were tent makers *by profession*. I already knew that, and I also knew that Paul was also a tent maker by profession. I noticed a few people glancing at me while he was speaking. He used three tissues to stifle his emotion on that sermon.

Then Lois came to another Bible study, and the study that night included the phrase that *we have believed in Jesus Christ, that we might be justified by the faith of Christ, and not by the works of the law*.[2] I can't remember my exact words, but the point I was making was about the advantage we have of being released by the gospel from the need to keep the Old Testament Law. I understood that to be Workers' teaching for at least the previous forty years. But when Lois spoke, she went to great pains to make the point that we *must* keep the Law. She said, "the Law [was] good, and necessary, and we must still keep the Law *in its entirety*." She went on to say that we must learn to love the Law because "it is our salvation". I wondered if she'd even read the chapter for the study – but perhaps she reads the same way she listens. I'll explain that later, but I felt like asking her after meeting if she'd ever eaten shellfish and ham, but of course thought better of it.

After another evening meeting that summer someone asked to see my Bible, so I showed it to him. I was using the New International Version. Jay Clark commented that the Workers didn't approve of that version. I told him my brother, who was a Worker, used that version with people who were coming to his gospel meetings. Mike Colson claimed that the King James version was the only one that was acceptable because it was the only one that was directly translated from the original. I said I didn't think so. So he grabbed his KJV Bible and began to read the introduction out loud, and when he came to the part where it said it was *carefully compared to other translations* his voice kind of tapered off and he proposed another topic of conversation.

At that point in my life I'd become somewhat impatient with college educated people who think Jesus wrote the Bible in King James English. But the most amusing part of that evening's discussion was that I was not the first person to quote from a different version in a meeting. The young Worker, Dan Nejely, had done so in a gospel meeting, and I recognized his quote to be the rendering in the NIV. But it was even more interesting that in the following Sunday meeting, the Worker Marilyn Denio said when she began to speak that she was going to read some verses, but they may not be the same as the verses in our Bibles because she was not reading from the King James Version.

Overall we were somewhat hopeful that our difficulties with the Workers were over. After all, we'd not had a corrective visit between May and the end of that year. I remember sharing with the people in my email group that I was beginning to feel better about the whole scene. But that expectation was very abruptly shattered one Sunday in February of 2002.

That Sunday morning Lois came to our meeting. It's customary in Friends' meetings that the elder of the meeting is the last person to speak, but because Lois was there and was leading the meeting, Mike Colson spoke before I did. He mentioned in his testimony that there were people in Reno who'd stopped going to meetings, and this was evidence that they had no more love for "the Truth". On my mind that morning was the elder of a meeting in Canada who had continued to be compassionate toward someone the Workers had put out of fellowship. There was no denying that the Workers there disapproved of what he was doing, but somehow he'd managed to avoid a confrontation with the Workers that would have jeopardized his own ability to continue to host meetings in his home. So when I spoke I mentioned how I admired someone who kept a right spirit no matter who opposed him – Friends, Workers, outsiders – whoever. I guess that was offensive to Lois, but I didn't know it at the time. Not having yet figured out that people who critique others in their testimonies probably expect others to be just as "snarky", it might have been expedient for me just not to mention Workers.

But to be honest, I believe she was on a mission to straighten me out before she ever saw my face. Workers keep small books, one for each field, in which the Worker will record whatever important events occurred in the time they were in the field. When someone else is sent to replace them, they pass the book on to the new Worker, who will then know what needs to be known about the field. Of course, to many Californians northern Nevada was a den of iniquity anyway because gambling and prostitution are legal and advertised in neon lights. But I digress.

Near the end of the meeting, while Lois was speaking, Judy whispered something to herself. Judy is quite deaf – she wears two hearing aids and often whispers much louder than she realizes. I was sitting right beside her, and I didn't really notice that she'd said anything – even whispered. Mike Colson was sitting on the other side of her and he assured me that he hadn't heard her say anything either. But Lois, who was at the other end of the room, immediately stopped speaking and said, "Excuse me. Were you speaking to me?" Everyone was surprised and looked around. Then Lois said, "Did you want to say something?" She was looking directly at Judy. Because of her hearing problem, Judy had no idea what was taking place – all she knew was that Lois had a problem and everyone in the room was looking at her instead of Lois. Then Lois made quite an ado about losing her train of thought and getting it back.

When she finished speaking she asked Mike to express thanks for the bread. Normally, in Friends' meetings, the person leading the meeting simply asks for someone to volunteer to express such thanks. Lois was apparently afraid either Judy or I would volunteer to do that, so she chose Mike to do it. After the bread was passed, she expressed thanks for the wine herself.

As we were leaving the house Lois was standing by the door, wringing her hands, and didn't seem to know what to say. It was obvious Judy still didn't know what was wrong, and I hadn't yet had a chance to explain it to her. I really didn't know what Lois' problem was, and I couldn't think of anything that could have caused such an interruption to the meeting.

Monday morning there was a message on our answering machine. It was Harold Hilton, and he was alerting me that he was coming to town and he would like to see me on Wednesday evening after Lois and Marilyn's gospel meeting in Jay Clark's house. He said Lois had some concerns about the Sunday morning meeting. Judy was very upset, as was I.

Monday evening the telephone rang again, and I didn't answer because I saw it was Jay Clark's telephone number. It was Harold again. He left another message – he wanted me to tell our daughter Karen that he wanted to meet with her too. I didn't even bother calling her to tell her. Judy called her and told her what Harold wanted, and she said, "No way."

Tuesday evening the phone rang again, and I neglected to check the Caller ID before I picked it up, and it was Harold. He wanted to confirm that we could all meet after meeting Wednesday – and I said *I'd* be there. He told me again that he wanted Judy and Karen, but I made no promises. That night Judy had quite a spell of trembling through the night – she'd just recently regained enough strength to go out to meetings again. She didn't settle down until I assured her that I was not going to let Harold speak to her. That was the first time the Workers had actually sought out Judy and Karen for bad behavior, and I got the impression that Harold was just a bit too anxious to get at them.

Wednesday night came and I went to the gospel meeting. It was at Jay Clark's house, and it was only for the Carson City meeting and the Minden meeting. Lois and Marilyn sat at the front of the meeting with Harold. It was routine, as gospel meetings go, but Harold had an unusual topic for his sermon: the four things you can do with a tent. He started by saying that, despite the fact that we don't use tents at a lot of convention sites any more, the mention of tents in the Bible is reference to conventions. So his sermon was about conventions.

The first thing he said we could do with a tent is sit *under* it. He elaborated on when he was small and sitting in conventions, under the tent. The second thing we could do with a tent is sit *on* it. And he told about waking up on a Monday morning after convention when he was small and finding the tent from Yountville convention folded up in their family garage, and he went out there and sat on it. The third thing he said we could do with a tent was *raise* it. He told us about when he was perhaps twelve, he went to Bakersfield with others when the tent was taken there for convention – and he got to help raise the tent.

Then the fourth thing he said we could do with a tent was *abandon* it. He said that some people just don't go to convention any more. He expounded on it somewhat, but that was basically the end of the sermon. Frankly, I thought it was the most ridiculous sermon I'd ever heard from a Worker. I was amazed at the enthusiastic response he was getting from everyone in the meeting. But I wasn't naive enough to miss the whole point of the sermon. I'd missed convention in California in 2001, for the reason I'd already explained to him in a previous visit. But the message in the sermon was for me. I didn't have to ask, it was his oblique manner of dealing with our absence from convention – no matter that we'd actually been to convention in Oregon that year.

After the meeting Harold asked me where Judy and Karen were. I said they were at home. He said he'd expected them to be at the meeting. I reminded him that Karen cannot go out at night, and I told him Judy wasn't well. He wanted to know what was wrong with her, and I said simply that she wasn't able for a visit with him. He suggested we wait until Saturday when they could both be available. I had to say quite emphatically, "No, Harold, Judy is not well enough for a meeting with you." He wasn't pleased, but said we could go over to Mrs. Bunch's house and talk there.

Mrs. Bunch let me in, and went upstairs and left me alone. Soon Harold and Lois came in. I thought we were ready to talk, but they never said anything. Shortly, Mike Colson and his wife Sherry arrived, and the visit began.

They arranged chairs in a circle around me. Harold began by asking me what had happened in the Sunday morning meeting. I told him it was obvious that when Judy whispered something that it distracted Lois, and she lost her train of thought. Then Lois wanted to know why Judy was whispering in meeting – her voice dripping with sarcasm. I said I didn't know, but I'd been sitting beside her and I didn't even hear anything she'd said. Lois said, "Judy was in meeting – she should have been listening instead of talking." I told her Judy is quite deaf, and she doesn't know how loud she whispers – deaf people can whisper when they think! I thought it was pretty interesting that none of them knew Judy well enough to know she is that deaf. But it appeared deafness wasn't an excuse for anything anyway.

Then Harold said that Judy and Karen had a bad attitude toward the Clarks. I said that surprised me. I told them that Nancy had been blatantly snubbing both of them continuously for a couple of years, but we'd never complained about it. I could have added that there seemed not to be a woman in the area who'd never gotten the same treatment from Nancy at one time or another. Instead, I told them I did *not* want to hear of any of them suggesting we'd ever badmouthed the Clark family. But they persisted. Harold said that one of the Clark kids had seen Karen rolling her eyes at Nancy one Sunday. I remember seeing the kid watching Karen do that – it was Karen's response to another routine snub by Nancy when Karen attempted to shake her hand. That turned out to be their whole case against Karen. Ironically, neither Lois nor Harold had witnessed that, and Karen's accuser wasn't invited to confront her with it. There's a saying: *Whoever tells the story first controls the spin.* That is particularly true when hearsay goes unchallenged. A lot of that goes on among the Friends and Workers.

Then Sherry spoke up and said she'd heard Judy whispering once in another meeting and it made her "sick to [her] stomach". I happened to remember that incident too. Mrs. Bunch was speaking, and as usual she was taking far, far longer than her share of time. When she reached ten minutes, Judy whispered to me, "She's preaching again." I told them that, and Lois had to acknowledge that Mrs. Bunch had received suggestions many times that she try to keep it down to five minutes. But Sherry repeated, "It just made me sick to my stomach." So Harold said, " It has to stop. It's disturbing the church." Considering the condition of Judy's nerves, I was so glad I'd told her not to come to that meeting.

Then Harold said the church had been upset by what I'd said in meeting Sunday morning. I asked them what was upsetting, and Lois said it was my reference to the Workers putting people out of meetings. I told them I had not even mentioned Workers putting people out of meetings. Then Lois really fired at me "Oh yes you did. I remember distinctly that you said the Workers didn't approve of someone." I said, "Yes, I did say that but the man I was talking about wasn't put out of meetings. He still has meeting in his house. He was just told that some Worker didn't approve of what he was doing." She didn't believe me, but didn't know how to say it. I knew what her problem was – she found out I wasn't even talking about Bill Frost on that occasion, but she didn't dare ask me who I *was* talking about.

Then Mike said, "You talk about those people all the time. We know who you're talking about." And Harold added, "I've heard you pray in meeting for people who've been put out." I said I never once used those words in prayer. "But we know what you mean," he explained.

So I explained that the real reason I mentioned the man I did on Sunday morning was because Mike had mentioned some people in his testimony who had stopped going to meetings. I said I actually wanted to inject some positive remark into the meeting – the man I was talking about continued to be professing. At that Lois fired again, and almost lost her cool trying to tell me what I had meant. I think she waited for me to respond, but I'd decided at that point not to even acknowledge her comments about what I'd said – not to be rude, but to prevent her from making some even more hostile interpretation to something else I might say.

Then Mike said, "You prefer fellowship with people who've been put out of meeting to fellowship with us." He sounded so childish. I asked him who he thought I was having such fellowship with. He said he didn't know, but I'd talked about it in meeting. That really surprised me. I actually was not having fellowship with anyone but that meeting, and I didn't make up stories to have an impressive sermon. So I asked him what I'd said about that.

He proceeded to tell me about the time I'd said I'd begun getting thoughts from Sunday meeting the night before. He said that was proof I was having meeting with someone else on Saturday night. I remembered the occasion quite well. He had no idea how much I remember of what I say in meetings. I explained to him that I'd been chatting with Fiona, one of the Friends in Tasmania, on Saturday night – already Sunday afternoon in Tasmania. She'd passed on some thoughts from her Sunday morning meeting. The look on all their faces was priceless – they were staring with their mouths open. At that point, if they truly didn't believe me, they must have thought they were dealing with a top-notch smart ass. I also write fiction, but the truth comes to me much faster than fiction.

They mentioned a couple of other times I'd made comments that they interpreted to mean I was having fellowship with people who'd been put out of the Truth. I happened to remember every occasion very clearly. It turned out that every suspicious contact I'd mentioned was someone who actually was professing, including relatives – a cousin of mine in the ministry, my brother in the ministry in West Africa, my brother who was a meeting elder. Lois then tried to return to the recent Sunday morning mention, but I refused to respond.

Then Harold must have decided to get to the real problem. He asked, "Do you have a problem with the Workers in California?" I knew a version of that question was coming the minute I saw them making a circle of seats around me. In such cases the question usually is, "Do you support the ministry?" It's usually the last question asked before an excommunication. The preferred answer is, "Yes, I do, and unconditionally" – or you're booted with no further discussion.

So when asked if I had a problem with the Workers in California, I immediately said, "Yes, I did have a really serious problem with one Worker, but I got a written apology for that and I am not going to address that matter again." They stared at me again – they hadn't anticipated anything like that. Mike was so shocked he popped forward in his chair and yelled, "What did you say?" So I repeated it verbatim. He checked the expression on Harold's and Lois' faces to see if they were as shocked as he was. They just looked stunned – but

Mike couldn't contain himself. I knew why – in his line of thinking, possibly Lois' and Harold's too – I'd just blasphemed.

Mike jumped right out of his chair and stood in front of me. He pointed his finger in my face and yelled, "I want to know, and you tell me the truth. Do you submit to the ministry in California?" Aha, the *submit* word had come out. I nearly laughed at him – I actually thought to bite his finger, but thought better of it. So I answered, "What is the ministry going to ask of me that they would need my prior consent?"

Mike didn't understand. He said, "What do you mean by that?" So I really went out on a limb. I said, "I suppose you want me to tell you what I'd do if a Worker told me to do something that offended my conscience."

Harold said, "What do you mean by that?" So I explained: "You know, in my lifetime I've found Workers, even Overseers, have had greatly differing opinions on some very important matters. What's your advice when you get the opposite advice from two different Workers?"

Their mouths were all open. Finally Harold stammered, "Well, Workers are all human."

It was worth my effort – he'd just made my point for me. That brought an abrupt end of the conversation. All Harold added was, "This all has to stop." And he wanted me to assure him that Judy, Karen, and I would stop disturbing the church. I'd probably put him in the predicament of having to defend one Overseer Worker on the continent over another, and my gut reaction is that he wouldn't dare acknowledge that he disagreed with any of them.

I was angry. I was glad I was angry. I'd withheld any display of anger for so long that if I weren't able to appreciate my anger at that point I'd have been be in serious psychological trouble. Anger is a healthy indication that one has been abused in some manner. That doesn't mean a person is justified in "fighting back" – the healthy response to anger is to eradicate its source. The unhealthy response to anger is to stifle it and submit to further abuse. It makes no difference whether one's abuser intends to abuse, or whether he believes he's being charitable – it's the effect on the target of his treatment that identifies it as abuse.

First of all, I was angry that Harold would even suggest Judy and Karen disturbed anyone. He'd just recently proclaimed loudly after a Sunday meeting that we were his great friends. Secondly, I resented his intimation that the sentiment of the others in the circle that night represented the opinion of the whole church. I knew better, and I'd been told so by others. Furthermore, Harold had still not assured me that I'd no longer be reported to the police – he'd never assured me of anything, except that he'd believe anything anyone else told him about me. Yet he wanted me to assure him that I wouldn't disturb the mind sets of my accusers on that occasion.

At that point I felt like I'd first of all been used – my name was used inappropriately to kick someone out of fellowship. And then I was abused – for no other purpose than to protect the reputation of Workers. I already realized that I could have chosen to say nothing to anyone and possibly had no problem with the Workers at all.

But then it dawned on me – there was nothing new about what had just happened in that little tribunal. The kind of treatment I'd been getting from the Workers that evening was the same kind of treatment others had gotten before I ever made my first protest about it. Before I mentioned anything to anyone, we'd all been misled, even lied to, and forbidden from communicating with people who could tell us anything different. That is all abusive treatment in itself.

What surprise should it have been that my name was used to substantiate something I didn't know about? What had become clear was that I could be dispensed with as easily as anyone else. Lois didn't become so belittling and sarcastic just because she heard Judy whisper one morning in meeting. Harold didn't begin compromising truth for the comfort of the ministry just because I disagreed with anyone. Mike didn't begin yelling at people and pointing his finger in their faces just because he had a problem with me. It just amazed me beyond measure that Harold not only let him off with it once with Bill Frost – he'd let him do it with me as well.

I'd never been treated as such a miscreant in my life. They made no pretense of striving for the moral high ground – their concern was entirely about preserving the reputation of the ministry as beyond reproach. To put it succinctly, they expected me to change my thinking to accommodate their priorities – but there were people who were trusting me to be an example of honesty, and I would not let them down. The workers had presumed for too long that I'd go along without question with whatever they wanted to tell people, and I would have none of it. I promised myself that I'd never again participate in such a meeting without counsel.

He who endeavors to control the mind by force is a tyrant, and he who submits is a slave.

~ Ingersoll, Robert G.[3]

CHAPTER 11

In The Beginning

As I mentioned in Chapter 2, I'd never been told anything about the history of the Truth fellowship, though I did deduce from things people said that it originated with Jesus *in his time*. However, I was aware that no Workers, and thus no Friends, had been in North America prior to 1903. Many stories circulated about the sacrifices and courage involved in the first Workers' coming from the British Isles at the beginning of the twentieth century. As late as the mid-1990's the media was actually being told that this *true* form of Christianity had been passed down through an uninterrupted line of succession *from the apostles of Jesus Christ*.[1] And it was apparently being preached by Workers. Mike Colson told me what clinched his decision to convert from Catholicism was Harold Hilton's assurance of that uninterrupted line of succession.

Growing up, I heard many times that the Truth had no human founder, as all other religions did. I remember Bill Bryant, the Overseer of the Workers in the Maritime Provinces, saying at a convention that the Truth is the product of seed planted by the Workers who came before us. He was building on the Workers' teaching that no one receives the Holy Spirit except that they hear the gospel preached by one of the *sent ones*, i.e. the Workers.[2] The analogy of the seed was to demonstrate the certainty of this uninterrupted line of succession – without living individuals to pass on seed to another generation, a species becomes extinct. I know Jurassic Park suggests that may not be the case, but there was certainly logic in the analogy. It served as an admonition for us to assure that the Truth did not at any time die out in the world. It impressed me – we each had a role in assuring that all succeeding generations would have access to salvation.

But it's well documented, and commonly enough known, that a man named William Irvine was the person who orchestrated the founding of the Truth ministry and fellowship – often referred to in the beginning as a movement. Irvine was born in Scotland in 1863, and worked in the coal mines from age ten until 1893. At the age of twenty-one he became a Freemason, and later fathered an illegitimate child born in 1886.³ *Then, Wm. Irvine was born again or professed faith in Christ when he was about 30 years old in a meeting held at the Town Hall of Motherwell, Lanarkshire, Scotland, through a well-known traveling Presbyterian evangelist named Rev, John McNeill.*⁴ His profession led him to attend classes at a Bible college in Glasgow. Incidentally, John McNeill was never affiliated with the Truth founded by Irvine.

Mr. Irvine then abandoned his bright future in his occupation, and on June 14, 1895 joined Faith Mission, an organization devoted to evangelism. In 1896 he was sent by Faith Mission to Ireland, where he inspired conversions from among the citizens. But his relationship with Faith Mission didn't flourish, and he was put out in 1897/1898 for not following their disciplines.⁵ However, he continued to proselytize independently until he officially left Faith Mission in 1901. By that time he'd gained further converts, and over time a number of Faith Mission *Workers* left and joined ranks with William Irvine – retaining the title *Worker* as it was used in Faith Mission.⁶ One of them, Eddie Cooney, wrote:

> *Through the preaching of William Irvine who was at the time an Evangelist in connection with a well known mission called the "Faith Mission" I decided to become a disciple of Christ when about 32 years of age. Shortly afterwards I decided to go forth and preach in fellowship with the said William Irvine and others in fellowship with him.*⁷

One can imagine how greatly shocked and surprised I was to learn that Mr. Irvine died in the same year that I was born – 1947. That meant my grandparents had professed in a religion that at the time was perhaps only twenty-five years old, and they were surely unaware of that fact.

Irvine maintained two cardinal principles in organizing his ministry. One of them: he'd send out his Workers in pairs as Jesus had sent out his disciples,[8] which undoubtedly gave the Workers the nickname *Two-by-Twos*. The other principle he took from the same chapter: he'd send out his Workers without *gold, silver, or brass*, and to *freely give* what they had to deliver.[9] To this day, any semblance of soliciting a collection at a meeting is taboo. Irvine's boast in 1922 was that he'd not spent more than $10.00 on clothing in any year, and his bicycle was often all he had for transportation.[10] Shirley Doolittle's message that I mentioned in Chapter 3 was certainly not in keeping with that principle. But because the group enjoyed so much success in gathering converts in the early twentieth century, they attributed this poverty and contempt of comforts to the virtue of their faithfulness to the practices of primitive Christianity.[11] I, however, perceived that the praise of ministerial poverty began disappearing from the fellowship by the late 1960's.

Irvine not only preached against wealth, he also disliked the clergy and the rich – he told his congregations that learning could prove a hindrance to truth.[12] He also spoke disparagingly of his supporters who were not selling everything they owned to be preachers, and even *publicly reproved the preachers who had allowed in the non-preaching members*.[13] Concerning the doctrine of Irvine and his followers, a March, 1913 newspaper article reported them to be much like any other sect in their doctrine, and somewhat similar to the Society of Friends in manner of life in the extreme simplicity of their observances and practices. It also reported that they had no doctrine or practice that any other Protestant sect might not profess.[14]

In July of 1913 Irvine submitted a statement of his beliefs to a court in a case related to the group's practices. In that statement he said he preached and practiced *Evangelical Christianity* following the pattern of Jesus and his apostles. He said he preached the evils of drunkenness, fornication, and adultery. He claimed that *Chastity, Charity, Righteousness and Integrity* were basic to all Christian life, and that the *Blood of Jesus Christ is our only plea for the forgiveness*. He said he sent his preachers two by two, two women or two men or a married couple, and they were to preach freely.[15] On the contrary, some of Irvine's followers claim he had no use for *Calvary ranters*, preachers who taught that to *trust in Christ as redeemer of men*, and he believed people should become like him and go out preaching.[16]

From the beginning, Irvine held to the communal practice of all the Workers living from one community purse. All the Workers' money was handed over to Irvine, with the intention that it would be shared for the common good. Over time, however, the practice became that of the preachers taking care of their individual needs. In today's world this means that Workers, because they are not gainfully employed, normally live in the homes of the Friends and at the Friends' expense.[17] The exception is that Workers in places where there are no Friends to depend upon may rent living quarters called *baches* and find gainful employment to live on.

But with structure comes power, and by 1913 or 1914 the senior Workers got together and ousted William Irvine from his position of leadership. By then what is referred to as the *Living Witness Doctrine* had been developed – the belief expounded upon in the seed analogy mentioned previously. The acceptance of that doctrine elevated Irvine to an *all in all* position, he being the seed from which all the others received their access to the Holy Spirit. But not only did the senior Workers decide not to submit to him any longer, they conducted a purge that removed as many as one hundred Workers and one hundred Friends from the fellowship, either by excommunication or by defection to remain loyal to Irvine.[18]

It is speculation on my part, but from some of Irvine's writings in the late 1920's and later it is apparent that Irvine had come to believe he was the prophet Moses mentioned in Deuteronomy.[19] He didn't believe Moses was referring to Jesus, but to the prophet God would raise up for the Judgment Days. He believed what Moses meant by the phrase *like unto me*, was a man born to two human parents, unlike Jesus who was born of a woman and God. He believed he was chosen to be the prophet of Restitution and to give the message of Revelation to the world. The following are some of his quotes regarding his calling:

I am The Prophet whom Moses speaks of in Deut. 18:18-19 ..... and his words will mean life or death to the whole world according to the way people receive them; to put them in order and put an end to a world full of false prophets.[20]

..... whosoever will not hear That Prophet shall be destroyed from amongst the people ..... his message is the pure River of Water of Life.[21]

If you read the Bible where and when it has been opened to you, by MY Reading and His Spirit, then it will help you, otherwise it will hinder you.[22]

For if we let Him come into us by His Spirit, we will soon find out that the Spirit will give us words, understanding, and wisdom. This is the only way we can be sure I am the Prophet.[23]

People want to know what authority I have for being the Son of Man and Prophet, I know, and no other is supposed to know, but such as hear my words and obey them can know by the results in themselves.[24]

Your letter to Ollie will do more to convince her that I am The Prophet than anything else could do.[25]

Nothing gives me greater joy today than to know that Jesus is on His Throne and I as His Angel, Servant and Prophet in Jerusalem to end all the abominations on the earth and give honest people, good or bad, a chance to hear my witness, follow my leadership and obey my commands and so have right to the Tree of Life...[26]

But Edward Cooney did not believe in the Living Witness Doctrine. According to him, it was a heresy heavily promoted by Joe Kerr[27] and he attributed that heresy to Irvine's error of taking preeminence over the rest of the Workers.[28] Following Irvine's removal as Overseer, Cooney began to *separate between the wheat that came from God through him and the chaff that was only flesh and blood revelation savouring not of God but of man.*[29] The irony, however, is that once Irvine was gone, the senior Workers assumed similar preeminence in territories they carved up among themselves – this time leaving Cooney alone in his opposition to the heresy. Cooney lamented that the freedom he had in the beginning to express the revelations *God made clear in [his] heart* was being taken away from him.[30] His nonacceptance of the policy became a problem for the other senior Workers, because he did not accept that his mission was confined to the borders they had set among themselves. For a time, he claimed, he acted contrary to his conscience in an effort to cooperate with his fellow Workers, but in the end Cooney *confessed [his] sin to God and he has forgiven [him].*[31]

By 1928 the *apostles among the people of God,* as Cooney referred to the twelve senior Workers, decided something had to be done about Cooney. A meeting of the twelve was called, and they met in October of that year at Clankilvoragh, Lurgan, Ireland. John (Jack) Carroll and James Jardine presented to the group a verbal agreement which was to serve as *a basis of fellowship for all workers.*[32] They were asked to agree with two principles. First: *No worker would teach or preach anything contrary* to what the Overseer Worker in that territory believed, *without his permission.* Second: *If a worker decided to preach anything which the workers as a whole did not agree with,* he was expected to go to a country where the Workers had never gone to preach.[33] It was to be treated as a *binding solemn agreement* among the Workers, but Cooney refused to be bound by it and vowed to continue preaching as William Irvine had first instructed them. Jack Carroll immediately left the meeting, saying he would have no more fellowship with Edward Cooney. Shortly, nine others also left the room, leaving Cooney alone with only one fellow apostle, Thomas Elliott.[34]

Oddly enough, it was pointed out that this demonstration was not considered an *excommunication,* but rather a *withdrawal from a brother walking disorderly.*[35] In my lifetime I've never heard of any person being *excommunicated* from the Truth – *put out, disfellowshipped, banished,* yes; but never *excommunicated.* But Cooney was not the only person affected by this event. Those who continued to communicate with him or leave their homes open to him were excommunicated, and hundreds of Friends and eight Workers were separated with him.[36] Cooney continued to preach, however, and the congregation of believers who followed him continue to this day in several countries – occasionally referred to as Cooneyites, but also taking no official name.

But Irvine's and Cooney's cases were not the only disruption among the senior Workers in the time between the two World Wars. A rift had developed between George Walker, Overseer of Eastern North America, and Jack Carroll, Overseer of Wester Canada and the U.S. states west of the Rockies. An attempt was made to settle their dispute, but by then they'd each achieved preeminence in their own territories, and rather than resolve their issues it only strengthened the policy of territorial jurisdiction made binding in the 1928 agreement at Clankilvoragh.[37] Though Walker and Carroll have now both passed, the division remains to this day, and evidenced in painful situations for many of the Friends who move from one jurisdiction to another. It's not exactly a tacit acceptance between Overseers that they disagree – it creates serious complications, most notably concerning families with issues of divorce and remarriage. I once had a twelve year old in California tell me that all the Workers on the East Coast were *wrong* – the kid had never been outside California, so one knows that children are being told this at home. I will add, however, that I've never heard such a comment made by the Friends on the east coast about the Workers on the West Coast.

Certainly there's nothing unusual about someone founding, or organizing, or even reviving, a church – there are thousands of denominations and non-denominations. And there's nothing unique about how Irvine came to found the Truth. Neither is there anything unusual about the founder being excommunicated from the group he founded. What's unusual is that it became an embarrassment to the leadership, who could have at least claimed credit for kicking him out to keep the ministry in order. One possible explanation is that the ministry had adopted the doctrine that they alone held the key to salvation, and the fact that they had a nineteenth century founder, no matter what his reputation, could not explain how salvation could have been accomplished in the centuries between the time of Jesus and the nineteenth century.

What's remarkable are the measures they took to obliterate William Irvine's existence from all records. At the time of his expulsion it was impossible to say he never existed, because he'd traveled extensively around the world preaching and converting individuals to his faith. At the time of his expulsion people were simply told not to even mention his name, and they were to *do away with the old songs, etc., so there will be nothing to bring his name into remembrance.*[38] People were asked to burn letters they'd received from Irvine,[39] and some photographs were cropped to exclude Irvine, and later Cooney as well, from the picture.[40]

Interestingly, George Walker recorded that he and two other Workers were the first ever to come to America in 1903 – but he never named the other two. I've never heard of anyone ever asking who the other two were, but, knowing what I know now, people should have been asking. The other two were William Irvine and Irvine Weir.[41]

What typically happened among people who actually knew Irvine is that they just didn't say his name – even when they were talking about him. A good example of this comes from the 1964 testimony of Fannie Carroll at a California convention in 1964: "Jack was having his vacation and one of the Workers came with him to our home." That Worker was William Irvine,[42] but who would ask which Worker – all that matters any more is that it was a Worker.

Edward Cooney disapproved of the Workers' attempt to erase Irvine from people's memories. He wrote: *"An attempt has been made to give an account of God's dealings with us, ignoring William Irvine. This is not honest. William Irvine was born again when a Presbyterian, through hearing John McNeill preach the gospel.*[43] George Walker, on the other hand, may have had quite a different reaction. Willie Edwards related the thoughts George shared with him concerning Irvine's expulsion:

"They were so delighted to think he [William Irvine] was gone, so they might get the Vineyard. How well I remember G. W. [George Walker] telling me of their plans. Everything was going to be different. They would not even sing the old songs. Nothing that would bring back old memories, and he says 'in two years, his name [the name of Wm. Irvine] will be forgotten and new people will never know that such a man lived.'"[44]

All of this history – and all *I* had ever known was that the Truth had been around since the days of Jesus, it is not organized, the Workers are led entirely by God – and they cannot differ on matters of doctrine because the Holy Spirit teaches all of them. I heard once at convention that the local Workers had no fear of a visiting Worker coming and delivering a different message, because the Holy Spirit taught them all. As I grew older, I didn't have to learn anything about the history to suspect all of that was not necessarily the case. But I made a good believer – I didn't investigate anything. One newspaper writer summarized it thus: *Here's a group that systematically got rid of its founder and erased his memory when he began to 'get crazy,' as they call it.*[45]

CHAPTER 12

The Church Today

What Irvine and his followers unofficially referred to as the *Testimony* in the *early days* is by most unofficially referred to as the *Truth* today. They emphasize that they're not an organized religion, take no name other than Jesus, and when asked to identify their affiliation will most frequently say, "nondenominational Christian". However, *nondenominational* now refers to any number of religious communities, and the term *Christian* in many circles no longer applies to Catholics, Protestants, or Mormons – just evangelicals and fundamentalists. In my experience, identifying myself as a Christian became most problematic when the person asking would reply, "So am I." It normally turned out they were Pentecostal and I was confronted with the greater difficulty of convincing them that I wasn't at all Pentecostal.

There's really nothing unique about the Friends' Sunday fellowship meeting. The testimonies are for the most part inspirational thoughts meant to encourage others, not at all unlike many other religious groups – except that Friends and Workers may insist that the *Spirit* is absent from all the other similar groups. There are thousands of such Worker organized Sunday morning meeting congregations to be found in most countries of the world.

Ironically most outsiders have never heard of the group. This is probably because members of the Truth are not conspicuous in their communities – they own homes and go to work like everyone else. One journalist best described it thus:

This 80-year-old church has no formal name, no incorporation papers, no tax-exempt status, no headquarters, no elected officials. It owns no property, publishes no literature and operates no schools. It advertises neither its weekly services nor the conventions. [It is a sedate church, not given to] stereotypical, highly emotional, Bible-thumping, sawdust-trail revivals.[1]

Ben Johnson, a professor of sociology of religion at the University of Oregon described the group thus: *Their theology is not particularly way-out. They're not dangerous politically. They don't brainwash or kidnap. It's a typical turn-of-the-century conservative Protestantism.*[2] Gordon Melton, editor of the Encyclopedia of American Religions, describes the *Two-by-twos* as *an old-line, 19th-century Christadelphian sect,"* an isolated *subculture of non-Trinitarian Christians. They are not a cult because there's [sic] no real threats or violence.*[3]

For those familiar with the group, however, it can be easy enough to identify the members in public – particularly the women. Hair wrapped in a bun, the absence of makeup and jewelry, and a skirt is a good bet, and worth an inquiry. The usual inquiry is: "Are you a friend of Dale Shultz?" – or whoever the Worker Overseer is in that jurisdiction. I once asked that question of a party of four at the table next to me in a restaurant, and ended up joining them for dinner. But then one can make the occasional mistake. One of the Friends approached a group of plainly dressed women and said, "Excuse me. Are you friends of George Walker?" One of the women answered, "No. We're Mennonites."

The inside reality of life among the Friends is that televisions are virtually banned. The closest form of acceptance I've witnessed is that the Workers will consent to visit in a home with a television, but they'll refuse to accept money from the residents. The true exception is a home where one of the couple isn't professing – presumably the husband – in which case the professing wife could be presumed to have no say over what's brought into the house. Movies are seriously frowned upon and preached against, although one Worker assured me, as he was chiding me for having gone to see a movie, that it was not cause for me to go to hell. In much of the world participating in sports is frowned upon, except in the unusual incidents when the local high school hockey team adjusts their game schedule to accommodate the meeting schedule – because they depend so heavily on the professing team members. Or the case of some professing person winning a medal at the Olympics. When I was in college I was advised that it was inappropriate for me even to go to a public skating rink with a companion. I went anyway.

As is common to most fundamentalist groups, *smoking, drinking. dancing and card-playing are out, and abortion and divorce are prohibited.*[4] One journalist claimed that the Friends compared closely to the Amish,[5] but I reject that comparison because the Friends are neither as radical in their appearance, nor as isolated from the larger society, nor as abusive of family members who leave the group. On the other hand, the Amish dress code is uniform. The Friends' dress code can in most cases be used to modify the usual styles of a society without creating a uniform look. The surprising thing is that if one asks any of the Workers and most of the Friends what the rules are concerning all these lifestyle matters, the answer is that there simply are no such rules. But one should not be surprised, at the same time, to get a short speech about how the Holy Spirit has revealed to all the Friends that such appearances and activities or refraining from activities are what God finds pleasing. And privately, among the Friends, one realizes that there are consequences, frequently severe, for not conforming to the *Holy Spirit's* guidance in these matters.

There may be an explanation why there's the claim of no official rules, yet the unwritten rules are so obvious, strict, and even arbitrary in many cases. Alfred Magown addressed this matter in a letter:

> *There were no regulations and no asserting of authority. The Lord had mercifully set us free in spirit to worship and serve him under the guidance of the Holy Spirit through a good conscience; and there was neither machinery nor any of those things that religious people think necessary and which are necessary in sects under human control. There was nothing in the vision we had of 'the way in Jesus' that would have led us towards another kind of sectarianism, nor did we ever anticipate a time when we would become a strong people in an evil world.*[6]

Magowan's concern was not different from that of Edward Cooney, and he described what he witnessed of that freedom from regulation being taken away from the fellowship.

Afterwards, dominion began to appear, and God's answer was the casting of it down in the person of William Irvine. That ought to have been the end of it, but it was not taken to heart by those who exulted under him. And the same spirit that had set him above his brethren began to be seen in them, so that in a little while they had divided the earth among themselves as rulers over little kingdoms, exercising authority after the way and according to the spirit of Rome, and doing violence to the consciences of men in the name of the 'Truth' or the 'Testimony'. When the anointing ceased, authority took its place, and then cruelty had to be resorted to in keeping people under control.[7]

The evidence that the original freedom of conscience was disappearing was confirmed by Magowan's accusations of tactics being used to control the flock. Magowan wrote this in 1931, but it describes precisely tactics that have been used through the years and into the past two decades to control the flock.

People are forbidden to visit friends, and some have been excommunicated on that miserable ground. Letters have been intercepted and sent to others or destroyed and the person to whom they were addressed never saw them. Pressure has been brought to bear on struggling souls to compel them to deny the truth that was in them. ..... But for some strange reason, when the same spirit is revealed among ourselves we justify it because the welfare of what we call the 'Testimony' is at stake. ..... No godly end justifies cruel means, and persecution is always wrong no matter how 'holy' the cause may seem to be in which it is used as a weapon. If the work of God seems to require dominion and cruelty so that a 'Testimony' may be preserved, then the sooner it is dissolved the better. ..... They have entered into a conspiracy of secrecy and fear, and have set the approval of one another above the approval of God.[8]

The membership of the Friends and Workers today accept that it's within the authority and right of the Workers to accept or reject individuals as members, and to direct attitudes of members on matters they consider important to preserving that authority. Recall from Chapter 11 that William Irvine found fault with Workers who allowed non-preaching people into fellowship – while in the beginning he did not reject such people. And recall that in Chapter 3 I learned that Jack Carroll claimed it was the Workers' role to "keep the wrong people out." Jack, recall, was one of the ten at Clankilvoragh who expelled Irvine from his position because Irvine had gathered too much power to himself.

It's not commonplace for Workers to bring attention to the extent of their authority, especially in the area of controlling the attitudes of individuals. But if one questions something involving a Worker or the ministry, one can be bluntly ordered into line. The following is the reply a young man received when he asked a question about a Worker's sermon – the Worker being the Overseer for the state of New South Wales.

Dear Ross, I have before me a letter that contains nothing edifying, but rather questioning the message that God gave me to share with His people. A letter that I would be more than ashamed to sign my name to. It has caused me to pray earnestly to God for you, because when the Pharisees spoke against the work that Jesus was doing and questioned His authority, He told them that it was a sin [sic] could not be forgiven. And while you think you may have done this to me, Jesus said forasmuch as ye have done it to one of these the least of my brethren, ye have done it unto me. Just as God said to the children of Israel, ye have not spoken against Moses, but you have spoken against me. I sincirely [sic] hope that you will be able to change your attitude and approach to those who have been willing to sacrifice all so that they might follow Jesus and obey His call. Unfortunately while you remain as you are I feel that God would not be able to accept your offering.

Yours sincerely, Clyde MacKay."

One other aspect of the Workers' teaching that has obviously changed over the years is how they place themselves on the spectrum of mainline religions. In the beginning they didn't consider themselves part of the sectarian world. I was in elementary school when an elderly Irish Worker explained to me that we were obviously not Catholic, but we weren't Protestant either because we *protest* nothing. However, among today's Friends I perceive that most of them consider themselves Protestant. Magowan recognized that shift of approach by the ministry, and indeed suggested it was a return to secularism.

> *We breathed the atmosphere of Orange Protestantism as children and later on when we heard the gospel were willing to break with all tradition and become a people neither Catholic nor Protestant. You know the history of Rome and how cruelty was her characteristic under the cardinals and the popes. The persecutions and the martyrdoms of the early Christians was only a testimony to the insatiable desire for dominion, not only over the bodies of people, but also over their souls. ..... Now, if the things that we have heard here and elsewhere are required by those among us who are looked upon as leaders, then I say we have ceased to be disciples of Jesus and have joined the ranks of his enemies.*[9]

This concern also relates to the organization of the ministry. One of Cooney's *problems* was that he insisted on being led to preach where the Spirit led him. And the ministry to this day distinguishes itself from *organized* religions, promoting itself as neither an organization nor a sect, but a *body of which Christ is the head*.[10] From my earliest memories, that is what I heard Workers telling people – they were sent by God to where the Spirit led them. It was their explanation for decisions to move on and hold their next series of gospel meetings in another place. Ironically, the ministry that descended from the Workers who expelled Cooney soon became a highly, tightly structured ministry. Each geographical jurisdiction has an Overseer who, according to the Clankilvoragh agreement, cannot be contradicted by any Worker in his jurisdiction. Also, all Workers in his jurisdiction are assigned to a specific geographical field, and are expected to confine themselves to that area and stay there until permitted or asked to go somewhere else – even for a visit.

Among the Workers on an Overseer's staff, there is a hierarchy that is religiously respected. One senior Worker once told us at convention that his young companion had to be chastised because he'd decided on his own to sleep one night at a home he wasn't assigned to. The senior Worker assured us that his companion had learned from that error how to be obedient. On one occasion when Harold Hilton came to Nevada alone to *reason* with me, he confided to me that he was there without the Overseer's knowledge. I was surprised – a mid-fifties aged man 105 miles away from where he was supposed to be for an overnight weekend visit!

Not only are the Workers held on a short leash, the Friends are as well. What can be best described as membership lists are kept in many jurisdictions. Such lists are updated annually, and for each Sunday meeting in the jurisdiction are listed the names of each professing person, along with their phone number, address, and frequently their e-mail address. They also indicate who is the elder of the meeting and the alternate elder, and can even indicate which members of each family are professing or not professing. The regular members aren't given these lists, but each Worker will have one as well as any person who's in charge of forwarding a Worker's mail. I've also learned that something like a *field book* is also kept – there's one for each field. It records whatever the next Workers assigned to that field should be aware of – such things as "John Doe has a very good heart but doesn't feel his need before God."

In the beginning, and still today, the Workers' claim is that they preach and live "by the Bible alone", or some will say "according to the New Testament". Oddly enough, the occasional older Worker will claim that because the Bible was written many years ago, the Workers have to add teaching and doctrine to ensure it's relevant for today's situations[11] – somewhat in the manner of William Irvine's revelations in his later days. I have heard Leo Stancliff, in California, preaching in gospel meetings that the Bible was a book of laws, and the Workers were responsible for additions necessary for our times. However, his Overseer at the time, Eldon Tenniswood claimed not to have such revelations.

Written communication between and among Workers and Friends has been widely used in the history of the group. I recall as a child that a Worker visiting in our home could receive volumes of mail – no doubt many envelopes contained monetary donations as well as news and well wishing. But the written communication has accommodated control over the flock as well. An excommunication in one jurisdiction can immediately be reported to another jurisdiction should the excommunicated individual be considered a *flight risk*.[12] In today's world e-mail and cell phones have become virtually invaluable for Worker communication. On one occasion it happened that a Scandinavian was excommunicated in Chile, and his family and the Workers in Norway were notified of the fact before the man himself had the opportunity to inform them of his plight.

When I was a child it was understood that the Workers focus was on proselytizing, and they stayed in people's homes while they occupied themselves with evangelizing. It was not unusual for Workers to have three gospel meetings a week for any number of weeks. Alfred Magowan recalls that purpose in his letter.

> *We had only one commission and that was to make disciples as we had been made; and we had only one authority, viz., if the Lord was with us we would so live and speak that He would use us in getting people saved. And as they listened to us they would recognize the voice of Him because of the anointing. That was the simple outline in the days of our beginning.*[13]

But in Nevada that has never really seemed to be the case. The usual seemed to be one gospel meeting a week, primarily for professing people. Harold Hilton did make the effort to advertise his gospel meetings, but some other *gospel* meetings were even restricted to Friends from specific areas. One ex-Worker has claimed that the *days of evangalizing are over, at least for most of North America.* For Workers sent to Africa, South America, and Asia, their work is primarily *pioneering and evangelical,* but in more developed countries their duties are mainly to the professing people in their field.[14]

This doesn't mean that gospel meetings don't serve an evangelical purpose when they're open to the public. The Worker Jim Knipe explained that, because the Friends don't hide their light under a bushel, when *somebody is seeking, the Lord will lead them. and where He leads them is the place they should go.*[15] Muriel Erickson invited "All who would like to embrace the faith of Jesus stand to their feet."[16] Despite the minimal outreach beyond families already converted, David Kennedy, a California Worker, reported that the group is slowly growing.[17]

The burning question always is: How does everything get paid for? A collection at any meeting is taboo – though some voluntarily slip an envelope containing money into the hands of a Worker.[18] But in today's world, the twenty-dollar handshake is no more than a drop in the bucket. Still, people are never asked to tithe or solicited for donations. But rent for halls for gospel meetings has to be paid. Attendance at a four-day convention, with meals and board provided, is free. Airfare for two or three visiting Workers from anywhere in the world to over one hundred conventions in North America has to be paid for. Living costs for Workers in many pioneering countries are financed from industrialized countries. In the United States, medical care and surgeries for Workers are not free. The bills obviously get paid – by someone. In contrast, who knows how many of the Friends have had to declare bankruptcy because they couldn't pay their own medical bills?

But then, I am in possession of a copy of the codicil format provided by the Workers to those who want to will property and money to the Workers. I was of the belief that such a thing was taboo among the Friends and Workers, but I now know of elderly people who've been approached by Workers suggesting that it's time to consider remembering the ministry in their wills. Whole estates have been left to the Workers. I also know that when Dale Shultz visited with a young lady offering to go into the ministry, the only question he asked was how much money she had.

Undoubtedly for the sister Worker, Terri Marsh, it works as she told a reporter: "When they need medical care or a plane ticket for missionary work in Australia or Eastern Europe, *the gift* always appears

– the Lord provides the way in every century."[19] Tharold Sylvester's response was that financial affairs "are left in God's hands."[20] But that's not the answer to the *real* question. People want to know how a *poor* ministry can sustain such an expensive operation.

The fact is, Overseers control significant bank accounts and trust funds, but take care not to have their own names on the accounts. Undoubtedly the Workers rely heavily on the support of wealthy Friends. Tharold Sylvester acknowledged that "There [was] one member who ... put his personal plane at [Tharold's] disposal whenever [he wanted] it."[21] Some people have claimed that Workers also have significant capital investments, but I'm only aware of the exact details of one such discovery. In any case, one Worker, Willie Hughes, said he "didn't have to tell anyone" about his banked funds.[22]

One aspect of the Truth fellowship that does not incur an expense is the regular Sunday meetings and the Wednesday evening Bible studies. They are all held in private homes. Most conventions are also held on private property, which has the added benefit of allowing the Workers to control who is and who isn't invited to the venue.[23] In fact, the church claim is that they own no properties at all because, as Jim Knipe politely reported, *church buildings are not sanctioned by scripture and thus are a route to Hell.*[24]

But convention properties are a far more complicated matter than they used to be in the early twentieth century. At that time most conventions were held on working farms, and they relied on tents when the standing structures were not adequate for the numbers of people. Today such properties are far more expensive, and far fewer people make their livings on working farms. For the Workers it matters greatly that when an owner has to abandon the convention property that the property be purchased by someone who will allow the convention to continue in the same place. Today's convention facilities have become more sophisticated and comfortable than at early conventions, and it's a very expensive and labor-intensive task to move a convention to a new location. Because they cannot own property, and because they also need control over the continuing availability of the property, they have come up with creative arrangements with the owners that will guarantee the property will remain available to them, with a resident of their approval, for an extended number of years. New convention properties today are purchased and constructed primarily for the purpose of hosting conventions – but never as true convention centers. One of them was constructed as a horse arena, on the property of a man who to my knowledge owns no horses. The ministry has become dependant on Friends who are wealthy enough to provide such properties with such facilities – all for a convention held once or twice a year, each lasting only four days.

Workers who have to retire are normally cared for in private homes by some of the Friends. Occasionally one will find a rest home that is owned by one of the Friends and they can care for a number of retired Workers. Probably what is considered the most unusual and outrageous Worker retirement was that provided for Bill (William) Carroll, a past Overseer in the state of Victoria, Australia. He was a married man (not unheard of decades ago), and each year one of the brother Workers would be assigned to be his servant and groundskeeper, and one or two sister Workers would be assigned to be cook and housemaid for them – instead of preaching in a field with a companion.[25]

Another common question that is asked about the Friends and Workers is whether it is a cult. I hesitate to answer that question because I have no idea what any reader will believe to be the definition of a cult. The word has lost its original meaning because it is now commonly used as a derogatory term for minority religious groups, conjuring *images of brainwashing, coercion, deception, exploitation, perversion, and religious fraud*. I prefer to use the word in a more exacting fashion – i.e. relating to the manner of worship. In that sense, the Friends and Workers have their own *cultic* practices, or style of worship, as do all other religious groups.[26] I will not pretend that the term *cult* is never applied to the Friends and Workers because it is – it gets common enough use among some ex-Friends. I personally believe that what those people are referring to is personal abuse, which I will discuss in Chapter 17. I also will discuss why I won't consider prevailing on anyone to leave the church – despite the fact that I personally do not wish to return.

CHAPTER 13

Disentangling Myself

³ "Therefore, son of man, pack your belongings for exile and in the daytime, as they watch, set out and go from where you are to another place. Perhaps they will understand, though they are a rebellious house. ⁴ During the daytime, while they watch, bring out your belongings packed for exile. Then in the evening, while they are watching, go out like those who go into exile. ⁵ While they watch, dig through the wall and take your belongings out through it. ⁶ Put them on your shoulder as they are watching and carry them out at dusk. ..."

~~ Ezekiel 12 – New International Version

When I arrived home after my *tribunal* that night in early 2002, Judy took one look at me and knew how it had gone. I made one comment, "We have to stop disturbing the church." She replied, "Then I'm not going back again." She called Karen and Karen concurred with her.

Needless to say, I was distraught. I'd begun taking a night class on Thursday evenings to get my mind off our difficulties, but the next night when I went to class the subject matter wasn't distraction enough. A couple of times I found myself miles away from the instruction and, by the end of the threehour class, I'd taken in virtually nothing. After the others left, the instructor commented that I'd been a "long distance away tonight". He seemed worried about me, so I made the excuse that my father was terminally ill with cancer. That was actually true, but that wasn't my problem that night. A couple of days later I decided I was just not going to be able to concentrate on the course, so I dropped it.

It so happened that Greg Olson, a young engineer who had joined the other engineers in the Minden meeting, was launching into the ministry that weekend. So a special gathering was planned for that Sunday for all the meetings in Northern Nevada in celebration of his debut as a Worker. Harold Hilton was already in the area to deal with me, so he was there with Greg as his companion Worker for the event. It was an easy event for me to miss, so I didn't go.

But at that point I'd actually come to the realization that I was going to have to leave the fellowship. I didn't exactly make that decision, it was more like an acceptance that I was not in safe territory with respect to the ministry, and I was above all painfully disappointed. My entire life had been spent with my family in the comfort of the community of the Friends and Workers, and the last thing I ever expected was to become the black sheep. I was abruptly lost.

It wasn't unlike the sense of loss one experiences upon losing a lifelong companion, I expect. Unlike being lost yet hopeful of finding your way again – this is the loss of something being taken from you that will never be returned. A person is left with only two choices – live your life under the illusion that it could be returned to normal, or make plans for another future. Unfortunately one cannot do both, so I had to contemplate what to make of the rest of my life. I also decided that I wasn't going to let my feelings of loss impel me to make any quick fix to my situation. Instead, I'd leave on my own terms, and when I felt comfortable and prepared to leave so many friends behind.

What I didn't feel was a sense that a door had been slammed behind me. If they'd just outright excommunicated me, or if I'd shown my anger and abruptly left, I'd not have had the opportunity to see from my new perspective how people interpret the sudden disappearance of others from fellowship. I'd witnessed such disappearances over the years, and it always seemed similar to witnessing a ship sinking and the sea returned to normal – and no one said a word or investigated the cause. It's strange that such a thing could happen, but among the Friends and Workers such a reaction seems to be appreciated for the appearance of peace it maintains. I've never heard of a search party attempting to rescue such *capsized vessel*, nor a mission to find out why a person left and lessons to be learned from his departure. In fact, it's discouraged, sometimes vigorously, with warnings that associating with the one who disappeared is akin to exposing oneself to evil influence. Any consideration of failure by the *system* is simply taboo.

What followed that week of evaluating my situation was every bit as insightful and exasperating as anything that had happened previously. I'm sure it was because I kept showing up occasionally, and never where I was assigned to meet, making it obvious that I'd neither been kicked out nor left of my own accord. But among the Friends and Workers such behavior is disturbing because it threatens the order of things. Individuals have been excommunicated for not attending the meetings they've been assigned to. I could have been taken to task for that, but I'd already demonstrated without words that there was *a problem*, and I'm sure they weren't going to risk what I might do if they confronted me again about something.

But as it turned out, I didn't get off that easily. Days later I received an email from Mike Colson. He wanted to talk to me alone, so we met at a Mexican restaurant. We ordered, and he said he was at a loss for words. But he wanted me to know that everyone loved us and missed us in the meeting.

But I was primed. I told him I was quite fed up with being harassed. I asked him when was the last time I'd been absent from a fellowship meeting, and he said he couldn't remember. I told him I didn't appreciate his saying that I preferred fellowship with outsiders to fellowship with the meeting. I told him I also didn't appreciate being told about my prayers, and asked him if he'd ever heard me thanking God for those I could have fellowship with. He told me I prayed about that frequently. I asked him who he thought I meant when I said those words, and he said he just assumed it was other people I was having fellowship with and not the meeting. I assured him it was the people in the meeting that I was referring to.

I said, "I expect you were sent to our meeting so you could keep track of the disturbing things I say in meeting." He looked shocked. Then he stammered, "Well, no – no, I'm sure that's not what was said. But I forget the exact words." He was so transparent. He went on to explain that he does everything the Workers tell him – and never questions it. And he gives them all the support he can afford, because they were the only way to heaven and he didn't want to miss it.

He even told me that between 5:00 p.m. on Friday and time to go to work again on Monday morning, he has no dealings with nonprofessing people – so he would not be tainted by the world. He even told his relatives (he has no professing relatives) not to call him between those times unless there was a death in the family or something equally important. He said he'd begun taking his kids to ski at a different ski slope because that's where all the other Friends went skiing. He was getting quite carried away with his own righteousness.

So I brought him back. I asked him if he knew that Nancy had been snubbing Karen and Judy continuously for years. Of course he hadn't noticed. I asked him if he thought he could have fellowship with someone who wouldn't speak to him for years on end. He wasn't sure what the answer was. I reminded him he didn't even know that Judy was deaf. I asked him if he would take his wife to a pot luck in the home of a woman who would not speak to her. He shrugged his shoulders.

Then I said to him, "Speaking of the ministry, what is this business you are harping on about me not supporting the ministry?" He explained that Linda Passage had told him that Bill was evil and should be shunned, and I hadn't shunned him. I pointed out that since Bill was allowed to go back to meetings, he (Mike) had accepted him in his own Sunday morning meeting. He stuttered again. Then he explained that when Harold had come to him to ask if he had any objection whatsoever to Bill going to his meeting, he realized that Bill was going to be allowed back to meeting and if he (Mike) wanted to be "on the side of the Workers" he was going to have to be supportive of that. So he told Harold he had no objections. That also was a revealing statement, though not at all surprising.

I said, "So I was right all along – Bill has returned to meeting. Why, then, am I still being hounded for disobeying the Workers on this matter?" He launched into a long explanation of times appropriate for various different things, and about the Workers having *unctions* from God. I'd indeed heard of such unctions – the term undoubtedly comes from the scriptural passage: *But ye have an **unction** from the Holy*

One, and ye know all things.[1] Among the Friends and Workers *unctions* typically refers to the *hunches* Workers get when deciding disputations, but I never accepted their interpretation of that passage. Considering the dictionary definition of the word *unction* and its grammatical placement in the biblical passage, I understand it to mean that the layman has the *comforting anointing* of such knowledge in himself, and did not need a preacher to tell him.

I reminded Mike about the way the Friends had behaved when we'd had our visitors in the area the summer before. He told me the Workers had told everyone it was for people who'd been put out of fellowship. He questioned me on who was at the get together, so I told him exactly who they were and where they were from. He was quite surprised to discover they were people who went to Worker approved meetings. I assured him I had indeed told the Workers who the people were who were coming, and asked him if he thought what the Workers had told him was true. He didn't know what to say.

He eventually got around to the standard lecture. He told me I had to obey the Workers because that is the only way to salvation. I told him, "Salvation is not equal to membership in this religion." That set him off, and it was quite revealing. He launched authoritatively into a fullfledged sermon. First he explained the history of the church. He said there was an uninterrupted line of Workers from the first twelve apostles until today. I asked specifically, and he assured me it was two-by-two *every* year – since Jesus. I asked him where he'd learned that, and he told me the Workers told him. He told me it was that *fact* that most convinced him that this is the "only true religion". I almost laughed, but I didn't want to miss whatever else he thought I should know.

I told him I'd been around Workers a lot longer than he, and I could tell him things that would destroy his faith. He said, "Oh no, oh no, oh no. I know where my faith is based." So I let him go on. Remember – this from a man who'd been a devout Roman Catholic until just recently, and still the novice among the professing men in the area.

He explained all the laws of submission to me. Young Workers must obey old Workers, women Workers must obey men Workers, saints must obey Workers, and the people in the meeting had to obey the elder. So I thought I'd try something. I said, "Mike, the Bible says we are all to submit to each other." And he said, "That's what I'm telling you." He told me he used to believe my way of thinking was OK, but Andrea Gronley (a Worker) had explained the *pecking order* to him, and he now understood that we had to submit to that – "or else". So the conclusion of the matter was that I was supposed to obey him because he was now an elder. No wonder he was so greatly frustrated with me.

I hadn't expected to make any progress with him anyway, but I did take advantage of the meeting to find out as much as I could about where he was at. I wasn't surprised about anything, but at least I knew that I was not misreading him as he'd been misreading us. I was glad I still had my tape recorder in the pocket of my sports jacket. I used it because that's what one does when he can't trust people to either believe him or quote him accurately. And I didn't want to forget or misquote anything he told me.

The next Sunday, ten days after the tribunal, was Union Meeting, so I decided I would go. That meeting was at Jay Clark's house. It was a big meeting, and Lois was there. Judy was not with me, of course, so I found a seat beside Bill. I was in no condition to either pray or speak – so I did neither. When the meeting was over I made my way rather quickly to the front door. I talked briefly outside with our good friends, the Lynches, from Sparks, and gave them an inkling of what had been going on with us. They said, "Come to our meeting," and I thanked them.

As I turned to leave I noticed Lois approaching me, running, from around the end of the house. She'd apparently gone out the back door and ran around the house so she could intercept me before I got in my car and left. She wanted to have a visit with Judy and me. I told her Judy was not up to that. She wanted to have a visit with me. I said I'd have to think about it. She said she'd email me, and let me go.

I was really torn about what to do. I was in no mood to have anything to do with her, but I decided I needed a one on one talk with her. I'd never had a personal visit with her, so I didn't know what to expect. We met at a restaurant for coffee, and she had her companion, Marilyn Denio, with her. She really didn't have much to say except to cordially tell me that she hoped we were all going to be all right.

I was flabbergasted by her audacity. She'd just given me a clear insight into the mentality I'd been dealing with – not just hers, but the ministry collectively. Days earlier I'd been treated like a trouble maker and a liar, say nothing about how my wife had been embarrassed in front of the church – and now I was supposed to be comforted by nothing more than her hope that we were going to be all right. In plain language, it meant that any Worker could treat me any way deemed effective and I was expected to find it edifying. So I discussed our chances at being all right.

I told her I didn't have much hope that things were going to be all right. I told her we were quite tired of being harassed, and that I was really upset that Karen and Judy were being called on the carpet for something so trivial. She acknowledged that what Judy had done did seem to be quite a trivial thing, but gave no hint that she may have overreacted, much less offer an apology. I told her I thought we'd gotten a real kick in the teeth, considering everything else that went on in our meeting in the last few years. So she offered, "Oh yes, we have all been upset about Bill. It will be so nice when he won't have to deal with the probation any more." I decided she was either terribly stupid or trying to bluff me, but probably both.

So I told her, "I'm not talking about Bill. I'm talking about Nancy Clark openly snubbing Karen and Judy in meetings for years, and now getting this response from the Workers. I'm talking about learning from the Friends that the Workers have been warning our local friends to stay away from our professing company. I'm talking about learning that Workers in Texas were warning the Friends there about the evil influence it would be on them to come here to visit us. I'm not pleased to hear that Overseers were consulting each other about the 'unconvention' I was supposed to have planned for people who were put out of fellowship, especially since I'd told them on two occasions that I was planning no such thing. I didn't like the way the Friends came and watched us have a picnic from afar. And I really don't like to be yelled at by the elder for ninety minutes straight."

Her response was priceless, and classic. She agreed that "sometimes the Friends get carried away with their gossip and it can be very hard on other Friends when they do." So I corrected her, "This gossip didn't come from the Friends – it came from Workers in all cases, and I've been given the names of a number of Workers in a number of states who've discussed me. Aside from being reported to the police by Norman Dunn, I'm not really afraid of what any of the Friends can do to me."

That really set her off – I finally had her attention. She said, "You know, if you aren't going to take part in meeting, we'll have to reconsider your qualifications for being the alternate elder." Ah-hah, my forfeiture for being honest. I didn't respond to that – I knew she'd soon enough find out what I'd decided on that matter.

I told her I'd come to the conclusion that I was going to have to "disentangle myself from some relationships that [were] distressing me" – that I was beginning to suffer physically and I had no more energy to invest in trying to keep peace with them. She seemed delighted to hear that. She said, "I think that's a good thing for you to do. You really don't need to be exposing yourself to people who are going to disturb your spiritual peace." It was quite an impressive little speech, but her enthusiasm for my proposal told me she had not a clue what I'd been trying to tell her. I didn't have the nerve right then to tell her she was at the top of the list of people I was going to cool it with.

At that point I decided the conversation would be over and made moves to put my coffee cup aside. Marilyn spoke up then and said she'd be in the Carson City meeting in the morning, and asked me if I could be there too. She was extremely kind about it, and I suspected she was not pleased with a lot of the rest that had been said in the visit. So I said I'd see in the morning whether I could handle it.

The next morning I did go to meeting – at the Bunches' house. When I went in everyone was looking at me, of course. There was an empty seat beside Marilyn, so I sat there. I don't remember much of what was said in that meeting. I do remember my own testimony. No wonder. In the last four weeks I'd been both blasted for what I said in meeting and threatened for what I didn't say in meeting. But I wasn't afraid of Marilyn.

When the meeting was over I got up and shook hands with a few people between my seat and the door. I hadn't intended to make a full tour of everyone in the room, but Mike Colson wasn't going to let me off so easily. I saw him push people aside so he could make his way to me. He shook my hand and gushed about how good it was to have me in the meeting. I never went back to that meeting again. Our very best friends, Bea and Ernie Rabe, were in that meeting, and I hated to not go to fellowship meetings with them there. But I couldn't deal with the rest of that scene any more. After that day I did go to Sunday meeting in Reno area at Dave and Sharon Lynches on occasion, but never on a regular basis.

I went to Bea and Ernie's for Bible Study a few times over the next couple of months. By that time the Colsons had been moved out of that Wednesday meeting, so I expected they'd no longer be there. Then one evening I walked into the room and the Colsons were sitting there – and I had a sudden feeling of nausea. If I'd known they were going to be there I'd have stayed home – I had no intention of wasting my medication for nausea producing stress on Mike Colson. After the meeting they announced that they'd be temporarily at that Bible Study a few more times, so when I saw their car in front of the house the next time I turned around and went home.

Then, one evening soon after that, Norman Dunn's family came into the meeting, and I learned that they'd been reassigned to that Wednesday evening meeting. I realized I wasn't emotionally well enough to deal with Norman's presence either, so I signed up for a college class on Wednesday evenings rather than take a pill. I was just divorcing myself from relationships that distressed me.

It turned out to be a good move. I had always enjoyed studying, and since I no longer needed credits for any professional qualifications I was free to take any course I wanted just for interest sake. Since then, as often as I could I have taken such courses because they've been so comforting to me. A three-hour evening with a large cup of coffee and a stimulating lecture has been a regular source of enjoyment, as well as the accompanying study and assignments.

On March 15 I got an email from Mike Colson:

I need to ask you a couple of logistical questions about Sunday Mtg. The first is if you decided to continue to come to the Mtgs, do you have any problem with leading the singing? ... We struggle when you are not there, but even with that, you should feel no pressure to do that it you'd rather not.
The second is a little more touchy to express...I hope that I can share my thought and help you to understand my concern without hurting your feelings ... We will be making several trips in the next 5 months and will not be at Velma's a good number of Sundays. How do you feel about leading the Mtgs, or do you want me to ask for a different alternate elder?
... Again, I am in no way trying to push you out...on the contrary, I have been praying very heavily daily for you and the others...I sincerely hope that you will continue to be in the Mtgs and to lead the singing and also be willing to lead the Mtgs in my absence. Please advise.

I decided it was time to clarify how I felt about being the alternate elder of that meeting. So I sent the following email to both Harold and Lois:

March 18:
I have decided that it would be best for everyone if I were no longer the alternate elder of the Sunday meeting at Bunches. I am physically and emotionally unable to deal any longer with the atmosphere of suspicion and distrust that I have been confronted with. It has also been disconcerting that the elder can presume to literally scream at me and tell me he can no longer have fellowship with me whenever he disagrees with me. I am sure you will be able to replace me in that role.

The next day I replied to Mike's email: *I have already told Harold and Lois that I will not be the alternate elder anymore, so they will be looking after that.* A few days later Harold replied:

March 22:
I received your email stating that you are not able at this time to continue as alternate elder of the Carson City Sunday morning meeting. We will ask [Jay C.] to take the meetings when Mike is out of town. I am sorry that neither Judy or you are presently feeling well. I had a bout with my health two years ago, but am grateful to now be back on top. Bob, I am pulling for Judy and you to recover. Hopefully, you will be able for Mtn. Ranch convention. I'd love to see all of you there.

Harold H

About the end of March I received a letter from Lois. She said she wanted us to know that our "brethren love" us, and that we should be diligent in going to meetings because that's where we acquire our sense of peace. I remember saying out loud, "Yes, except when you show up and embarrass someone." She said that if she were to return to the area after conventions she'd do whatever was necessary to help us, so I decided I'd tell her in plain terms what she would have to address. The following includes excerpts from the letter I wrote her:

April 5, 2002
Dear Lois
Thank you for your letter .....
Harold made a special trip here to tell me that he didn't want to hear about what was distressing me, and he didn't want me to speak to anyone else about it. It is no wonder our brethren do not understand us – I have been expected to cover for workers who have abused my name, insulted my wife, and scandalized us and others among professing people; and the whole thing was reduced to "the Bill matter"! It is demeaning and disrespectful of workers to speak so about the friends, and yet gag the friends so they will not speak about the workers. I felt betrayed, because I knew full well that if I ended up in court on this matter that the workers would be there to support my accusers! ..... I also have to add that, since Bill has been restored to fellowship, it has to indicate disapproval of me personally that I am still being criticized for standing by him when everyone else was forbidden to speak to him.

..... What transpired in the meeting in February where you were so upset with us was just the straw that broke the camel's back. And to be perfectly honest, when I consider that you have been a worker for so long, I cannot imagine that anything she [Judy] did in that meeting should cause you to lose your train of thought. It appears to me that you were looking for an opportunity to take her to task and took advantage of the situation. Whether you did it on purpose or as a practiced tactic, what you did in fact was embarrass her in front of the church to make her behave. In the best of circumstances that is a demeaning thing to do and does not reflect the spirit of a shepherd. Embarrassing someone in front of their friends is an exercise in control, not correction. .....

..... the fact of the matter is that I become physically ill at the prospect of facing some of the friends and workers, and it does not help one bit to know that workers are suspicious of my intentions and warning people about associating with me. It seems strange to me that you would recommend more exposure to these distressing things as a source of comfort!

..... I really don't expect any worker to have the guts to tell anyone exactly why Judy cannot go to meeting now. I am wondering how a worker could be honestly willing to help people understand what is going on with us. If you can appreciate this predicament, I would be more than happy to discuss this further with you.

..... Again, thank you for your letter. It would not surprise me, and I will understand, if you find that you can do nothing more for us than to express sympathy.

Yours Sincerely, Bob

I let my own physical revulsion keep me from my abusers, which is why I went to Sparks occasionally for meetings. I also found I couldn't handle large gatherings of the Friends, and it reminded me of others I've known who had also developed such a problem as I – one of them my ex-Worker cousin. I'd long wondered why it was that most adults who'd suddenly and unexplainably left the Truth, were normally reported to have developed a *bad spirit*. I was beginning to understand what could be included under the bad spirit umbrella.

After Mike decided he couldn't accomplish anything with me, he apparently decided to work on Karen. He sent her an email asking her to return to his meeting. She was quite upset by it, because his appeal to her was all about her *only hope of salvation*. Interspersed with his comments about her *despising the ministry*, he berated her for *disrespecting* my brother's sacrifice as a Worker in West Africa. He also reviewed for her how greatly his own personality had improved since he professed, as he frequently used to do in his testimonies in meeting. Coming from a professional salesman, it was strangely threatening and accusative as a sales pitch. I volunteered to answer for Karen because she didn't want him pestering her with emails.

May 20, 2002
Mike .....
I recognize it as your effort to encourage her [Karen] to return to your meeting. But you seem to be forgetting why it is that she (and Judy) isn't going to that meeting. It was the direct result of your (and Sherry's) complaints that they had a bad attitude and were disturbing the meeting. Before you ever had a clue to understand their behavior you made a major case about it with the workers. That's not how friends "deal" with each other. That's not how gentlemen do business with each other. That's not how the Scriptures tell us to deal with our brothers. .....
..... She does not hate anyone, but she does hate deception, manipulation, and abuse – especially sexual abuse. This is not hypothetical ravings about workers on her part, and it is not something that happened once in some other place. It has also happened in California – and recently.
..... Your mention ... of my brother was somewhat of a low blow. There is nothing but a longstanding, honorable, loving, and trusting uncle niece relationship between Karen and Armand. I resent that you would intrude on that relationship by attempting to align him with yourself in this discussion. .....
I think you went much too far overboard with your evaluation of my brother and his ministry. While he was in "the depths of Africa" he had ... ready access to the best medical care in the world, with no insurance hassles like we have to cope with. And about his

ministry – he is part of a ministry that was founded about 100 years ago by a man from the Faith Mission and a couple of others from the Methodist church. We even inherited the word "worker" from the Faith Mission. .....

... it doesn't really impress me or matter to me what you were before you professed – my experience with you is that you can still scream at me for 90 minutes straight (I timed you), until I thought you were going to have a heart attack. I have never in my life had anyone talk to me in such a manner – you were outrageous and abusive, but I suspect you still thought you were going to accomplish something by yelling at me. And to finish up you said you couldn't have fellowship with me any more. What a childish threat! I don't really know what you expect from me, except that I "just melt into submission" to you like you do with the workers. No, Mike, you are not going to get your tongue on either my wife or my daughter. You are perfectly welcome to talk to me, but until there is more of the spirit of the Dove in you I do not want you talking to them.

Sincerely, Bob

It took him a while to respond. My guess is that he spent a couple of days on the telephone before he did reply. Here is his answer:

May 31:
... There are a number of things that I could say at this time. There is apart [sic]of me that would defend and counter your thoughts. But I am not going to enter into this game. You have thrown many stones my way and they shall lie on my doorstep. That is what Jesus did when persecuted...I will not be able to visit or correspond with either of you any more. I have found that it serves to make the division wider and absolutely only discourages me exceedingly. I've decided that I am going on. I surely invite you both, and Judy too, to come along. If you do that would be great. If not, that is fine and certainly your choice to make. I simply cannot continue to deal with the situation as it is and it is very obvious to me there is nothing I can do. It is in your hands. I just do not want to read or speak about the negative things that you are involved with. I

am fresh with convention thoughts and am no longer going to be entangled with the negativity. Jesus only and always uplifted people...that is what I am striving to do. If either of you want to talk/write in a positive manner...or discuss things in an uplifting manner...you will have my complete attention. Otherwise, let us just part company. If you choose to be at Mtg..I will extend myself to you as best as is humanly possible. I will not shun either of you in any way. Again, that is what Jesus would do. I won't be communicating with either of you any more. I suspect that will please you both. I wish you the best and harbor no ill feelings and hope you feel the same.

Mike Colson

Poor persecuted fellow.

CHAPTER 14

And There Is More

In May of that year I went to New Brunswick for a week, primarily to see my father who'd had cancer surgery and came through it with a questionable prognosis. I knew it was going to be my last time to see him, so I didn't burden him with my difficulties. But he did have an idea of what was happening with us. In the beginning he warned me against saying anything to the Workers. But as events unfolded and I told him of occasional incidents, all he would say was that I'd done the right thing, and I'd been "put there for a reason." He was never one to involve himself in anything controversial, but my mother had this to say about me: "You're just like your grandfather Williston – when something is wrong, it's not right." Anyway, I realize I have a low tolerance for bullying, having been bullied a lot as a child.

When I returned from New Brunswick I started a new job – this time in Reno. It was a switch from anything I'd done before, but it gave me a decent raise and the challenge of being in a management position. One of the benefits was that it meant at least a half hour commute each way, and that did something for me psychologically. I had the commute time to meditate without interruption – barring a wreck on the freeway. But I was still suffering from the sick anxiety that would wash over me from time to time. My family was extremely good to me. I was the only one still going to meetings, and I had the decency not to agonize them with an invitation to go with me. Of course, they didn't understand why or how I could continue to go to meetings – even to the meetings in Reno. I had by then decided that I'd soon leave the meetings altogether, but in the meantime I intended to attend meetings as a *visitor*. I felt I'd earned the right to leave on my own terms, and I wanted to see what insights I could get in the meantime.

But what had become of Alice Dunn, Bill's *victim*? Some time in March of that year she was married to a young fellow who'd come to work in the area. The Workers enthusiastically announced that they were going to the wedding, and referred to it as a "joyous occasion". By June we learned that she was pregnant, and we were hoping that might get her over her obsession with Bill.

Lois returned to the area that June, and I had my first contact with her since I'd answered her note about helping us. I went to meeting that morning, and seeing no suspicious looking car parked on the street, I went in – and Lois was sitting in the meeting room. I considered leaving, but changed my mind. After the meeting was over she shook my hand and said simply, "It's good to have you in the meeting." She seemed quite subdued from her normal self, and that was a relief.

When Special Meetings came in late September, I got another worried phone call from Bill. He'd received a summons from the court to appear for a hearing concerning alleged violations of his probation. Alice had reportedly complained to the court that Bill had arranged for the Special Meeting pot luck to be in his housing complex, and that meant she couldn't go to it – it being held too closely to Bill's residence. She also said she wanted to confront Bill in court with her husband so she could properly impress on him how much fear she lived with that he would further harm her after his probation was lifted.

Incidentally, we all knew that Bill had not made the arrangements for the pot luck. Everyone everywhere knew he wasn't even allowed to go to such gatherings, say nothing about arranging it for everyone. In fact, it was Alice's cousin who'd made the arrangements. I could have gone to the pot luck myself, but I didn't. I'd checked the names of Workers who'd be at Special Meetings, and decided to go only for the morning meeting because there was a visiting Worker. It was obvious that the only man left to speak in the afternoon was Harold Hilton, so I left at lunch time.

A week after Special Meetings I went to court with Bill on a Monday morning. I had a couple of friends visiting from western Canada that weekend, so they stayed over through Monday morning to go to court with us. I was glad we were there. Alice arrived, obviously many months pregnant, with her husband. Her husband didn't know me, and she seemed not to recognize me – I'd grown a full beard during the previous six months.

Besides Alice's complaint that Bill had arranged for the Special Meeting pot luck, there were several other charges. Among them was her complaint that Bill had been distressing her by showing up at meetings – but she omitted the fact that he'd never been in any meetings she attended. She also said that Bill was using the Internet to access child pornography. She obviously had no idea how Bill was being supervised as a "sex offender".

Then it got more interesting. The judge asked the probation officer for an update on Bill's probation. The probation officer, I remind you, sits on the side of the district attorney and is normally there to substantiate the accusations of the D.A. with specifics from his investigation of the charges. But instead, he described Bill as a model probationer who had cooperated in all ways with the probation office. He also said that, as required, he had investigated every complaint that had been made about Bill and found them all to be unsubstantiated. The judge displayed great interest in the inconsistencies between what the D.A. had presented and what the officer reported.

Then the judge asked Bill's attorney for his comments. He gave an impassioned summary of events – Bill was a model probationer, the probation officer confirmed it, and the *victim* on several occasions had made complaints to the court that "could not be substantiated". He suggested that Bill be discharged from probation so he could get on with his life and put this event behind him.

The judge then asked the probation officer what his recommendation was. The officer responded that he would make the "standard recommendation" for Bill – that he complete his probation. Then the judge asked him specifically if he would recommend an early honorable discharge from probation. The officer kind of stuttered, and said he would not. The judge asked him why not, and the officer told him that his agency would not allow him to recommend early discharge for any probationers convicted of a sex offence. Then he added, "But a judge may intervene and order a discharge on his own." It sounded very much to me like the probation officer was doing everything legally possible for him to help Bill. At this point I will take the liberty to note that where my daughter worked, in parole and probation the consensus was "Bill got thoroughly shafted."

So the judge turned to Bill's attorney and told him that *he wanted* a petition to have Bill's probation discharged. He went on to say that this case had been going on for five years, and from what he could determine it was much more about an internal conflict in the church than it was about Bill. *That* comment was a startlingly insightful comment on the judge's part – not simply because he perceived the strife within the church, but evidenced by the fact that he even asked to have Bill's probation discharged early. It is virtually unheard of that such a discharge would be granted. So the judge instructed Bill's attorney to take two months to collect letters from church members who could support Bill's bid for a discharge, and prepare a petition for the court to consider.

That was great enough news, but the judge went even further. He ordered that Bill be allowed to attend all church worship and social functions that he chose, and Alice was directed to inquire before she went to any such event to see if Bill was going to be there. If she did not want to be there with him she was ordered to stay away. That ruling turned the tables completely.

One of my Canadian friends did not sit with me in the courtroom, so when we all came out to the lobby he stood around and eavesdropped on a conversation among the D.A., Alice, and her husband. She was upset because she didn't get to *speak personally* to Bill in front of the judge – she obviously still didn't know what court is about. She cried for a while, but the D.A. proceeded to give her a lecture. He told her she couldn't have Bill locked up for the rest of his life. She had to even accept the fact that Bill was probably going to get an early discharge, and it wasn't going to do her any good to continue to pursue this case.

I sent the following e-mail that evening.

October 7, 2002
Harold and Lois,

I was in court today in Minden to see how the hearing for Bill Frost went, and some decisions were made that I thought you should know about. According to the District Attorney the victim had complained a number of times about him violating the terms of his probation, the most recent violation being that Bill had organized the Special Meeting potluck in his community. Bill's probation officer reported that this accusation could not be substantiated, as could a number of other accusations not be substantiated. In the court today the victim also expressed an interest in confronting Bill with her husband, but the court did not consider that request.

At the conclusion of the hearing the judge asked whether the probation officer would recommend that Bill have his probation discharged, but the officer said that his agency did not allow him to recommend a discharge regardless of Bill's manner of compliance. The judge recognized that fact, and said that judges have the authority to intervene and order a discharge. The judge expressed an interest in receiving a petition from Bill's attorney to have Bill's probation discharged, but it was pointed out that there had not been enough notice given for Bill and his attorney to have a petition ready for today. The judge then advised that, because of his exemplary record, Bill's attorney should obtain in the next couple of months the documentation necessary for them to make a petition for January, 2003. The judge expressly pointed out that this case was as much a church issue as anything else, and he asked that letters be obtained from people in the church who could attest to Bill's appropriate behavior since he was let out of jail. Since the ministry was quite intimately involved in Bill's arrest, and since the onus now is on the church to confirm the judge's conclusions about Bill's behavior, I am presuming that you would be interested in providing such letters for Bill, since you have worked in this field and had ample opportunity to visit with him since he was arrested.

In the meantime the court has ordered that if the victim wishes to go to any function of the church membership, the victim is to inform Bill's probation officer ahead of time so that "she" can avoid going to that event. Otherwise, Bill should be allowed to attend functions as he chooses.

I should also tell you that if you could do this for Bill, it would lift a legal restriction from my family as well, since Karen is required to have prior permission from her supervisor before she can visit with Bill or any member of his family.

          Thank you. Bob Williston

A few days later Harold sent me a short reply. He said this was no real emergency, so he would let Lois consider the matter. He just confirmed my suspicion that the only emergency was making sure *Bob Williston* gave appropriate praise to the Workers.

A couple of days later I got a response from Lois. She told me that until she *had a chance to read the court record all the restrictions on Bill would remain in place.* I was not in the least surprised by her reply.

I found it interesting to learn that Lois had told one of the Friends that she was very worried about what was going to happen after Bill was off probation and Alice was free to approach him as she pleased at any time. Having that concern, what was wrong with me that she couldn't share that mutual concern with me?

In November we had the misfortune of losing my mother in law. It wasn't an unexpected event – she'd not been well for some time. But it was a great loss nonetheless. I appreciated the fact that Lois sent Judy a sympathy card, but I wondered about her wisdom in including the next year's Bible Study list and convention list with the card.

About that time we also learned that my father wasn't doing well. They'd found cancerous growths in his lymph glands when they'd operated earlier in the year, and it hadn't allowed for a lot of hope.

Christmas time came, and we did get to have our usual special family celebration of fun together. But for me the celebration was dampened by a bad case of shingles on my face – I narrowly escaped the disaster that comes with getting it in my eye. I did have lesions on my eyelid.

It was my second bout with shingles in this time period. I'd previously had shingles in the summer of 2000 after the fiasco over the picnic for our visitors. About the same time, one of the few Friends I felt I could confide in advised me that he'd notified the parents of Bill's new girlfriend that Bill had an unsavory character and history. I felt betrayed by that development, much the way I felt betrayed when Linda Passage decided to use my name to kick Souza out of fellowship. Fortunately, the girlfriend's family already knew more about Bill than the *Friend* could tell them, and the two have since married, and according to my last news of them have two children.

Soon after New Years of 2003 we got the news that my Dad had passed away. I'd have liked to be with my mother and four brothers for the funeral, but I was still recovering from the shingles and I couldn't handle such an ordeal. I was sad, of course. But it brought me to the full realization that my experience of the past 5 years had left me quite numb to emotions that I would previously have had. I really did not weep over my father's death, and that concerned me greatly.

That wasn't the first time I'd noticed this response in myself. Following the fiasco of February 2002 I found it impossible to weep over anything that had happened. I recognized that I'd long enough set aside my emotions to deal with what I had to deal with, and that I'd come to the sad, lonely, and empty place where one is all alone – no matter who still bothered with me. I had gotten so I could do little more than go to work, try to do my job, and return home and eat my meals and sleep. I began losing weight because I got so I couldn't finish most meals I sat down to.

Soon after my father passed away, Bea Rabe passed away. Then it was only a couple of weeks later that Ernie passed away. It was a very sad time for us – we felt like we had no more friends left in Carson City. Our relationship with Bill became complicated – we didn't want to make things difficult for him because he remained so friendly toward us. There remained one couple we could comfortably enjoy visiting with or eating out together – Ken and Mary Hornady.

Letters of recommendation for Bill were to be sent in by January and Bill's attorney received a number that he included with his petition. Harold and Lois decided they wouldn't write letters for Bill – I don't know that they ever gave a reason why. For a while it looked like the judge was not going to get a satisfactory recommendation to discharge his probation. But by then it appeared we should not have worried about that because the judge had apparently figured out exactly what was going on among the Friends and Workers.

One day Bill got a letter from the judge saying that he was being honorably discharged from his probation, and all his civil rights would be restored. The judge went on to explain that he'd concluded that the *victim* would *never* be satisfied with what the court did with Bill, and he (the judge) had written her a letter advising her that Bill's case is closed and he was not interested in any more discussion with her about it. Interestingly, Bill's probation officer came to visit Bill and gave him a bit of advice: have nothing whatsoever to do with that family or you'll find yourself in legal difficulty with them again.

When it was learned that Bill's probation was discharged, Dick Middleton came to Nevada and had a visit with Bill and Lois. Dick apologized for not coming to the area when the first complaint was raised about Bill as early as 1998. But if he'd done nothing more at that time than he'd done for Bill in the five years since then, it wouldn't have changed anything anyway. Before Dick left, Bill asked him if he could now go to Special Meetings and Convention. Dick's answer was, "I don't know." Is there not something wrong when the highest authority in the church hierarchy doesn't know whether someone can attend services or not?

With Bill's discharge came his opportunity to leave the state, which he did. He's doing well. I had occasion to meet people with whom he has fellowship in the state he moved to, and they assured me he is much appreciated where he is.

It was some time during 2003 that I went to my doctor and he informed me that my two daughters had been to see him. They'd told him they were worried about me because I was depressed, and not behaving as my normal self. He'd already prescribed medication for my anxiety, and it was helping. But he was very insightful – he said, "You're not telling me what your real problem is. If you don't tell me I can't help you?" I have never before or since broken down in the doctor's office, but that day I did. I knew what was wrong with me, and I knew I needed help, so I told him exactly what had happened to me. "You have to get out of that church," he warned me. He said he didn't know what I believed or where I might want to go, but for my health I had to remove myself from the situation. I agreed with him. I was surprised to find that Judy had had virtually the same conversation with her doctor.

Just knowing that my response to what had happened was nothing out of the ordinary was a comfort in itself.

CHAPTER 15

The Other Matter

During the time that all of these happenings were taking place in Nevada, there was another serious problem being dealt with in California. I made mention of this in Chapter 7 when I was visiting with Dick Middleton, the California Overseer. It was my concern about why Bill had been treated so contemptibly when a Worker who had done far worse had been vigorously sheltered from the law.

It was the case of Ruben Mata. Ruben was a Worker in the California jurisdiction, and easily old enough to be a grandfather. I'd met him a number of times and found him a pleasant enough man to visit with, but he was a serial child predator – and from what I could gather he had a history of offending for as much as two decades. To deal with his proclivity, he'd been on occasion moved away from his victims – once being assigned to work in Mexico. Finally he was put out of the ministry, at which time he went to live with his mother and was assigned to attend a meeting in that area.

I had twice been accused to my face of "promoting immorality", and most certainly discussed by many as defending a *child molester* – despite the fact that my concern was first of all about the untruths being promoted by the Workers. The fact of the matter was, I possibly knew more about child molestation than most people who were discussing my activities.

Once, upon reaching the age of puberty, I went with friends of my family to a convention in another province. I found the area of the sleeping quarters where some of my young friends were sleeping, and I claimed the only space left. The bunks were arranged side by side with the heads against the wall and the feet on the aisle. A close friend of mine was in the bunk on my left side, but when time for lights out approached that night a strange looking middle aged man arrived to occupy the bunk on my right.

To make a long story short, a hand slipped under my blanket in the dark, and I was too startled to move, I was too afraid to draw anyone else's attention, and I was ashamed of how my body had responded to his attentions. He got what he was after, but not without explaining that what *we* were doing was perfectly normal – it was just not polite to talk about it with others. Everyone did it, I would come to understand, and the more I did it the more I would enjoy it and it was going to be the most wonderful experience of my life. I wasn't impressed – I thought I'd suffered a seizure.

Some years later I learned the reason the bunk beside horny Harold (not Harold Hilton) was vacant – the other kids all knew what he liked to do. It turned out he was an ex-Worker, and parents had complained about him to the Overseer. The Overseer didn't believe he'd do such a thing – until Harold made a pass at the Overseer himself. Then the Overseer sent him home, and that was all that was ever done about it. Harold appeared later at a convention in my own province and people flocked to welcome him because he was an ex-Worker ... who had to leave the ministry because of his nerves, or maybe his health. The sight of him made me ill. I've not forgotten how a molested child feels about such unwanted attention.

Through my teens I learned of a number of other incidents of sexual indiscretions committed by Workers. Most of them occurred between consenting adults, and it seemed the remedy for those errors was that they left the ministry and married. Incidents of child molestation I believed were rare, always revealed in whispered confidence, and normally resulting in the offender being sent to another area – or sent home with his expulsion being attributed to health or nerve problems. I used to believe the Workers had a blanket policy of advising the Friends not to report each other to the police. But over the years I've discovered that the most commonly mentioned Worker policy was that they consider each case on its own merits, which didn't do anything to increase my confidence in Workers' decisions.

It was after Bill got out of jail that I began hearing of Friends' concerns in California about what should be done about child molestation by Workers. At the time I treated the concerns as hypotheticals. However, as a teacher, I'd been amply tutored on how to deal with any evidence or *suspicion* of child abuse. It was absolutely never to be ignored – the most convincing argument: outside the legal and justice systems, no one has the means or the authority to enforce corrective measures in those cases. Because of that, I wrote a detailed article explaining how parents could deal with the ministry to assure that they had the help of the law in dealing with the problem.

I soon scrapped that approach when I began studying the problem from the legal perspective. Mandatory reporting had by then become the law, and I learned how law enforcement investigates such crimes. So the critical correction to my article was that anyone who suspects abuse should report it to authorities immediately and without consulting others or questioning the victim him/herself. I firmly stand by that advice still, and I understand the article has been shared among Friends all over North America and perhaps elsewhere.

It was in 2002 that I began a discussion with 'Lloyd Smith', one of the Friends in California. He was the elder of a meeting, and he had both a minor child and a couple of minor foster children in his home. He told me the Workers had assigned Ruben to meeting at his house when he'd been sent home from the ministry, and Lloyd had to refuse to have him there – not simply because there were minors in the house, but because he had to abide by Child Protective Services regulations regarding foster children. According to Lloyd, the Workers then decided to ask Ruben go to a different meeting, but I've never heard whether he ever went to any other meeting.

In further discussions with Lloyd he told me that Ruben, accompanied by a Worker and one of the Friends, had gone to the District Attorney in Tulare County and turned himself in. Lloyd was told that the D.A. decided not to prosecute Ruben because none of his offenses had been committed in Tulare County. Lloyd seemed to accept that at the time – but I didn't, and still don't. It is unthinkable that a D.A. would not act on such an admission by a *mandated reporter*, no matter where the offenses occurred in the state.

Lloyd had also been told that Ruben had been receiving counseling as a result of his visit to the Tulare County D.A.'s office – and the counselor was one of the Friends who had something to do with the D.A.'s office. But what startled me was the advice the counselor was supposed to have given Ruben – it was that he should turn to pornography portraying adult women, which, he was advised, would turn him away from his obsession with children. I told Lloyd at the time that the counselor was obviously a quack. It was then that I decided something was terribly wrong with what was going on.

I became most concerned when Lloyd shared with me that Walter Pollock, an older brother Worker in California, had been visiting with parents and telling them that they should not report Ruben to the authorities. Whether Ruben had committed any such crimes or not, Walter was himself a mandated reporter and should have reported Ruben to the police himself, certainly not advising parents to refrain from reporting.

I agonized over how I should feel about that situation. When I was a child I never felt comfortable being alone with a Worker, not because it ever led to molestation, but because they asked me questions I didn't want to answer. That was why, in Carson City, I refused to let a brother Worker take my young grandson out for a walk – on principle. What began to trouble me were things I remembered happening in Carson City.

Ruben Mata had come to town and stayed for a time with friends of ours – who had two teenage children. Seemingly unrelated to the visit, we learned that Harold Hilton had advised the parents not to report their *son's* misbehavior to law enforcement, citing the fact that it would result in a criminal record. Then puzzlingly and without notice, the couple sold their house, left their good jobs, and moved with their children two states away. I insist that I have no idea if any of these three events are connected in any way. What concerned me was the chance that my young grandchildren needed protection against a ministry that sheltered such a predator. And yes, it crossed my mind that it was the epitome of duplicity that the ministry would shelter a child raping predator, while telling me I was promoting immorality.

In any case, I knew something was terribly wrong with Ruben's case, and I knew I was unable and incompetent to investigate the case, and unauthorized to do anything about it except report it to the police – the police were the ones with the authority and the know-how to do a proper investigation. I also knew that law enforcement had a legal obligation to investigate any suspicion of child abuse. So in late 2003 I called the police in Fresno, California. They asked me for a written complaint, which I provided, along with the names and addresses of people they needed to talk to. I never heard anything more, not even about Ruben's arrest, until the time of his trial in San Jose in 2006. Then when I checked into the court record, I found the complaint that led to his arrest was the precise wording of the complaint I'd filed with the police department.

It appears that in 2005 it was no longer a secret that Ruben had several times sexually abused a five year old boy. But according to the time line of events it was undoubtedly time for the Friends in California to realize that there was an intense investigation underway. I've since been told that it was on the strength of the evidence of that molestation that Ruben was arrested in May of 2006. I wasn't told about that at the time, because I'd already moved away from Northern Nevada and was not on the list of people to be trusted with Truth scuttlebutt. I did learn at the time of Ruben's trial in December of 2006 that he'd been convicted on several counts and sentenced to thirty-six years to life.

One of the Friends who was very concerned about this matter told me personally: *Walter Pollock told them that 'one day they learned about allegations, the next day he was out of the work,' the point being that they removed him from the work as soon as they knew about allegations.* It's obvious Walter Pollock was at least ingenuous when he claimed Ruben was immediately dismissed upon first suspicion, but it was certainly interpreted by the Friends as evidence that the Workers had reported him. The truth was that in the 1990's Ruben was moved away from Mexicali because one of his victims had complained about him to another Worker.

I doubt the Workers had any idea where the formal complaint came from. I discussed my decision with no one ahead of time, and I've not even mentioned it, except with a small number of confidants, since then. Despite the great difficulty I had in deciding to report Ruben, I'm satisfied that the matter got settled in the appropriate way. I don't know that any Workers were ever reported to the police for such an offense before my report, but a number of Workers have been prosecuted for this crime since then – and at least two have been prosecuted for failing to report such abuse. Now that I've been made aware of the official response of the ministry to Ruben's arrest, I feel some comments are in order.

I was not wrong over the years when I assumed that such offending Workers were simply reassigned, or sent home. Despite my earliest encounter with a molester, I never really believed it was just something everyone did and never talked about. Indeed, Workers have gone on public record as claiming that the church will not tolerate pedophiles.[1] But when it comes to reporting pedophiles, Workers have been reported as saying that child sexual abuse, or CSA, should not be reported to authorities but dealt with within the church; and that the main priority should be to prevent false accusations instead of report allegations. One Worker even said he wasn't even free to talk about this matter with people. It's often been said that sexual crimes among the Friends don't get reported in order to protect the victim from embarrassment, which is outrageous by any moral standard because it forced both criminals and their victims to live their lives pretending nothing ever happened, prevented both victims and their criminals to live without any emotional and psychological help they needed, and prevented parents from knowing they were exposing their children to predators. Worst of all, the real purpose for not reporting a Worker's crime was to bolster the good reputation of the ministry, and to *protect the kingdom*.

This reluctance to report such crimes to the authorities undoubtedly arises from the passage in the Bible that warns against taking one's brother to the law[2] – but it's an abuse of that passage when it comes to CSA. Some Bible versions are more explicit than others, but those verses do not refer to crimes, they're about suing one another over private disputes. Ironically the same people who would refuse to inform on a child molester would undoubtedly have no problem reporting a murder – but then the disappearance of a well known human being cannot be hidden quite so easily. A friend of mine suggests this teaching of not reporting may even distort people's understanding of what constitutes a crime, and when confronted with something such as CSA - *they don't understand it as a crime being committed, rather they are devastated by the breach of a moral code or moral ethics.* Which segues smoothly to the realization that among the Friends and Workers human rights are virtually never mentioned, except to condemn efforts to advance one's rights. And despite the severity of the crime, the *culture* of the Truth most often shrugs off any responsibility to report, using the defense that *The way is perfect, but the people are just human.*

There's another reason why such crimes are kept hidden from authorities. It's understood that the ministry is the undisputable core of the faith, and because it is the earthly representation of the will and plan of God, the perfection and integrity of the ministry or any part or member of it are sacred, and to question anything about it is to blaspheme. I say this, truly, in an effort not to accuse the ministry of being self-centered – but in so many ways it has damaging effects on abused individuals in the group. John Sterling, a Worker from the Pacific Northwest, once explained why exposing CSA offenders was not a priority: *"As you know, 'the truth' is not orthodox, and this could destroy 'the truth' as you know it. So we have to be careful that this information does not get into the wrong hands."* [3] It's worth noting that John used the word *expose*, rather than *report, punish,* or *deal with* it in any way that anyone would hear about it. It's a mystery why Workers can even think that the Friends won't share their woes with others anyway.

Ruben's arrest, even though he was by then an ex-Worker, would have been an event that demanded recognition. The ministry was abruptly faced with an *exposure* – the proverbial broom had swept under the twenty-year old rug, and out came their most odious of errors for media distribution. This was fitting, of course, because in the long run we owe the benefits of living in a free society to the openness of the judicial system and the freedom of the press. And it was equally fitting that the Overseer address the Truth community on the matter.

Dale Shultz had become the new Overseer for California following the passing of Dick Middleton. Dale was in his new position in 2006, and composed two letters to the flock, one addressed to the Workers and the other addressed to the Friends. In his letter to the Workers he instructs them on how to use his attached letter to the Friends, or to *Whom It May Concern*.[4] The letter was not to be distributed – to anyone. In my next chapter I will explain why Dale wouldn't want the *to whom it may concern* letter being *exposed*. The Workers were not to make copies of the letter, but show it to any Friends who *asked* about Ruben's case. The Friends were to read it in the presence of the Worker and give it back, *because it is hard to say who all might read [it]*. If the *rare occasion* arose where a Worker felt it should be shown to an *unprofessing person (e.g. a victim)*, the Worker was advised to *consult with us [sic] before using it this way*. He cautioned that if they were not careful with such letters, they can appear on the Internet, and *arouse concerns in those who never were concerned*. The stated *purpose of the letter is to help those who have concerns, not to advertise a kingdom problem to those who either do not know about it or are not having a problem with it*.[5]

Despite its gentle tone, this letter is nothing less than an unmitigated demand for *don't ask – don't tell*. Over the years it's become a widely recognized feature of the Truth community, such that one of the earliest books published about the group was titled *The Secret Sect*. This letter to the Workers was written less than two months after Ruben's arrest, so it appears that Dale at that point was hopeful that somehow the media, including the Internet, could be eluded. In the end not only the complaint against Ruben, but a comment by a juror, circulated through the Internet.

The attached letter, which the Friends were allowed to read, confirmed that the ministry knew about a half dozen cases where Ruben had molested young boys over at least a twenty year period while in the ministry, and admitted they were not sure how many other times he had offended. According to Dale, none of his companions were aware of what Ruben had done. In 1996, though, one of his elder companions was told about a molestation, but the companion didn't think it was a serious enough matter to report. Then a sister Worker was made aware of another molestation incident, and did nothing about it. Another sister Worker then heard of another incident, and reported it to Dick Middleton. That time, according to Dale, Ruben went to the Tulare County District Attorney's office in his failed attempt to turn himself in.[6] I, in the meantime, had reported Ruben to the police in Fresno County, which report led to Ruben's prosecution in Santa Clara County for crimes he committed in at least one other county – and it appears Ruben was arrested in Tulare County anyway. Perhaps the Tulare County D.A. was just lazy. But then, no one really knows what Ruben told the D.A. I understand he could have claimed he'd committed his crimes in Mexicali and he'd have been telling the truth – a safe admission because California has no jurisdiction in Mexicali. In any case, Dick could just as easily have told Ruben to turn himself in to the county where he offended – except that Dick had admitted to *me* that he had sheltered Ruben from prosecution.

As well as the letter to the Friends and Workers, Dale provided his Workers with a document entitled *Guidelines Regarding Incidents of Child Sexual Molestation.*[7] I cannot be sure if that document has since been amended, but as a guideline for Workers in the year 2006 it is a condemnable document. Most of it was devoted to when and how *not* to report to the police. He summarized his options with the statement: *In more severe cases, there may be instances when option (d) seems preferable.* Option (d) was the option of reporting to law enforcement.[8]

The document accurately points out that the Workers in California are mandated reporters of sexual abuse of minors. However, Dale's document *required* that no Worker report any such incident unless given permission by *Overseers*, which is nothing more than a skillfully argued plan to keep everything as it always was – secretive and unreported if at all possible, and under control of the Overseer. The first egregious instruction is that the mandate to report only applies if the abused individual *is still a minor at the time the workers learn* of the allegation. I've been unable to find any indication of that exception to mandated reporting in California. He does suggest that a

Worker *may* still have a moral obligation to report – which is a rather hollow standard of morality for those who consider themselves moral authorities dealing with sexual crimes against children. Furthermore, he makes no mention that California law provides a ten year statute of limitations, which can even be extended if reporting circumstances merit it.[9]

He does acknowledge that California law requires that CSA suspicions be reported within thirty-six hours of learning about it, but he believed that *the law would be flexible regarding the time factor*.[10] It's true, he would need more than thirty-six hours for the report to pass from the younger companion to the older companion, to the regional Overseer, to the general Overseer, then have discussions about which option to choose – but a judge would have a much better understanding of why a thirty-six hour requirement is in place.

Dale's option (a): find counselors for both the victim and the perpetrator, and family members if necessary. Option (b): report alone to a counselor if the victim or perpetrator will not cooperate, thus relieving the Workers of the responsibility of reporting themselves. Or option (c): report to Child Protective Services, who will keep the name of the reporter confidential, and *does not put the responsibility of determining the validity or severity of the case on the workers*.[11]

The man is abysmally naive, not only about CSA, but about what constitutes competent investigation and prosecution of such cases. Overseers with discretion realize they are, because of their position, incompetent to direct any part of such matters. Unless such an incident is reported first of all to law enforcement, the whole case immediately becomes prejudiced and far more likely to be impossible to prosecute. For a Worker to assume the role of counsel to both the victim and the accused is an intolerable conflict of interest. Furthermore, when a Worker then decides how the case should be handled, he has assumed the role of both counselors and the judge – the foundation of tyranny. Workers need to understand that serious crimes against children are crimes, even if one of the Friends or Workers is the perpetrator, and crimes are not adjudicated outside the legal justice system.

Point (8) in Dale's instructions is that Workers may inform the parents that through the California Victim Witness program funding for victims and members of their family is available – *if a police report is filed*. However, he prefers that a police report not be filed if at all avoidable. Translation: He prefers protecting the child molester ahead of counseling for the victim. I can say with virtual certainty that the ministry will *not* be paying for counseling under his options (a), (b), or (c) – an indication of who he intends to help most with his instructions.

For all parents of children, my advice has always been – if you do not have the will to protect your own and your friends children from sexual predators, you can expect no protection from the state – except, perhaps, to be prosecuted for child endangerment.

Mr. Shultz, however, is no longer typical of all Overseers. A friend of mine passed me a note about instructions Barry Barkley, the Overseer of much of the Eastern United States, gave at a gathering of Workers in his jurisdiction:

You are mandated reporters, regardless of what your state law is. You will report in a timely manner, what you see, what you suspect, what you hear and what you are told. You will make that call to the authorities and you will get a log number to keep on record. When asked what about reporting it to an overseer it ... is your choice. You can if you want, it's not required, but regardless you will report it to the law.

Hopefully, for children, this will become the standard for Workers everywhere. Without a doubt the reason CSA never got reported among the Friends is because of fear – fear of Worker condemnation, which for most Friends is paramount to blasphemy. But fear is a wicked enemy.

CHAPTER 16

The Shultz Edict

In the late 1990's Dale Shultz, the Worker Overseer for Saskatchewan, prepared a letter for circulation among the Friends in that province who were troubled and concerned about what was happening among the Friends and Workers in Alberta. Without even knowing what was happening there, it's still possible to identify many points of Truth doctrine (at least according to Mr. Shultz' perspective) from reading it. This is a summary of what a person studying it from a neutral, or academic, point of view would conclude about the doctrine of the Truth. In the absence of a recorded history, this is how a history of the Truth in our times would be deduced by future generations.

Following the summary is the actual letter written by Mr. Shultz. Each statement in the summary is indexed to the supporting phrase in the letter that follows. For example: for the phrase in the summary, *vision that others do not share[24]* , the number "24" refers to the supporting phrase in Mr. Shultz' letter, *[24]they are seeing some things in the picture that some of us are missing.*

Summary of Doctrine

This Way of God is presided over by a small number of high priests, possibly three.[3] They have vision that others do not share[24], and/so God has called them and is using them to guide His work in the earth.[17] These priests, though generally not greatly communicative, visit the provinces[2] and hear complaints from both their Overseers and the people.[14] They approve venues for study,[1,5] and advise on land sales.[4] They are respected, not for their deeds, but for the work they have to accomplish.[20] They appear charged with and successful at maintaining the status quo.[9] Their full access to a person's house is a condition for preferred status for the home.[33]

The high priests are represented in the provinces by Overseers, who owe their positions of oversight to the high priest.[11] It's not clear that these Overseers make decisions on important matters, and they may be overruled in conference with the high priests.[10] Indeed, they appear not to be intimately knowledgeable of the decision making process,[12] though they do seem to be free to speculate on it.[13] They even appear on occasion to expect changes inappropriately.[8]

The role of the Overseers appears to be to encourage obedience to the high priests[15] rather than to evaluate right and wrong.[23] They acknowledge their fallibility, but this can be compensated for with respect for those above them in the hierarchy, by praying for them, obeying them, and esteeming them highly in love for their work's sake.[19] And despite their limited understanding of matters, they are confident in advising the people to follow their example in these activities of obedience.[37]

Their *people* are those who welcome any in the hierarchy of the priests, Overseers, and other servants to their homes. This is an occasion for them to demonstrate an acceptable spirit.[34] In this way they can be taught to be realistic[16] and practical,[27] which can be generally interpreted as submitting to anyone above them in the hierarchy, considering that they come into great danger when they do not so submit.[29]

The people are prone to lose confidence in the high priests and Overseers,[6] and often have inappropriate expectations of change.[7] They need to be reminded that, for them, to implement change is to be out of their place.[32] Their struggle apparently is to learn to live within the high priests' judgments, the best way they possibly can[22] and no matter what their thoughts are on the matter.[26] Apparently this means to accept their losses in judgment, because those who learn to cope with that and do it graciously are upheld as *real* examples.[35]

One concludes that the theme of doctrine is not a question of right or wrong, but a question of doing the right thing[30] which is satisfied by unquestioning submission in the hierarchy.[36,38] And it is always right to respect the judgment of the high priests.[21] It is the right thing to do *because* the decision is from the high priests.[25] Again, this applies at all times in a comprehensive way, and is not dependant on the correctness of the judgment.[28] The people are enjoined not to suspect that this means obeying men, because one's thoughts about the high priests are one's thoughts toward God.[18]

Real questions of right and wrong are not a matter for the people to consider. That is a matter for God to concern Himself with.[31]

Dale Shultz' Letter

Saskatoon, Sask.
CANADA S7K 3N9
April 12, 1999

Dear_____,

I want to send letters to a number of people in Alberta who have been communicating with me by letter and/or phone. I have followed the developments in Alberta with interest and concern over these past months. Some of the more recent developments that I am aware of being the court case in [1]Edmonton, the Wednesday study removed from the home of 'Tom & Bonny Carlson' in 'Riverside', [2]the visit that [3]Eldon Tenniswood, Ernest Nelson and Sydney Holt made to 'Gary' & 'Frieda Martin' at 'Willowdale', [4]the sale of the Willowdale convention farm which followed that visit and the removal of the [5]Wednesday meeting from the home of 'Bert' & 'Olive Mercer' in 'Georgetown'.
I do know that those of you to whom I am writing have felt, for various reasons, that [6]your confidence in the oversight in Alberta has been eroded to a larger or lesser extent in different cases. [7] You have hoped and, at times, expected that some change in the oversight would be implemented. A year ago now, [8]my own expectation was that the overseers as a group would have seen fit to have implemented some changes affecting the province of Alberta. However, as you know, [9]the decision coming out of

the meeting of overseers last July was to support the status quo in Alberta. [10]That was not the thinking of everyone there; but it was the decision of the meeting. With Eldon, Ernest and Sydney coming into the province in recent weeks, it remains very evident that [11]the overseers generally are fully supporting Willis and Jim and their oversight in the province.

[12]We could wonder why the support remains so solidly behind Willis and Jim, and [13]it would be possible to advance a number of possible reasons. We know that this stand has been taken after [14]hearing a number of concerns expressed from both workers and friends. [15]I would just like to encourage you to accept this support that Willis and Jim have at the present time as a [16]reality and to respect that decision because it comes from a group of men whom God has called and whom God is using in [17]guiding his work in this part of the earth. [18]If our attitude towards them becomes disrespectful, it is a reflection on our attitude towards God as well. We realize that the fact that we are servants of God, or even very responsible servants of God, doesn't make us infallible. However, [19]something that is very much a part of being a child of God is to respect those who are over us in the Lord, to pray for them, to obey them, to [20]esteem them very highly in love for their work's sake. Their judgement may not always be right, but [21]it is always right for us to respect that judgement [22]and to work with it in the best way that we possibly can.

So, there are two possibilities regarding the decision of the overseers to maintain and support the status quo in Alberta. [23]One possibility is that the decision is a right decision for the province. That would mean that [24]they are seeing some things in the picture that some of us are missing when we look at it. Another possibility is that it was not the best decision for the province. But, whichever is the applicable possibility in this case, [25]it does remain the right thing to respect that decision because of where it has come from and to [26]work with it no matter what our own thoughts might be on the subject. [27]This is a very practical area where we can exercise the teaching of II Corinthians 10:5, "- bringing into captivity every thought to the obedience of Christ." We may think that we are "obeying men" and not "obeying Christ" when we submit to something that seems wrong to our own thinking. However, the scriptures teach so much about submission e.g. to the government of the land, wives to husbands, children to parents, the Lord's people to the ministry, etc. [28]That teaching doesn't just apply when the governments, husbands, parents or workers are 100% on the right track, but it applies in a very comprehensive way. We also know that a point could be reached in these different relationships in which submission is generally expected where, because of some deep conviction before God, we would feel that we could not submit to something that is being asked of us. However, [29]there is also great danger in "not submitting" and in taking a rebel attitude when the situation doesn't warrant that extreme position in God's mind.

So, I would like to encourage all of you to accept the present situation, knowing that quite a bit has been done to bring concerns to the attention of the overseers. The present situation remains in spite of these concerns having been very publicly expressed and drawn to the attention of the overseers. [30]Whether the decision is right or wrong, the right thing for all of us is to respect it because of those who have made the judgement. [31]If the decision is wrong, I am sure that the Lord will have ways of correcting that over time. He still is very much on the throne. In the final analysis, there are some things that we just have to leave in his hands. [32]I believe that for anyone to try to force changes now, after all that has been done to bring issues into focus, that it could mean just being very much out of our place.

[33]It is evident that when any stand is taken to restrict the welcome of any workers to your homes that your home will then be considered unsuitable for a meeting. I would certainly encourage you to make the workers welcome in your home. [34]It has been pointed out that this would give you opportunity to show the spirit of Christ to them. We don't want to add to the building of walls in the kingdom; but, rather, be amongst those who are building bridges. The polarization and division that has become so evident in Alberta is extremely dangerous and gives Satan a lot of territory in which to work. Many people tend to be caught up in it and to form camps. It would be wonderful, and very much in

keeping with the spirit of Christ, if we could all desire to reach out and begin to build bridges that would span the gulf of division that has evolved. Most of the people on the other side of this gulf are people with whom you would have never had any problem had it not been for this issue which resulted in you taking different sides. When we can get into the presence of the Lord in prayer, find bread for our souls, be influenced and motivated by his spirit, then our influence can be as Ephesians 4:1-3, "I therefore, the prisoner of the Lord, beseech you that ye walk worthy of the vocation wherewith ye are called, with all lowliness and meekness, with longsuffering, forbearing one another in love; endeavouring to keep the unity of the Spirit in the bond of peace."

I have appreciated a few visits by phone with Gary & Frieda Martin before and since the day that Eldon, Ernest and Sydney had the visit there. I marvel at their spirit of acceptance and the gracious way that they are handling this matter that could have left them feeling very bitter. [35] They are real examples. It will be people like them that will be contributing to a solution rather than promoting a further problem. The spirit of the lamb, the spirit of a little child, the spirit that can [36] take loss graciously without resentment or fighting back - this is the spirit that will not only preserve the kingdom (and preserve our salvation individually) but will also, in time, unite the kingdom.

I can understand your concerns and your feeling of perplexity. I do want you all to come through this experience with your faith deepened and your spirits enriched. [37] In light of the present situation and the understanding of it that I have (which is limited, of course), I have felt that I would like to exhort you in the way that I have expressed in this letter. I think that you know that [38] I am writing to you in this way because of concern and love and a deep interest in your future and the welfare of your souls. I hope that these few lines may be of some help. I have appreciated your communication in the past. I would welcome your response to this if you care to respond.

Yours in Him
SIGNED: Dale Shultz

The situation Dale Shultz was writing about is addressed in Chapter 23. Dale has since succeeded Eldon Tenniswood and Dick Middleton as Overseer of the California jurisdiction, and it's been observed that his influence has now become important in many jurisdictions well beyond his own. I take the liberty to opine that he is now one of the Overseers of Overseers he mentioned in his document discussed in Chapter 15.

CHAPTER 17

Who Abuses Whom ?

Following my described devastating experiences, I needed to find out what had caused me such psychological trauma. I came across the expression *spiritual abuse*, which conjured up images of notorious apocalyptic religious cults. But I learned there's no difference between emotional abuse and spiritual abuse, except that spiritual abuse is practiced *in the name of God*. Whatever Lois and Harold were trying to accomplish with me, I presume, was thought to be in the name of God and/or for my benefit.

Life among the Friends and Workers is quite free of domestic and violent abuse. However, emotional abuse is prevalent throughout the group – as it is in society at large. It isn't hidden – it's quite visible, and it's effective enough that it's frequently applauded. Much of it is ignored, and much more of it is accepted. Abusive tactics such as put-downs, sarcasm, and the ability to outsmart the unsuspecting have come to be valued as comedy. The tragedy is that, unless we give diligence in educating ourselves about such abuse, we have no defense against it, and no awareness of our own abusive habits.

Emotional, or psychological, abuse involves any behavior, verbal or non-verbal, that negatively impacts a person's emotional or psychological well-being. It frequently occurs as a consistent pattern of unfair and unjust treatment. Victims are most often led to understand that such treatment is for their own good – tough love, so to speak. But when an individual is degraded and controlled he is being abused. In other words, punishment is not correction. All abuse is about control, and emotional/spiritual abuse is no exception – whether the abuser recognizes that or not.[1] Such abuse can occur in any relationship, but especially where a power difference exists – perpetrated by spouses, intimate partners, parents, siblings, friends, teachers, employers; and in spiritual communities by the clergy and others in positions of influence.[2] Importantly, spiritual abuse is not just a symptom of cults or deviant doctrines. *All that is needed is a pastor accountable to no one and therefore beyond confrontation.*[3]

Abusive people use a variety of styles, some of which I've recognized in the occasional Worker, as well as an occasional Friend. There are even labels for each style of abuser.

The **Overbearing Critic** has an opinion on everything, and treats his opinions as unquestionable facts. He interrupts and corrects you when you express your opinions. Such arrogance will pass as evidence of wisdom and authority, and among the Friends it can effectively prevent another from being recognized as a worthy fellowship example, and destroy his self esteem as well.[4] I've met people who cannot restrain themselves from critiquing others, and most people don't have the wherewithal to object to such treatment.

The **Person Who Is Always Right** – is always right, and everyone else is wrong. Even if it turns out he's wrong, he will still be right. He sifts through events and information for proof of his rightness, and he's the person who always has the last say. Unlike normal people who admit their errors, he always finds a way to justify his decisions. For him, *what* is right is not as important as his *own rightness*.[5] I remember a visiting Worker from western Canada saying that Workers don't apologize for the decisions they make. Indeed, I've never known a Worker to apologize – except the one from whom I demanded an apology for my wife's sake.

The **Judge and Jury** abuser delivers decisions that are final, and he grants no appeals. Unfortunately for others, there's no reliable standard by which to measure his decisions. His condemnation of others is *as persons*. His *teaching* strategy is to produce guilt and shame to force another to reform.[6] He's the authority who withdraws privileges from another until he learns his lesson – this childish action despite the fact that all concerned are mature adults. A prime example is that of Clyde MacKay's judgment of Ross that I mentioned in Chapter 12. Telling Ross he had a wrong understanding of scripture was not enough for him – he had to condemn Ross as an individual.

The *Put-Down Artist* is the sarcastic, wise-cracking person who takes pride in outsmarting others. He's generous in his use of such adjectives as *crazy* and *stupid* when describing others. His choice of language and tone of voice is chosen to make a person feel valueless and entertain others. Unfortunately, the more skillful and creative he is with his use of verbal put-downs and sarcasm the more popular he may be as a comedian.[7] I've met Workers who took pride in their ability to outsmart people they actually wanted to offend. Andrew Abernathy, despite the god-like adulation he enjoyed from many, was perfectly proficient at putting others down. He laced his sermons with sneering remarks about people doing things he disapproved of. He disapproved of sandals, and preached frequently against *dirty hippies walking around in chains.*

The *Stand-Up Comic*, somewhat like the Put-Down Artist, uses sarcasm to address issues or make a point, and in so doing belittles individuals. He tells jokes to engage others in the ridicule of his victims. This type of abuse leaves a deep sense of outrage in the victim for being used for another's entertainment[8] – and with no opportunity to rebut. I heard a Worker from the Pacific Northwest recite, in a gospel meeting, the rhyme: "Once I was a monkey, climbing in a tree. Now I'm a professor with a P-H-D." He got his laughs – but it wasn't the way to welcome a Ph.D. to the fellowship.

The *Guilt Giver* uses unrealistic and undeserved false guilt to control the behavior of others. Unlike the Stand-Up Comic, who delivers his abuse like a ton of bricks, this person delivers it a brick at a time.[9] I well remember many sermons about the shame people can and do bring on themselves. Shaming is a common enough method of maintaining control over the flock. One Worker told a young man he was not to speak in meetings for a year, during which time he would "recall [his] shame every time the rest of the people in the meeting spoke and [he] couldn't." I cringed after one Sunday meeting when the

Worker turned to an elderly lady who was suffering from Alzheimer's disease and said, "We didn't hear from you in this meeting."

The *Historian* remembers every bad thing his victim has ever done, or that he thinks he's done. He tells him he's forgiven, but proceeds to bring up past issues over and over again. This he does to shame the victim once again into accepting his decisions and feelings.[10] He's the one who says nothing until it's time to pass judgment, at which time he'll bring out a full litany of accusations that support a condemnation of the *person* of the victim rather than a condemnation of any specific act. The historian will never deal with your problems – he will address your errors instead.

The *Commander in Chief* likes order. For him life is not something to be enjoyed but something to be controlled, and discussions are just messy affairs. He attempts to control every aspect of another's life, from his thoughts to his actions, by displaying rigid behavior and expectations.[11] For him a chain of command is indispensable. He's the reason, but ironically never the excuse, for the guilty person who pleads, "I was only doing what I was told!" A Worker in his late twenties undertook to advise us on how my four year old autistic grandson should be made to *act normal* – fortunately my daughter did not abuse the child in the manner the Worker prescribed. And such things as my daughter's inability to attend Wednesday Bible studies caused one Worker to fear for her soul's salvation. These types prefer automatons to individuals.

For the *Screamer*, yelling and name-calling are the weapons he uses to control others.[12] One's first response to the Screamer is to just comply in some way to appease him; but that's the trap. It only encourages him to scream again so he can again be further appeased. My favorite screamer of all time was Mike Colson. All my life I thought of Workers as the meek and mild examples of behavior, then I learned about a couple of brother Workers having a full blown shouting match on a roadway. I was further shocked to learn that one sister Worker who, when yelling wouldn't work, physically attacked her companion. I've come across a number of Workers, both brothers and sisters, who spare no words to *straighten someone out*.

The *Intimidator* uses threats. There are two types of intimidators: the ones who are all talk, and the others who back up their threats with action. The threats are not necessarily blatant, but however they're delivered they're understood. By creating intimidation, fear, and anger the intimidator gets his way.[13] His threats are commonly introduced with the phrases: "I love you, but ....."; and "If you do ..., then I will .....". *In a healthy relationship, threats are not necessary because trust and love provide the motivation for behavior.*[14] In the Truth fellowship the threat of being excommunicated can be taken seriously. And in the absence of having the authority to excommunicate another, I've been told such things as "I can't have fellowship with you!" or "I can't say 'Amen' to your prayers!" I know of one young man who was asked not to speak in meeting because he'd been speeding on the road leading to the convention property.

The *Dr. Jekyll and Mr. Hyde* personality is sometimes referred to as the *street angel, house devil.* He has a gentle public persona that is distinctly different from his harsh private persona, the public person being the false front for the true nature.[15] The person who has to deal with him is expected to deny one aspect of his relationship with this abuser while functioning under the pretense of another kind of relationship.[16] This practice has most notoriously been used when sexually abused children are required to sit in meetings or at the table with his/her abuser and behave as though nothing happened.

The *Person Who Plays Favorites* is easily recognized even by children. Suggestions that start with, "Why can't you be more like someone ....." are a clear indication to them that they don't measure up.[17] To abuse adults in this way, one has to be much more subtle about it, but this style of abuse proliferates nonetheless. What draws frequent concern among Friends is the sometimes blatant duplicity in meting out consequences to various offenders. When confronted about this, the normal Worker response is that "each case is handled on its own merits." But that's really not an answer – all it says is that a political decision was made. Someone somewhere used criteria that he hasn't shared to make a decision that can't be overturned, and the Friends are left to speculate on what the criteria are. That appears to be why a child predator Worker can be protected from prosecution and a young Romeo can be sent to prison for making out with his fiancée.

The **Role Reverser** forces others into roles without their consent, or into roles that are inappropriate for them. He commonly uses them as informers, couriers, enforcers, performers, or even lovers. They are expected to inform on one another, deliver and/or enforce someone else's judgments against each other, or encourage each other to accept any form of abusive treatment. I've never heard of a regular tattler being chastised for reporting anything about anyone else to the Workers. None of these expectations are compatible with friendship or fellowship – they are, in fact, virulently destructive. In role reversing fashion, this abuser himself departs from his role as *minister* to the fellowship's health and assumes the role of investigator, prosecutor, judge, or lord. This is why the Friends worry so much about what other Friends are going to tell the Workers about them.

The **Little White Liar** values conformity more than truth. He has no misgivings about saying whatever is needed to control the situation, even if it requires a *white lie*. The liar's real intention is to mislead in some manner, but coming from an *agent of truth* it changes the little white lie into a full fledged lie. And a lie is an abuse, it's the opposite of truth and the archenemy of trust. The Little White Liar should be warned that a lie, when exposed, is still a lie and honest people will recognize it as a lie. The most blatant and damaging lie that's ever been propagated among the Friends and Workers is the claim that this presently organized ministry began in the first century C.E. Equally guilty is any Worker who permitted such a lie being repeated without correcting it. In truth, this abuse has been foisted upon most late twentieth century Workers as well as the Friends, because they were all born and raised after the decision was made to deny the beginnings.

To characterize the culture of the Friends and Workers as riddled with liars and abusers is not accurate. Among the Friends it's common enough, as in our experience, to trust *stranger*-Friends with such things as the key to one's house – a custom that would never survive in this day and age if the Friends had no reason to trust the integrity of one another. But what really exists in the group is the separation of trust between the upper hierarchy of Workers and the rest of the Workers and Friends. This lack of trust is not simply a suspicion of dishonesty, but a lack of trust that others can be trusted with and use knowledge responsibly – or as some would say, "We aren't trusted with the secrets!" I've even seen treaty-like documents signed by numerous Workers as promise to respect agreed upon boundaries of their individual territories.

What exists is a system of skillful and artful manipulation. In Washington it's recognized and respected for what it is: politics, the pursuit and maintenance of power. But there's nothing democratic about the system of the Friends and Workers. The Friends largely respect this practice as part of God's *plan*, which is frequently praised for its perfection – somewhat in the way parents are justified in sheltering their children from knowledge they believe children cannot handle – "the way is perfect, but the people are not." As well as representing God's planned way, it facilitates each Overseer's regulating his own domain as he sees fit, according to the agreement made at Clankilvoragh. But the effect is to negate the validity of the individual's experience with the Holy Spirit – ironically because the Holy Spirit often tells the *individual* something the *Worker* doesn't agree with! The majority of the Friends have a sycophantic relationship with the Workers, so whenever someone has a grievance with a Worker he's effectively alienated from the plan. A suitable analogy may be that those who have grievances against the star of the show are an embarrassment to the rest of the fan club. An aggrieved individual is not just alone, he disturbs the peace of the community.

With this kind of totalitarian oligarchy in place, any perceived abuse by the leaders is expected to be appreciated as corrective guidance by *the authority from which it came* – as clearly explained in Dale Schultz' letter in Chapter 16. Workers' sermons are frequently laced with correction – rarely explicit, to be sure, but *the willing heart will be chastised by the innuendo and will obey.* That being understood, the concept of abuse is never entertained, and the suggestion that any Worker has abused anyone is virtually taboo. Instead, tolerance of harsh treatment is highly respected, and it's considered a *virtue* never to speak of it. The idea is that because we are human we need constant correction, and the truly humble are forever diligent in pursuing it. I know of a situation where a Worker mentioned the vanity of wearing wedding rings in his sermon at a convention. Taking it as a cue, women lined up after the meeting to throw their wedding rings into a nearby stream.

Still, to say that all Workers are abusive is wrong. Probably the majority of Workers are not abusive at all. Many Workers are themselves abusively treated by their superiors, and though one rarely hears about it, many of the Friends are aware that it happens. I was quite young when I heard it whispered that a young Worker had gone home after her first year in the ministry because her companion was so difficult to live with. More than once I've heard older Workers describe their relationship with new young Workers as one of "breaking them in". It reminded me of breaking a horse. One middle aged sister Worker described her earlier years as almost impossible to bear, but after a while she just "seemed to learn how to accept it." At the same time, new Workers are fawned over by the Friends and treated like royalty. One wonders at the disproportionately high percentage of Workers who have to leave their calling because of *nerves* – or in more specific terms, complications of excessive occupational emotional stress. In my mind, something has happened to Jesus' yoke that is easy and burden that is light.[18]

The shock of all shocks remains the blatant lie by a Worker. One can excuse the Worker who innocently repeats the lie of someone higher up in the hierarchy, but the fact that he accepts it as truth doesn't change the fact that it's a lie. I now have no illusion that a Worker will not lie, but unless you challenge something one of them says you'd probably never even suspect it. In my experience, because I asked annoying questions, I *inadvertently* discovered that more than one Worker has flat out lied to me. This is disconcerting, to be sure, but understanding the history of the Truth it shouldn't be a surprise at all. So many Workers have made a fraudulent claim to the legitimacy of their ministry that it defies all reason to suggest that it's not abuse on a systematic scale.

The most explicit account of *non-consequential* lying by a Worker appeared in an account of a major upheaval among the Friends and

Workers in the province of Alberta. Apparently someone had refused to have a Worker come to his house because the Worker had been spreading lies about him. The Worker who came to chastize him for that advised him that "lying has nothing to do with doctrine" and was, therefore, "not any basis to deny the Workers the right to come to their home."[19]

All this being said about abuse among the Friends and Workers should not be interpreted as an indictment of the fellowship. Most abuse can appropriately be attributed to the individual perpetrators themselves. Neither should anyone conclude that the Truth is unique in its level of abuse of members – every church is subject to the human natures of its leaders, and their leaders are no less vulnerable to the seductiveness of the power they can exercise because of their position of authority. What makes the Friends' and Workers' community more susceptible to internal abuse is the strict totalitarian structure of the group. Certainly every Worker who's ever practiced any of the above mentioned abusive tactics would defend it as necessary for some positive end. I reject that explanation outright. In my mind the essence of being a good Christian is not about accomplishing goals, but rather practicing the virtues consistent with the Golden Rule. And abuse is still abuse – it's still about control and it's neither necessary nor becoming of ministers of truth to mature adults. Most abusers are too impressed with the results of their abusive styles to even understand it as abuse. Neither am I inclined to excuse most Workers for any of their abuse. They're plenty sensitive to any hint of disrespect from the Friends, and they have a strikingly low tolerance of it. That's a clear indication that they do indeed recognize abuse. That being the case, I believe they should treat the Friends with the same dignity as they demand for themselves. But then, what consequences can a Friend prescribe for an abusive Worker, besides leave?

This became the determining factor for why I left the fellowship. Most of the kinds of petty abuse I mentioned above never fazed me much – undoubtedly because I had enough self esteem to consider the pettiness of it all. I was always sympathetic to people who collapsed under it because of their inability to deal with it. But when it came to the ongoing degrading episodes that resulted from my innocent attempt to expose a misinformation – then I had more self respect than to accept such indignities from such abusers. Further, the reasons I had for staying no longer outweighed the reasons to leave, and once I left I was given scarce incentive to return.

Undoubtedly I'm now referred to by many Workers and Friends as a *bitter ex.* That's the phrase used for people who just up and leave for some suspicious and/or assumed reason. With the Workers, *bitterness* is considered an iniquity – individuals are advised to patiently endure and live above the bitterness. But Workers can renounce their commitment to the ministry on a moment's notice and face no consequences. Even if they end up having a seriously abusive companion, they can look forward to moving on to another companion. But I know of one Worker who told a woman that she had to stay with her husband despite the fact that she feared for her life. That is outrageous advice, and serves nothing more than to demonstrate the control of an Overseer over his people. It reminds me of the passage that reads: *For they bind heavy burdens and grievous to be borne, and lay them on men's shoulders; but they themselves will not move them with one of their fingers.*[20]

It's interesting that when there's no apparent abuse among the Friends and Workers, there remains a distinct air of secrecy within the community. Aside from the fact that the finances and political concerns of the Worker Overseers are intentionally kept secret, there are two areas of concern to the Friends and outsiders that also remain shrouded in mystery – doctrines and regulations. I've heard many remarks over the years by people who were not sure what the doctrine of the Workers really was. A great number of the younger Workers, when asked a question on doctrine, can't give an answer. This is curious, because it may not mean that the Worker has no thought of his own on the matter – if he doesn't know what the Overseer believes on the matter he isn't free to speculate.

Until I was forty I wasn't that concerned with doctrine. I knew perfectly well that the Workers had a greater knowledge of the Bible than I did, but I felt comfortable that I at least knew what I needed to know. And as far as Truth morality went, I believed I knew enough about that to explain to anyone. But that all had to be learned anew when I arrived in Nevada. The one thing I've learned about doctrine among the Workers is that it's not consistent, despite claims to the contrary.

What's equally curious is how outsiders are attracted to the Workers' gospel, and how truth becomes *revealed* to them. In the beginning, according to those who joined with William Irvine, people were free to live as the Holy Spirit taught them. [21] That's exactly what the Workers adamantly claim today, and many of the Friends repeat it. Ironically, no one today who was raised in the Truth really believes that. They all know televisions are forbidden, long hair on men and short hair on women are forbidden, pants on women are forbidden, jewelry and makeup are forbidden, dying hair is forbidden – the list goes on and on and on. Frankly, born and raised children know *all* those rules whether the Holy Spirit ever taught them anything. Neither have I met anyone who professed as an adult who believed the Holy Spirit taught them those things. The closest they have come to that explanation is that they've observed, or heard someone say, that some certain thing is not acceptable, so they conformed to the standard.

Someone shared an amusing story with me about a Worker in Australia who was asked by an outsider attending gospel meetings about the rule on hair styles. She'd concluded accurately that some kind of bun was the norm, and asked the Worker if that was so. He replied no, that we don't have any rule about that. Then, to impress the outsider that he was right, he asked a number of teenage girls to let their hair down for the next gospel meeting so the outside lady would believe him. Leo Stancliff, however, was an exception on that matter as he was on many other matters. When a woman from a non-Truth background professed, he went to her house the next day and *read the rules* to her: no television, no pants ... the whole *no-list*.

This withholding of guidance from new recruits may be more than just a tactic to attract new members. It may be serious doctrine. One Worker once explained to a friend of mine that when he was a young Worker he was taught how to *not* answer questions: "I was taught that the unbeliever has no right to receive the answers to everything." One of the passages that apparently was supposed to support that policy was, *neither cast ye your pearls before swine, lest they trample them under their feet...*[22] The approach appears to be to attract people to the fellowship, have them come to like the style of fellowship, become committed, then when they can handle it they will learn how things really work.

Unfortunately, that's not the *honest* way to tell the truth to intelligent, responsible adults. Even when I was a young child, I felt the same way. If someone is mature enough to ask the question, he's mature enough to deal with the answer. I see no virtue in ignorance, and those who promote it are abusers.

CHAPTER 18

What To Do About Me?

By the year 2004 I was left with my family intact and a job to go to, but little more – and no idea where I was headed. I rather liked my job, but I was uncomfortable there. I was suffering from depression, and I basically had to learn my job through a never-ending series of *faux pas* with upper management. My subordinates' complaint was that I'd not been treated professionally. They several times reminded me that my predecessor had just died at quitting time one day, from no apparent cause other than stress. That wasn't helping my depressed state of mind.

My doctor, who was at the time coaching me through my depression, asked about my job. I told him about my unmanageable circumstances. His advice was to quit my job and take a complete rest. I didn't quit immediately. But when my supervisor announced in March that I was suspected of mismanaging the office's money, I resigned. Then, because it was a state office, the Attorney General's Office had to investigate the unresolved accusation, and it was concluded that everything was accounted for, to the very penny. So the case was closed. In late April they invited me to go back to work, but I declined the offer. The Attorney General's conclusion was comforting, but not surprising – I knew perfectly well they'd come to the conclusion they did.

But I hadn't refused to return just because of the investigation. In the meantime I'd had an extensive medical checkup, and my doctor referred me to a urologist who informed me that I had a growth in my bladder that he suspected was cancerous. That was a shock. I had surgery in late April, and expected to have a month long period of recuperation before I went looking for another job. It was a relief to learn a week later that the growth was not cancerous, and not even precancerous. I considered that my second blessing of the year, following my release from the stressful job.

At the same time, Karen had gotten a transfer to the High Desert State Prison in Indian Springs, outside Las Vegas. She sold her house in Carson City and moved to Las Vegas on the first of June, but she wasn't happy about moving there by herself. Since I was out of work, and we had no more circle of Friends in Carson City, Judy and I decided it was a convenient time for us to move too. Conveniently, Judy and Heidi also worked for the state, and both could be transferred to offices in Las Vegas.

I joined Karen in Las Vegas that June, but through the summer I didn't recover from my surgery. I wasn't suffering, I just never regained strength. Then, near the end of the summer I got another health shock. The doctor I saw suspected I was HIV positive. I was sure he was mistaken, but I let him draw a blood sample anyway. I had a laugh with Judy about it when I came home. Unfortunately, the doctor's suspicion was correct, and I was sent to the University Medical Center for evaluation.

There was no question where I contracted the virus. I'd encountered a doctor in Reno who turned out to be a drug addict who shared needles indiscriminately, and it was confirmed on one occasion that he was high on methamphetamine while treating a heart attack patient and misprescribing medications to him in the hospital emergency room. I thought the man was strange, but when I told some of my coworkers about him, they were horrified and told me about his reputation. I was stunned at the time to learn that I'd been given an injection by such a character, but it was hardly a week later that he suddenly disappeared and no reason was given. I soon forgot about it, probably because I didn't get sick at the time. But by the time I was diagnosed, Nevada was in a massive panic over doctors' misuse of needles. Thousands of potential victims were tested, the majority of them from an endoscopy clinic in Las Vegas. The most common casualty of such malpractice was hepatitis, and some have died from their infections. The prosecution of one endoscopic doctor found him guilty of 27 criminal counts, including second-degree murder. He died a prisoner in Reno in April, 2017.

My good fortune was that this wasn't a death sentence either. My doctor was encouraging. Because I'd had an otherwise healthy lifestyle, he assured me I'd respond well to treatment, and I did indeed. What exacerbated my condition by the time of my diagnosis was the severe stress I'd been under through previous years. I had an appropriate angry moment, then decided that I had to set the anger aside or it could consume me. I thought about my two daughters who were then single mothers each raising a young boy, and I determined I was going to be around to help them, at least until the boys graduated from high school. As the doctor predicted, I regained my general health to the point where I returned to work as a teacher and missed no more than five days for sickness in the six years before I retired. My diagnosis did, however, speed Judy's transfer to Las Vegas, and our daughter Heidi soon followed her. We have called Las Vegas home ever since. And my grandsons both graduated from high school and I am proud of the young men they have become.

In Las Vegas I began going occasionally to a meeting near where I lived. The elder, Keith Noble, was a very kind man, a wonderfully sensitive individual. The others in the meeting were also friendly, and it wasn't long before 'Mark', one of them, quietly let me know that one of the Friends from Reno had clued him in to some of what had taken place in Northern Nevada. Mark knew I'd had problems with the Workers. In fact, he expressed some of my own feelings about the Workers' abusive dealings with people. It would have been nice to have known while I was in Northern Nevada that I had such sympathizers there. But I realized everyone was in the same position I was – they had to choose between saying nothing and being in who-knows-how-much trouble.

'Eddie', whose wife never came to meeting with him, asked me about my wife. I explained that I'd gotten in trouble for disagreeing with the Workers and my wife couldn't handle the harassment any more. To my surprise, he told me that a similar thing had happened with his wife. She'd come to Nevada from overseas and was so disturbed by some things she'd witnessed that she stopped going to meeting as well.

At some time that year I read a verse in meeting from the New International Version of the Bible. When the meeting was over, Keith approached me and volunteered to get me a King James version of the Bible. He explained that there was a newly professing couple in the meeting who seemed confused by the wording of what I'd read from the NIV. My reaction alarmed me. I actually felt panicked – I just couldn't handle being confronted about that, or anything else for that matter. It demonstrated just how fragile my emotions were regarding comments about my *behavior*. I already had several King James Bibles, but I mostly read the NIV and my French Bible because they were easier to understand. I considered not going back to that meeting, but I reasoned that Keith probably knew nothing about my situation. A few days later I wrote him a note in which I said I was "declining to accept the Bible" from him. I assured him I had a King James Bible, but I was more comfortable reading the other one. The reason, I explained, was that I was recovering from "so much hostility" in Northern Nevada that I was having difficulty feeling comfortable going to meetings, and I needed to read the easier version. I assured him I wouldn't read passages from the NIV Bible in meeting. I knew it was a bizarre kind of letter for a mature person to write, but at least it helped me establish some control over my emotional environment. Keith never mentioned it to me again, which I appreciated a lot. I'm sure he had conversations about me, undoubtedly with the Workers in Las Vegas, but I never once detected any disapproval from him or anyone else.

That first fall in Las Vegas I went to special meetings. I knew almost no one there, so found myself a seat near the back of the hall. Before long I noticed that Harold Hilton was in the crowd, and the all too familiar nauseous uneasy feeling swept over me. I avoided encountering him, and I left during the lunch break.

There was one Sunday morning that, had I known ahead of time who was going to be there, I may have turned around and gone home. It was after the meeting began that I discovered Ken Forbes and his family from Carson City were sitting on the far side of the room. I was very uneasy. After my previous interaction with him in Carson

City, I wasn't interested in saying anything in front of him, so I didn't participate. But what I heard from them reminded me perfectly of what I'd confronted in Carson City. His prepubescent son expounded on the passage where Jesus' enemies *communed together and reasoned*,[1] and refused to recognize Jesus. Naturally, he had an immature understanding of the whole chapter – but he did what so many young kids do when they speak in meetings. In preparation for meetings they cherry pick for a passage that will support Truth doctrine, and expound on it. I did it myself when I was twelve years old. But what he said about it was something he'd undoubtedly heard many times. He said that when we meet Jesus, we must never use our reasoning, we must simply obey without question. His mother then rose and recognized the wisdom of what the kid had said. She went on to say that we should never ignore, question, distrust, or disobey any message that comes from the Lord. My problem was that I'd come to understand that the phrase "obey the Lord's instruction" was nothing more that a euphemism for "obey the Workers". After the meeting I quickly sneaked out before I could have shaken hands with everyone in the room.

A few times I went to social gatherings of the Friends in the meeting. When the weather cooled I went with them for a Sunday picnic in a park. I enjoyed their company, but it was always difficult because I never felt comfortable telling them much about myself or my family. With Mark and Eddie I had no problem, but I didn't trust that anyone else would be comfortable hearing my story. Despite that, it was an interesting and diverse congregation. They included a number of African-Americans, and others from such far flung places as Jamaica, New Zealand, South Africa, Guam, and Romania. Phyllis Munn and her sister Jeannette had retired from the ministry, and were being cared for by a lady in that meeting. Because Las Vegas is a big tourist and convention center, there were frequent visitors from other places.

There were some awkward times, of course. My mother and brother came from Canada for a visit, and I knew they'd be wanting to go to Wednesday Bible study. I hadn't been to Bible study in Las Vegas, but I decided to take them to one while they were here. On the Sunday prior to their visit I asked a lady what the Wednesday Bible study was for that week. She looked shocked, and said, "Don't you have a study list?" I said, "No." "How come you don't have a study list?" "I don't do Wednesday nights." "What do you mean, you don't do Wednesday nights?" "I just don't." She stared at me a minute, then got out her list and told me what the study was. It shocked her, because anyone who "doesn't do" meetings is a certain oddity.

The subject of convention was another interesting matter. I'd not been to a convention in California in the previous four years, and I didn't intend to go to one in the foreseeable future. There would be too many people there that I wasn't prepared to run into. But one Sunday morning a married couple who'd recently professed asked me if I was planning to go to the upcoming convention in Buttonwillow. I just said no. I don't know whether it gave them the notion that conventions were optional, but at least I wasn't going to lie to them. I left it to someone else to clue them in to the idea that everyone goes to a convention every year.

The second year in Las Vegas, during the special meeting week, the lady who was caring for Phyllis and Jeannette invited me to have dinner at her house. It was undoubtedly planned to be my special meeting time visit with Workers. A few others in the meeting were invited as well, and several visiting Workers were there. It was a wonderful meal, and I enjoyed the company. But one of the visiting sister Workers watched me like a hawk throughout the visit. Every time I looked at her, she was staring at me. I didn't know her personally, so I could only guess why she stared. Maybe she didn't approve of my shaved head, or my beard. Maybe she thought there was something unbecoming about the way the young African-American girl spent so much time talking to me – but the girl thought it was fun to talk to a teacher outside the school setting. Of course, it did cross my mind that she'd heard a lot about me before she ever arrived in Las Vegas. That time, however, I remember that the Worker's staring didn't bring on that sick nauseous feeling I used to get around such people, and I realized I was overcoming the effects of my ordeal. I felt good about that. I was becoming more used to the idea that there was nothing more they could do to me.

As luck would have it, my good friend Hinh had moved to Denver for his work, and he mentioned my difficulties to Leslie White, the

Overseer in Colorado. Leslie invited me to convention in Elizabeth, Colorado, and I arranged to visit Hinh and his wife and go with them to that convention. I made special note that the west coast doctrine of complete obedience to the Workers was tacitly breached a few times. I'd never have recognized it if the rigidness of the obedience doctrine in California hadn't been so forcefully impressed upon me. But there was one indication that the doctrine was alive nonetheless – not surprisingly, from a visiting Worker from the west coast. Lowell Stidolph spiritualized the contents of a firefighter's handbook, and concluded that all the rules of conduct it contained could be inspiring for us spiritually, with only one exception. That he identified as the rule that a fireman must be willing to disobey an order. His comment was that he couldn't imagine a situation where that rule would apply spiritually. He could have asked me! Actually, over the years I'd often heard it said that we must "obey the Lord's instruction". I had an understanding of that, but I'd just so recently been taught that the expression is a common euphemism for "obey the Workers".

Despite the fact that I felt there was so much I couldn't share with the Friends at that time, I can't say that I really wanted it any other way. As much as I appreciated those who helped me through my experience, I can't say they relieved me of the aloneness of the experience. There were so many things I needed to settle in my own mind, and I needed lots of time just to think. Unlike a lot of people, I don't look for advice on what to do. I ask questions to get information, and then I decide what I will do and I take full responsibility for my decisions. I learned very early on that some of the biggest mistakes of my life were the result of following someone's advice instead of deciding for myself what is best. To a great degree even my wife and I were in our own separate struggles. Even though we agreed about everything that was happening, we had our own private decisions to make.

There were occasions when we received visits from out of state people who had been through similar experiences – it turned out there are plenty of them to be found. We had visitors from as far away as Canada and Europe, and the chance to relax and enjoy their company without the fear of incriminating ourselves in some manner was refreshing. With one such visitor I shared the interesting fact that the majority of people who leave do so on their own, without any knowledge of or influence from others who have left. It was remarkable to discover after leaving that what we'd witnessed turned out not to be unusual after all. In fact, one man I visited with from Washington state had gone through a virtually identical court drama as we'd witnessed in Nevada, and been emphatically absolved by the court – yet he was never welcomed back in meetings. Learning of such struggles by others relieved the fear that perhaps I'd lost all sense of reason through the ordeal.

One noteworthy matter I had to deal with was the question of how I would maintain appropriate moral boundaries, given that the Workers had basically given up on me. Sorting through that matter was interesting. It gave me an insight into the extent of control the Workers actually have over one's everyday life – which surprised me. Yet, I also came to realize that most of the *moral* choices I'd ever made were not made on the Workers' moral guidance, but by my own sense of what was good and right which had been nurtured entirely by my parents. Mostly, for the Workers, what I'd maintained had been a comfortable accommodation of their individual personalities while they were around.

The real moral predicament I ran into with the Workers was still my inability to mistreat others at their request. In my mind that was the antithesis of morality, no matter what the rules dictated. I hadn't decided to leave so I could practice immorality – I left because I didn't accept being forced to compromise my hard-earned sense of morality.

Like many professing people, I often found it difficult to discuss my faith with outsiders. There were a few reasons for that. One of them was that it was common enough for outsiders to consider us weird. Being different in that way was not a problem for me. My school friends often enough made positive comments on my being different, most often mentioning my clean language. But I did find it difficult to be asked about *why* we were different. I was smart enough to know that I had nothing more to say about that than all the stock phrases I'd heard so many times – but that probably meant nothing to outsiders, and frequently meant not that much to me. When I finally achieved the freedom to discuss my distress with my *outside* friends, I discovered how universally horrified people were by what I told them. It was a bit embarrassing, when I told them things about my experience, that they would react like I was a refugee from a group like the Fundamentalist Latter Day Saints.

A lot of my thoughtful time was devoted to the matter of fear. I still marveled at how fearful I was the day I dropped that letter in the mail to the Overseer in California. In my mind I knew I was doing the right thing, but I was so close to fainting that I almost couldn't drop the letter into the box. For just a moment I thought of the people who'd been so ruthlessly shamed and destroyed, and reminded myself that those same people would be watching *my* life, whether the Workers paid any attention or not. And the letter just slipped out of my hand.

But I still needed to understand *why* I was so fearful. I'd never followed my conscience in anything in my lifetime that had created in me such fear of a Worker, and I wondered what evil I was dealing with. The fact was, I'd been so conditioned over decades by the panicked, almost terrified, responses of people when someone suggested complaining to the Overseer about one of his Workers. I now appreciate why it is that so many people refuse to come forward and defend someone who's being scandalized. Unfortunately fear is a tremendous motivator, either to act or to not act – fear of anything, whether a person can identify the source or not.

A friend of mine has made the statement that the Truth *has become the fellowship of moral cowards – where many people in the organization share these concerns but so few are willing to openly stand for them. Fear of reprisal is far greater than genuine interest in basic Christian values.* I would not expect any of the Friends to even acknowledge such a state of affairs, but there's a tell-tale sign that this is indeed true – it's their horrified reaction when someone else makes a complaint about a Worker. It was that insight that made me recognize the value of a good conscience, and the cost of keeping it clean. I think maybe that's how some people become wiser than others. Neither would I expect a Worker to say such a statement is true. Some Workers would undoubtedly respond with, "There is no fear in love;"[2] the point being intended as chastisement for fearing a Worker. But the relationship between love and fear is not a chicken and egg dilemma. Love does not develop in a vacuum – it develops from an evidence of trust. No one, not even Workers, can be loved if they cannot project a trusting spirit toward another. Then, if love is *perfected*, it "casteth out fear."[3] By 2004 I had reason to believe I couldn't trust the Workers for anything I, my wife, or my family needed – and that failed to arouse any affection in me for their care.

The practice of control through fear began early in the Truth. It was fear of banishment that suppressed the facts of the group's history.[4] If the threat was never real, the history would never have been squelched. I suggest, if Dale Schultz' teaching is correct, that senior Workers may alternately even treat such fearfulness among the Friends as a positive "fear of the Lord", as bizarre as that sounds. After all, he expects the Friends to consider Workers' decisions to be God's will.

Finally, there was the fear of hell – the greatest motivator in Christianity. I know all about the *good news* of the gospel, and the *love* of the heavenly Father. But the *sacrifice* of Jesus remains the only hope *in hell*, so to speak, of avoiding an eternity of cruel punishment – and that is never without condition, despite any claims to the contrary. I wonder if Christians really appreciate how much of a motivator fear is for them. How many people have endured unimaginable abuse as the price for their soul's eternal salvation? How many people live their whole lives dreading the possibility that they'll be found in the wrong frame of mind at the time of their last breath? Not every Christian lives his life in such a high state of alert, but the existence of hell can reduce any virtue to an exercise in self preservation.

I know perfectly well how many people believe I will now be going to hell. It's rather cut and dried, especially for a fundamentalist. This was loudly demonstrated for me one morning while I was working for the state. A lady in her thirties came into my office on business, but had a panic attack before anyone got to deal with her, and she was over an hour recovering enough to continue with her day. Her problem was that her father was dying – not that day or even that week, but his loss of mental facilities meant he couldn't avail himself of a Christian baptism. And the certainty that he'd suffer forever in hell was beyond his daughter's capacity to deal with. Ironically, according to the lady, her father had always been a very virtuous person, but lacking a baptism he was damned for eternity. It's enough to scare the *hell* out of anyone. How is one to claim that modern Christianity is not a remnant of a primitive blood sacrifice culture? Furthermore, we have no clear means of measuring to determine what level of mental ability or disability satisfies the requirement(s) for salvation.

I lost count of all the people who, when they knew I'd given up on the Workers, either invited me to their church or asked me where I was going to worship now. I had no intention of going anywhere. Aside from the intolerable treatment I'd faced, something else had been going on as well – I'd figured out that the Truth was just another religion, from its founding to its fully developed hierarchy. The fact that we were deceived about its origins was neither unique to the Truth nor its disqualification as a legitimate denomination. I'd decided I wasn't going to look for a religion or denomination. I was going to investigate what there is to know of historical and objective truth, what has been true and universal from the founding of the universe. I wasn't delusional – I didn't really expect to learn all there is to know about that. It just meant that I wasn't going to be distracted by any person's *inspired* definitive insight into truth. And in the process, I was not going to waste my life pandering to peddlers of doctrine.

What I specifically didn't want was proselytization from any religious thinker. The world is full of the writings of such thinkers and philosophers. I'll read almost any of them, but none of it is going to tell me anything more than what their human minds can comprehend and explain in their human vernacular – including the Bible. I didn't have the vocabulary for it at the time, but I'd come to despise any dogma that anyone could use to control my search for such truths. I wanted what there was to know without any religious presupposition. I never considered I was any chosen vessel intended to receive any special revelation. I just wanted to know what I wanted to know.

Dare I quote: *I bear them record that they have a zeal of God, but not according to knowledge.*[5]

CHAPTER 19

The Bible

I do not feel obliged to believe that the same god who has endowed us with sense, reason, and intellect has intended us to forego their use.

~ Galileo

After I moved to Las Vegas, I continued taking courses at a college near where we lived. I discovered that in the religious studies department there was a course in the Old Testament, described as covering *history, ideas, and theological beliefs of Biblical Israel,* from a nondenominational perspective and in the light of archaeological research and literary criticism. So I enrolled. I was pleased that it was a *religious studies* department, not a *theology* department. Theologians *ruminate* on God; religious scholars *explore how other human beings (theologians included) ruminate on sacred things.*[1]

Being a course on the Old Testament, it didn't surprise me that there were Jews in the class. There were also several Muslims who participated and appreciated the course as much as anyone else. But then there were atheists and other non-religious individuals as well. To say that I found the course interesting is an understatement. After the final exam a Jewess and I agreed that it had been more of an experience than just another college course. It's not possible to share everything from the course here, but in keeping with the reason for writing this book I will share a few of the most enlightening and transformative moments.

The first lecture was an astounding lesson in reading. The Old Testament was a required textbook for the class, and we started by taking turns reading verses from the first chapter of Genesis. As the lecture proceeded, we discussed what it meant, and more often than not we were told: "But that's not what it says." And indeed it *didn't* say what most people believed it said. Most people believed the chapter had something to do with the creation of the planet and the universe that we'd learned about in Science class – or Sunday school. But then, how was a person to know that the first verse of Genesis had nothing at all to do with a *planet* – instead, it was about the *earth*. To the ancients who told the story first, the earth in the first verse of the first chapter of Genesis was just a *formless and empty* bubble in the vast universe of water – there was no mention of land, but there was light and darkness, and God separated them on that first day. The sun, the moon, and land did not appear until the fourth day. According to the ancients' understanding of the universe, the chapter made complete and perfect sense.

Did I believe that story to be the truth about the creation of our universe? No – because what existed at the end of that week of creation was flat land, surrounded by water, with a huge dome overhead to protect it from the blue ocean of the universe above. What I *did* believe was that the person who originated the story was a wise interpreter of his environment. Why else would the rain have been described as what happens when the windows of heaven were opened? The lesson I took away from that lecture was that a lot of people had spent a lot of time trying to make the biblical story of creation relevant in a modern-day Christian's mind set. I was relieved, actually, because I never thought apologists did a good job at that.

The Old Testament turned out to be replete with inconsistencies and contradictions – much to the consternation of one outspoken Christian in the class.[2] What became telling was that every time she was introduced to another such inconsistency, she claimed there "had to be an explanation" for it, but she couldn't "imagine" what it must be. Also to her consternation was the discovery of God's promise to Ishmael, which was no less than God's promise to Isaac.[3] That promise is believed to be the origin of the Arab people and the foundation of Islam. Interestingly God, as all other gods that have existed, also has a name, though it is not mentioned in the Old Testament. An occasional Jew may tell you the name, but I don't know what it is because I've never met anyone who would utter it even once for me. It is obviously more taboo to utter God's name than it is to use obscene language on national television. No, none of the titles applied to God in the Old Testament are his real name!

Also problematic for devout Christians was the nature of God in the Old Testament, and that he was not the only god – most of the time. That isn't really a mystery. God was originally one of the ancient Pagan gods, the god of armies, or hosts, and Abraham chose to make a covenant with him alone. This accounts for God's Old Testament prejudicial and non-pacific attitude toward and brutal judgments against individuals and peoples. We read often of other gods of the time being called upon by Israelites for favors. They obviously were taken seriously, because it was an ongoing struggle to keep them out of Israelite culture. This Old Testament posturing of God has always been problematic for Christian moralists, but that is still the nature of God in Judaism today. Does it not seem futile to keep scouring the Old Testament for the peace-loving god of the New Testament?

The Old Testament is not history. Neither was much of the Old Testament even written by spiritual inspiration or for spiritual enlightenment. It was considered more a record of ancient Jewish culture and tradition than a book of spiritual guidance. It was not even compiled as a volume until a group of seventy Hellenistic Jews compiled a Greek version of it, known as the Septuagint, about a century before Jesus was born. Even then, not all of it was necessarily considered scripture by those who compiled it. Today that compilation is considered Old Testament scripture by the Catholic-Orthodox churches – but is not accepted by Jews or Protestants. The Tanakh (aka the Hebrew Bible, or Protestant Old Testament) was not officially recognized as the Hebrew canon until the second century C.E.[4], *but differs ... considerably from* the Septuagint.[5] The *Catholic Answers* website acknowledges that Martin Luther's *drawing from the Hebrew texts is more accurate than the Greek ... Septuagint,* but interestingly makes disparaging comments *of the all-too-human author.*[6]

The real kicker of the Old Testament course was to learn that Jews did not believe humans had souls separate from their bodies. This has consequences for understanding not just the Old Testament, but the New Testament as well. Jews did not die and go anywhere, except to the grave. Those who did go to heaven were very rare and were normally taken alive into heaven. For a long time I'd been aware that the terms *hell, gehenna, grave, hades,* and *sheol* seemed to be used interchangeably, and not necessarily to mean an eternal lake of fire. Of real concern to me was that fact that none of them actually represented a conscious afterlife for Jews. I've heard Workers preach about such characters as King David and Job being in heaven, and I somehow don't believe the Workers were the only Christian preachers who ever pondered such a possibility. I asked a few practicing Jews if Jews go to heaven when they die, and none of them even volunteered a *yes.* The answers varied from: "Heaven is not a relevant concern for Jews," to: "Well, that's a good question – I've never heard anyone talk about that."

I have no problem believing that much of Genesis was folklore passed down for hundreds of years and modified when needed to be explainable to whatever generation. I do have a problem with the attempts of supposed scholars to make science prove the *facts* of the Old Testament – or even the New Testament for that matter. It was enlightening to discover that for Jews there was never a need for a savior to save them from themselves – after all, they were God's chosen people. Logically, Christian theology is indeed blasphemous of the Hebrew God. It certainly wasn't the objective of the course, but by the end of it I was quite convinced that the Old Testament gave no support whatsoever to Christian theology. What became most disconcerting was not just the ignorance of ancient Jewish beliefs among Christians, but the efforts put forth to deny that Jews even understand their own scriptures. An objective evaluation of that attitude suggests that all the writers of the Old Testament were the equivalent of modern day science fiction writers – writing what will only be revealed to generations centuries later.

My study of the New Testament was every bit as soul-stirring as was the Old Testament. Reading it outside the framework of Christian theology and Sunday School style discussion, the study became highly offensive to many of the fundamentalist Christians in the class. They'd apparently been expecting the course to be an affirmation of their own fiercely held beliefs about the Bible. But the course wasn't a *revival service* – it was a study in *nondenominational literary criticism and historical background*. In fact, I was impressed by the absence of any suggestion that anyone abandon his faith – Christian or any other. The professor, himself an ordained mainline Protestant clergyman, had no problem acknowledging that his own church had mistaken interpretations of scripture. Perhaps I had an advantage, having been a history teacher. I was quite satisfied that he knew what he was talking about – I understood the difference between a fact claim and a faith claim.

The words of Bart Ehrman, a religious studies professor and writer, described my approach to what I learned. I decided that *any truth I learned was no less true for being unexpected or difficult to fit into the pigeonholes provided by my evangelical background*.[7] It was right about that time that I came to understand what getting out of one's cultural box really means. My notes from these studies would fill a volume much larger than this book, but the *raison d'être* of this writing is to share what I learned that forced me to reconsider what I'd previously thought or been taught.

So like a high school literature and history course combined, we studied the New Testament. It is, of course, the Christian scriptures. It's devoted almost entirely to Jesus and his role in the establishment of Christianity – though it's widely acknowledged that he probably never considered himself a *Christian*. Jews do not believe that Jesus was anything more than possibly a wise man. Muslims, on the other hand, believe that Jesus was a prophet as was Moses, though perhaps not *the* Messiah or *the* Christ as do Christians. Yet many Muslims believe Jesus will be judging the world at the end of time. Though Muslims don't recognize the validity of the Gospel of John, the *Qur'an* condemns those who are disobedient to the other Gospels.[8] There's a reason why they don't believe John's Gospel – for much the same reason that Jews don't accept any of the New Testament. It has to do with their belief in Jesus' role as a messenger from God.

It turned out that an understanding of the history and cultural setting of the New Testament era is absolutely critical to understanding the New Testament, and the Gospels. The first important fact is that the majority of Jews at the time did not live in Palestine, which at the time was just a problematic territory controlled by the Roman Empire. Not all Jews had returned from Babylon, and for centuries other Jews had been migrating throughout the Mediterranean region where they were losing contact with Jewish culture and language.[9] They became what are called Hellenistic Jews, speaking Greek and enamored of Greek culture. In fact, the Hellenistic Jews and the Palestinian Jews were somewhat less than enamored of each other by Jesus' time. Possibly the most easily available and readable overall picture of Palestinian life and politics of the day can be found in Reza Aslam's *Zealot - the Life and Times of Jesus of Nazareth*.[10] The Bible makes little mention of Jesus as a political figure, but the Bible does give adequate suggestion that his message had political consequences, regardless of the spiritual lessons he expounded. Lacking a decent understanding of these circumstances, it's not surprising that anyone would miss even the critical inconsistencies among the Gospels. Most Christians actually aren't aware of the obvious inconsistencies.

A major handicap for Christians in understanding most of both the Old Testament and the New Testament is that they hold the mistaken belief that *Messiah* and *Christ* mean the same thing. Unfortunately, many Bible translators were not aware of that difference either. *Messiah* is a Hebrew word meaning *anointed*. Every king in Israel was a messiah, literally anointed with oil. But others who were called by God for some high purpose were also called messiahs – for example, Cyrus, King of Persia, was considered a messiah because he was anointed by God to facilitate the building of the second Temple in Jerusalem.[11]

The Jews did indeed look forward to a Great Messiah. Jesus' problem with respect to that expectation was that he did not fulfill messianic prophesies, did not embody the qualifications of the expected Messiah,[12] and did not satisfy the Jewish belief that revelations are national in nature.[13,14] Further, their belief was that unless Israel was *inhabited by the majority of the world Jewry*, there could not be a prophet in Israel, and that requirement has not existed since the exile in Babylon. Neither did Jesus properly observe Torah[15], which identified him as a false prophet.[16,17] It's rare to find anything in the

Hebrew Bible that is explicitly rejected in the New Testament, but one such rejection was Jesus' remark concerning "an eye for an eye".[18]

It's no surprise at all that the Jews did not accept Jesus as a savior. The reason Christians accuse Jews of not appreciating Jesus is because they generally reject the Jews' understanding of a messiah. They instead retroactively project Christian theology onto Old Testament scriptures – and cherry pick for passages to support their Christian theology. The relevance of Old Testament scripture to Christian theology is somewhat like using the French Constitution to justify the British monarchy – you can find the words, but the foundations are different.

Because of their theology, Christians have since mistranslated Isaiah 7:14, using the word *virgin* for the *"alma"* who would give birth – presumably referring to Mary. However, the Hebrew word *alma* has always meant a young woman, not specifically a virgin. According to Christians, Jesus was born of a virgin[19] – an insurmountable problem for Jews. The Jewish Messiah was to be born of human parents, and to be neither *a demi-god nor ... possess supernatural qualities*. He was to be born a natural descendant of King David on his *father's* side.

Another noteworthy error of interpretation involves the use of Isaiah 53 as a prophesy of Jesus' suffering. The problem with that chapter is that it isn't a reference to a future messiah – it's a continuation of a discussion of the exile and redemption of the Jewish people in the chapters leading up to Isaiah 53. The nation of Israel is referred to as the *Servant of God* no less than eleven times in those chapters – *Servant of God* being a common characterization of the nation of Israel in the Old Testament.[20,21]

This doesn't sound much like a Christian's understanding of Jesus – because they believe Jesus is *the Christ*, and Jews never believed in christs. *Christ* is the Greek word for a child born of the mating of a god with a human female. There were many such christs in the ancient Pagan world, and common among them was their mission in life to prepare humans for an afterlife with the gods in heaven. Following their deaths, these christs would ascend into the heavenly realm – where their fathers resided. They cannot be copycats of Jesus because they were written about long before Jesus' time.[22] For Jews that was blasphemy, heathen nonsense. Jews did not believe that humans had immortal souls separate from their mortal bodies.

The New Testament, like the Old Testament, has many inconsistencies. As well, the text has frequently been edited over the centuries. A man named John Mill, while researching manuscripts for such variations, found many thousands of them.[23] Undoubtedly many of them were made accidentally, but some were intentionally made because the scribes felt they were supposed to be changed, not always for theological reasons,[24] but certainly so on many occasions.[25] Sometimes they believed the text contained a factual error.[26] Sometimes changes were made to improve the agreement among biblical authors.[27] Certainly not by accident was the insertion of the last twelve verses of Mark, which virtually changed the nature of the Gospel.[28]

Even Jesus, in Matthew, is recorded as rejecting an instruction in the Old Testament;[29] further damaging to the belief that *the Bible is the inerrant word of God,* that *it contains no mistakes* and that *it is inspired completely and in its very words "verbal, plenary inspiration."*[30] Interestingly, the original texts of New Testament originals vary much more than later professionally standardized copies.[31]

Christians for centuries have taught, and believed, that Jesus was killed by the Jews. More recently, more literate Christians have modified that somewhat to say the Romans killed Jesus to satisfy the Jews. But in the historical and cultural setting – it makes no sense at all. Simply put, and confirmed by the Bible, is that Jesus committed crimes against the Roman government, and was punished in the normal manner for those crimes – by Roman officials. The *Qur'an* agrees, and intimates an error on the part of the Jews in what they perceived the crucifixion to be: *They say: "We have killed the Messiah, Isa* (Jesus), *son of Maryam, the Rasool* (messenger) *of Allah." Whereas in fact, neither did they kill him nor did they crucify him but they thought they did because the matter was made dubious for them.*[32]

Jesus rode into Jerusalem triumphantly to the welcoming crowds – Jews, no doubt, who believed he could be the expected Great Messiah, the *one who would rebuild David's kingdom and reestablish the nation of Israel.* He was not the first self-proclaimed messiah to come to Jerusalem, and this he did in full view of the occupying Romans. As for all the others before him, the fanfare was *tantamount to declaring war on Rome*,[33] so the Romans suspected him upon his arrival in the city. Then, apparently, before the week was up, mention of his being the *Son of God* enraged the Jews as well. It was *still* blasphemous for a Jew to believe *anyone* was divine, as it still is today even for Muslims,[34] and the only recourse the Jews had for that crime was the Sanhedrin, the supreme council and court of Jewish religious matters.

There are two very curious questions to be asked about what happened there. Not mentioned in the Bible was the fact that if the Sanhedrin had a *Son of God* problem with Jesus, they had full authority to do with him as they pleased – but they did nothing. It's not mentioned in the Bible that it was routine for the Sanhedrin to collaborate with the Romans by delivering suspected traitors to the Romans. The Romans didn't care at all what the Jews did with each other, but in Jesus' case they did what was their usual. They curried their favor with the Romans by delivering a suspected traitor to the Empire for Roman justice.

Ironically, the insider who exposed Jesus went not to the Jews but to the Romans, who wanted him. It is curious why Pilate, first of all, even gave any attention to Jesus' recorded testimony – a matter that was strictly outside of his jurisdiction. It's just not credible that Pilate, as reported in the Bible, expressed sympathy with Jesus' predicament. Pilate was:

> *a man renowned for his loathing of the Jews, his total disregard for Jewish rituals and customs, and his penchant for absentmindedly signing so many execution orders that a formal complaint was lodged against him in Rome – ...* [35]

There are some very interesting discrepancies to be found in the New Testament, if one knew how to recognize them. According to Mark, Jesus was crucified *the day after the Passover meal was eaten*,[36] and according to John he died *the day before it was eaten*.[37] Luke says that Joseph and Mary returned to Nazareth after performing the rites of purification,[38] but Matthew reports that they fled to Egypt.[39] Paul claims that he did *not* go to Jerusalem following his conversion on the way to Damascus,[40] but according to the book of Acts *that was the first thing he did after leaving Damascus.*[41]

Much of the New Testament was forged, judging by the definition of forgery. There has been abundant research on this matter, but suffice it to say that forgeries are anything that are not written by the ones who are credited with writing it. Most obviously, none of the oldest copies of New Testament writings were written in Aramaic, the language of Jews in Palestine in Jesus' day. They were written in Greek. The writers of the Gospels can be excused, because the titles of their writings indicate that they are gospels "according to" the ones they're credited to. However, Peter and John were illiterate,[42] which calls into question who the writers of their words really were. Some of Paul's writings are questioned because the originals were not all written in the same dialect of Greek.

Quite aside from the above considerations is the actual history of the New Testament. It didn't just conveniently fall into place, but over time a huge number of writings appeared concerning Jesus. Very few of them made it into the New Testament collection. Some Jesus believing groups, who did not necessarily believe in the *christ*, accepted only Mark. The Valentinians, a group of Gnostics, accepted only the book of John.[43] The author of the book of Mark, for example, was writing for a Roman audience, and wrote it after Jerusalem was destroyed.[44] Jewish believers accepted only Matthew, it being the gospel that stresses the continuing validity of the Law. It was the Roman church that eventually decided on the contents of a canonized New Testament – in an effort to eliminate writings they considered heretical. The first mention of the present compilation of the New Testament as being the official canon of the Catholic church dates as late as 367 C.E.[45]

By the end of the first century C.E., after the destruction of Jerusalem, the focus of Christianity shifted from Palestine to Rome, and interest in the *Jewish* culture increased over time among many of the Roman elite. It was Pope Damasus in the fourth century C.E. who had the scholar, Jerome, produce an *official Latin translation* that would become the authoritative text for all Latin-speaking Christians. That version has been used ever since, and there exist *nearly twice as many copies of the Latin Vulgate as there are Greek manuscripts of the New Testament.*[46]

By the end of the fourth century C.E. most Christians, undoubtedly influenced by Roman authority, had agreed that the canon would include the *four Gospels, Acts, the letters of Paul, and a group of other letters such as I John and I Peter, along with the Apocalypse of John.*[47] Since then, and into modern times, the Bible has been translated many times, not all of them equally authoritative – or equally unbiased. Preserving original manuscripts has been a problem for Bible translators. One researcher, feeling certain that a library had a manuscript he wanted to study, discovered that the ancient manuscripts had been sold to a fireworks manufacturer because they were considered useless.[48]

For sure many will believe I've written this chapter to criticize the Bible. That's unfortunate, because I to this day consider the Bible in most of its versions to be very important literature. As an icon of Western civilization, it is indispensable. As a spiritually enlightening volume, it is satisfactory in many aspects. As a moral guide for living, it has its failings – which I will discuss later. But concerning all the authors of the books of the Bible, I believe they were honest and faithful to their *purpose* for writing – though not wise beyond their personal world view, intellectual level, and reasoning ability. Most of the Bible was undoubtedly inspired – but not all of it for the saving of souls. An appropriate summary could be: ... *a very human* book, with very human points of view, many of which differ from one another and none of which provides the inerrant guide to how we should live.[49]

I have to say that these courses did nothing to diminish the appropriateness of the Bible as scripture. They certainly did change my understanding of a lot of what I'd read in the scriptures. It also confirmed for me that I wasn't always so wrong when I thought others had misinterpreted what they'd read. Actually, I appreciated the Bible much more following the courses than I did before, because the impenetrable mystique surrounding the whole tome was lifted. What greatly distressed me was that so much of what I'd learned has been known for so long, and banned by people with theological agendas. The Catholic church quite satisfactorily explains it's variances from

Sola Scriptura – it's the exponentially multiplying interpretations of Protestants that belie their certainty that the scriptures are inerrant. I'm assuming, of course, that it's been intelligent and literate individuals who have orchestrated the fragmentation of whatever true following there ever was.

Most importantly, I came to understand just how much I never understood about anything religious. With my studying I had inadvertently opened a door to two millennia of church history since Jesus' time, as well as several millennia before that time. And I had only begun my journey.

CHAPTER 20

Christianity

The history of Christianity, I found, was as intriguing as my study of the Bible. It seems to me that Christians believe the Bible was used as a guideline for building the Christian church. But as logical as that may sound, that's hardly what happened. Also, noting that there are so many different denominations of Christianity today, it would seem logical to conclude that Christianity is fracturing in these modern times. In truth, it was probably as fractured at the end of the first century C.E. as it is today, and the various sects held to at least as broad a spectrum of beliefs as do modern Christians. The *Holy Bible* did not become *holy* until the Christian theology had been defined, after which writings were selected that conformed to that theology.

I begin this chapter by distinguishing between *believers* (in Jesus) and *Christians* – *believers* being those who believed Jesus to be a normal human being, rather than a *christ*. It's doubtful that the terms *Christian* and *Christianity* originated among any of Jesus' followers in Palestine. According to the Bible, the disciples were called Christians first in Antioch.[1] Interestingly, Antioch is the Greek city where Paul, a *Hellenistic* Jew and Roman citizen who had never met Jesus, had been preaching. There's significance to that event in that it occurred outside the influence of Jesus' Palestinian ministry.

We have evidence of meaningful differences between Paul and the original twelve apostles from the beginning. When Paul went to Palestine to meet with James and the others, they told him to take note that there were *thousands of Jews there which believed, and they* [were] *all zealous of the law.*[2] They obviously pointed that out because Paul had taught that the Law did not bring salvation, but punishment.[3] Further, they accused him of teaching all the Hellenistic Jews *to forsake Moses.*[4] He was instructed to purify himself, walk orderly, and keep the law.[5]

His reputation had preceded him, and as the apostles had warned him he was confronted by a mob of angry Jews – their reasons obvious. As it turned out it was the Romans who came to his rescue[6] because they recognized he hadn't offended any Roman law.[7] Paul, however, did confess to his Jewish *heresy,*[8] to his faith in *Christ,*[9] and that he *knew* Jesus *lived,*[10] a blaspheme when naming a dead Jewish *messiah.* There is no account of the apostles coming to his defense, and when he faced trial he claimed his Roman right to justice from none other than the Roman emperor.[11]

The New Testament doesn't address what became of the *believers* in Palestine after Jesus' crucifixion, but their influence spread even to other Jews throughout the Diaspora. Peter obviously went to Rome – he's reputed to have been the first bishop of Rome. He was possibly there before Paul arrived. Missionaries had been sent out from Jerusalem, and Peter wrote of his disapproval of converts who did not keep the Jewish law. He wrote in typically Jewish manner about the ministries of Paul and his followers, that *the dog is turned to his own vomit again; and the sow that was washed to her wallowing in the mire.*[12] His interpretation of Paul's perceived freedom from the Law is not unlike the traditional Jewish perception of gentile wickedness and uncleanness.[13] Peter's attitude on this matter was the norm among the original apostles, because it was on instruction from James, their apparent coordinator, that he separated himself and his Jewish followers from Paul and his gentile followers.[14]

It's commonly believed among modern Christians that the early Christians in Rome were persecuted. This is true, but somewhat out of context. Peter's followers, or *believers,* had already found respect, if not other believers, among the Roman elite; but Paul's *Christian* followers did not associate with them.[15] The *believers* in Rome had so negatively reacted to Paul's message that he decided to preach only to gentiles, *for they* [would] *listen.*[16,17] It was *those Christians* who were persecuted.

Paul in his own account described his resistance to the apostles in Jerusalem, how he felt about their interference with his followers.[18] This explains why *Saint Peter* became the first pope in Rome, and *Saint Paul*, who much later became the father of Christianity, was executed in Rome. The *Bible* did not yet exist.

Geopolitics played no small part in how Peter's religion became replaced by Paul's *Christianity* in the third century. It began with the Roman destruction of Jerusalem in 70 C.E., when the center of the believers' movement shifted from Jerusalem to the Greco-Roman cities of Alexandria, Corinth, Ephesus, Damascus, Antioch, and Rome. By the end of the first century, when most of the New Testament was being written, Rome had become a prime target of evangelism.[19] The first gospel of Jesus, *the beginning of the good news of Jesus the Christ*, was written in Greek for the evangelization of a gentile population.[20]

Evangelizing gentiles without a *Christian* bible was the challenge faced by Paul and his followers. Not only were they disrespected by the company of Peter's favored *believers*, they had to clean up for the gentiles the accusation that it was Romans who killed Jesus. Reminding Roman gentiles that it was they who'd killed the savior was not a palatable gospel message, and by the time the *Gospel According to Luke* was written the record indicated that the Romans were absolved of that responsibility, a guileless Pilate had scathingly reprimanded the Jewish religious leaders, and it was the Jews who killed Jesus.[21] That condemnation of the Jews prevailed among Christians until the embarrassment of the Jewish Holocaust during World War II. The twenty-first century doting by fundamentalist Christians on the Jewish nation is a startling reversal of sympathies.

Incidentally, the *Qur'an* states that the Palestinian Jews had accepted the *false* accusation that it was Jews who killed Jesus,[22] though it doesn't suggest who may have killed him. There seems no real question that it was the Romans who executed Jesus, but Paul was never inclined to defy Roman authority.[23]

Despite the fact that Paul was called to Jerusalem to answer for his deviant teachings around 57 C.E.,[24] he didn't abide by the instruction he received there. This is why the original Aramaic-speaking Jewish *believers* clashed with the Greek-speaking gentile believers in a christ, and divided the community of Jesus believers into two distinct camps.[25]

> *By the third century C.E. the Jesus believers were a loosely organized church, whose bishops based their authority on succession from the apostles and their faith on a large collection of sacred writings (far wider than the present New Testament) was in place.[26] .... There was no systematic theology, due to the great variety texts being used.[27]*

How the belief system of the Hellenistic followers of Peter became replaced by the theology of Paul was a long process. The further Jews became dispersed from their Jerusalem roots, the more they concentrated on converting gentile audiences. It wasn't long before the majority of the movement consisted of gentiles, who brought Pagan elements into their cultic practices and *discarded* [their] *Jewish past for a Greco-Roman future.*[28] Jesus is believed by all modern Christians to be *the* Christ. It's probably impossible to explain to most modern Christians that through history the christology of Jesus morphed from being a humble human being from Nazareth into *a divine, preexistent, literal son of God whose death and resurrection launch*[ed] *a new genus of eternal beings responsible for judging the world.*[29]

The eventual winner in the theological debate turned out to be the *Christian* gentile converts who eventually gained official recognition by the Roman government. Having become the predominant group of believers in Rome, their influence in the Empire ripened with the conversion of Emperor Constantine to *Christianity* about 312 C.E.[30] Paul's writings, largely overlooked in the West until the fourth century C.E., became what the *Christian* believers needed to support their gentile world view.[31]

> *The task of defining Jesus's message fell instead to a new crop of educated, urbanized, Greek-speaking Diaspora Jews who would become the primary vehicles for the expansion of the new faith. As these extraordinary men and women, many of them*

immersed in Greek philosophy and Hellenistic thought, began to reinterpret Jesus's message so as to make it more palatable to their fellow Greek-speaking Jews and to their gentile neighbors in the Diaspora, they gradually transformed Jesus from a revolutionary zealot to a Romanized demi-god, from a man who tried and failed to free the Jews from Roman oppression to a celestial being wholly uninterested in any earthly matter.[32]

This was the group that eventually decided what books got to be included in the New Testament, and what the Christian creeds would be.[33] They established themselves as *orthodox* – that is, they claimed to have the *right belief.* They determined *what future Christian generations would believe and read as scripture.*[34] Being *orthodox* demanded oversight, which required standardization, and this standardization of beliefs and acceptable readings was not exactly about the *truth.* It was the method by which the *orthodox* church would exercise control. In Christianity one is made to be a sinner, original sin being the inescapable sin, and the church provides the solution to getting past this sin. Hence, the revised concepts of both heaven and hell in modern Christianity.

By the third and fourth centuries, however, as Christianity gradually transformed from a heterogeneous Jewish movement with an array of sects and schisms into an institutionalized and rigidly orthodox imperial religion of Rome.[35] .... Peter's role as the first bishop of Rome and his status as the chief apostle made him the ideal figure upon which to base the authority of the Roman Church.[36]

This transformation of the Jesus movement wasn't really an unintentional drift toward Paganism. In an effort to expand their appeal to traditional Pagans, it's acknowledged by church fathers that an effort was made to portray *Christianity* as not that different from their Pagan beliefs, and extensively accommodated the calendar of Pagan festivities by injecting them with a Christian explanation.[37] This explains why so much of Christian cultic practices consist of Pagan symbolism combined with Christian events; e.g. Easter bunnies and eggs, and Christmas trees.

Jesus, according to the Hebrew scriptures, was unsuccessful as a messiah – that is, he was neither liberator nor king. That was a problem for the morphing church, so they effectively cherry-picked the various mentions of *messiah* in the Hebrew Bible to describe Jesus as one who *rose above such messianic paradigms.* But, ... *it does not appear to be how Jesus himself understood it. .... In the entire first gospel there exists not a single definitive messianic statement from Jesus himself*.[38]

It cannot be overlooked that Christianity resembles Mithraism much more than it does Judaism. Mithra, the god of light, was worshiped in what is now Iran many centuries B.C.E. Following the conquest of Babylon, Mithraism migrated westward, became the state religion of Armenia, and came to Asia Minor, with local adaptations along the way. However, with the Roman occupation of the Euphrates region the original Iranian elements of Mithraism successfully spread throughout the Empire, promoted by the Roman army from the Bosporus to Spain and Britain.[39] The practices of Mithraism were widespread in Rome from the first to the fourth century.

Mithra was known as a teacher who traveled with twelve disciples, and was variously called *the good shepherd; the way, the truth, and the light; savior; redeemer* and *Messiah.*[40] He was born on December 25, the day the rebirth of the winter sun was celebrated. The day of the sun, Sunday, was kept holy in his honor.[41] He was buried in a tomb and after three days he rose again. His resurrection was celebrated every year.[42]

A long series of analogies exists between him [Mithras] and Jesus. Mithras was born on December 25 in a stable to a virgin, surrounded by shepherds who brought gifts. He was venerated on the day of the sun (Sunday). He bore a halo around his head. He celebrated a last supper with his faithful followers before returning to his father. He was said not to have died, but to have ascended to heaven from where he would return in the last days to raise the dead and judge them, sending the good to Paradise and the evil to Hell. He guaranteed his followers immortality after baptism.

Furthermore, the followers of Mithras believed in the immortality of the soul, the last judgment, and the resurrection of the dead at the end of the world. They celebrated the atoning death of a saviour who had risen on a Sunday. They celebrated a ceremony corresponding to the Catholic Mass during which they consumed consecrated bread and wine in memory of the last supper of Mithras – and during the ceremony they used hymns, bells, candles, and holy water. Indeed, they shared with Christians a long series of other beliefs and ritual practices, to the point that they were practically indistinguishable from each other in the eyes of the pagans and also of many Christians.[43]

This is not an Old Testament prophecy – this is a very short list of the beliefs and practices of Mithraism at the time the followers of Jesus were becoming accepted in Rome. Curiously, if one cares to do the studying necessary, he'll discover that there's nothing in the New Testament story of Jesus that wasn't previously written about other persons in much earlier times. The closest Christian acknowledgment I've ever heard of this connection to Pagan origins was in a speech by Pope Benedict XVI, who stated that "Christians have a Greek concept of God, and Jews and Muslims have a Hebrew concept of God."

Undoubtedly the most significant period in the development of modern Christian theology was the fourth century C.E. In an adaptation from Greek theology (now called mythology), the belief that Jesus was divine became more widely accepted – the leap from Judaism to Christianity.[44] Probably the greatest catalyst for this transformation was the extensive influence Augustine had over the church, and his *obsession* with Paul's writings, though he never had access to the Greek originals.[45] Because Paul had been ignored in the West for hundreds of years, he hadn't been officially honored in Rome until the fourth century when he was portrayed in the fourth century Basilica of Santa Pudenziana, sitting to the left of Jesus – with Peter seated on Jesus' right.[46,47]

It was Augustine who introduced the doctrine of *original sin* into Christianity. He also introduced the modern Christian concept of *hell* as a place of punishment for all who did not accept God's saving grace.[48] This concept came to the height of its importance at the onset of the witch purges in western Europe in the sixteenth century C.E. The English word *hell* does itself have a Pagan origin, and the popular understanding of hell among Christians was best articulated by Dante in his 1300's epic.[49] Augustine determined that *the majority of mankind is destined to burn in hell.* He provided little evidence of that vision, *but it was accepted by the Church almost without debate and became embedded in orthodox Catholic belief for centuries to come.*[50] So desperate did the church become to control the population that Augustine concluded that heretics should be tortured, and Thomas Aquinas believed they should be killed outright.[51] These men are nevertheless appropriately counted among the fathers of Christianity for their influence in shaping Christian theology. Few have any standing to even dispute this Christian policy – *Martin Luther and John Calvin* [also] *advocated the wholesale murder of heretics, apostates, Jews, and witches.*[52]

The theology that developed during this period of time in Rome is the one that ultimately was called *universal*, or *catholic*. It was determined that their resulting doctrine and form of worship was correct, claiming that authority came to them from God through their first pope, Peter, to whom were given the *keys of the kingdom*.[53] The church ultimately canonized the New Testament to bring the rest of the Christian world into line with their theology. They selected documents that supported their beliefs from the vast number of writings being circulated among the congregations around the Mediterranean. Not surprisingly, half of the twenty-seven books that now make up the New Testament are either by or about Paul.[54] And as for the writings the Church disapproved of, the power of the Roman Empire accommodated their virtual eradication from existence.

Centuries later Martin Luther adopted the mantra *sola scriptura*, which became the foundation doctrine of the Protestant Reformation. *Sola scriptura* implies that all matters are *subordinate to and corrected by* the written word of God – in other words, the Catholic canon. Luther, believing in *sola scriptura*, observed that the Church was abusive, employing practices that were not supported by their scriptures. He protested that state of affairs, and because he would not recant he was excommunicated. Hence, he and his fellow protesters against the Roman Church have been called *Protestants* ever since.

In modern times it's common enough for Protestants to rely exclusively on the Bible, their criticism of the Roman Catholic Church being that it had strayed from its *biblical* foundations. But the organization *Catholics United for the Faith* offers the reasoning behind their church's objection to *sola scriptura*.

> *...we must acknowledge that Tradition and Scripture make up a single sacred deposit of the Word of God, which is **entrusted to the Church** (Dei Verbum, no. 10). We must further recognize that **the task of safeguarding** (cf. 1 Tim. 6:20) **and interpreting the Word of God**, oral or written, has been **entrusted to the Magisterium alone** (Dei Verbum, no. 10; 2 Thess. 2:15).*
>
> *The doctrine of Mary's Perpetual Virginity brings to light two distinct errors that are rooted in misconceptions concerning the nature of divine Revelation. The first error is the "sola Scriptura" approach that collapses the Word of God to merely that which has been written, thereby denying the role of Tradition and the Magisterium. Curiously, such a position, developed during the Protestant Reformation, is not taught in Scripture. Indeed, the testimony of Scripture conveys otherwise. For example, in 2 Thessalonians 2:15, St. Paul exhorts his followers to "stand firm and hold fast to the traditions [they] were taught, either by an oral statement or by a letter. . . ." In 1 Timothy 3:15, St. Paul further states that the Church is "the pillar and bulwark of the truth."* [55]

Not always recognized among Protestants, except by the congregations who routinely remind themselves of it, is that *Protestant* does not exactly mean non-catholic – it means a catholic church that protests the authority of the Roman pope over them. In Anglican, Episcopalian, and Lutheran churches they refer to themselves as catholic. It's not surprising, then, that they use the Catholic canon, the New Testament. Perhaps Martin Luther believed the *true* Church actually had compiled the appropriate scriptures and then strayed from them. But he was excommunicated, something he had not anticipated, for maintaining his belief in *sola scriptura*. In any case, all versions of the New Testament in common use today are descended from the original Catholic canon. Ironically, Protestant Bible churches today, who believe they have no connection whatsoever to Catholicism and even do not recognize Catholics as Christians, have a more focused faith in the Catholic scriptures than do even Catholics. Further, they tend to invalidate any evidence of differing teachings prior to or separate from the adopted Catholic canon.

The eventual disappearance of the original Jewish *believers'* community is undoubtedly due to the aggressive purge of the Roman government to rid the Empire of non-orthodox sects. But despite the power of the Roman government to promote Catholicism, not all early Christians lived under the influence of Rome. A missionary named Ulfilias is rarely mentioned, but he converted the Goths to Christianity in the 340's C.E. However, he didn't believe in the Roman church's Trinity. For that reason he was never made a saint in the Catholic church, and his followers were officially rejected by the church by 381 C.E.[56] In my experience with the teaching of World History, I've never heard mention of Attila's Christian affiliation. But history tells us that a century after Ulfilias' missionary success beyond the northern bounds of the Roman Empire, the pope in 452 C.E. appealed to Attila's Christian faith to persuaded him to retreat from his attack on Rome with a threat of the *eternal consequences* of his actions. [57]

Even more estranged from Western orthodoxy, to this day, are the millions of Christians living in southwestern India. They're not the converts of Western proselytizing – they're believed to have been converted by the apostle Thomas in the first century, and are known as Saint Thomas Christians. During the period of European expansion, the Portuguese missionaries destroyed most of their writings and imposed the Portuguese language on them, in true Western and Catholic fashion. But the outside intrusion of other Christian varieties appears not to have affected their beliefs. Today they're retrieving the remnants of their ancient scriptures, and *some liturgies are sung in*

Syriac, close to the Aramaic language spoken by Christ. Of course, they remain heretics from the Catholic community.[58]

Western Christianity, the dominant brand of the religion, is in all its various manifestations descended from its catholic theological foundation, perpetuated worldwide by the power of the Roman Empire first, and the power of European colonizers in modern times. To return to the matter of a Catholic creed – it was not the Catholic Church but Emperor Constantine who ordered the adoption of a universal *statement of faith* and the creation of a *monolithic church* – for the purpose of *marrying the church to the Roman state; and institute the practice of denouncing and excommunicating those who would not obey the church.*[59] Then:

> *By 380 A.D. the church bishops were integrated into the judicial system, with the power to torture witnesses of low status and imprison the accused and administer corporal punishment. Thus, the state gained power over* **aberrant Christian, Jewish and Pagan activity,**[60] *and the authority to* **champion the supporters of Nicea, over its rivals.**[61]

The Roman government was not terribly concerned about what the creed was in the end, as long as it *unified* the Empire. The Roman *church*, however, wanted it to be *their* theology, and that they accomplished by the Councils of Nicea where Roman pressures prevailed. This officially established them as the Catholic (Universal) Christian church. Those who disagreed with the Creed were *immediately banished from the empire and their teachings violently suppressed.*[62]

As it turned out, the Roman Empire collapsed anyway. Eventually the Eastern church, when the power of the Roman Empire to enforce the Creed was gone, separated itself from the Roman church. They'd never completely agreed with the Roman church on the meaning of the Creed in any case. The divided church became known as the *Roman* Catholic Church and the Eastern *Orthodox* Church – both titles indicating they are the *universally true* church. These things have always been known. None of this history was erased from the record, but centuries of censorship of what the general population would be trusted with or allowed to know has indeed dictated *orthodox* Christian theology on the whole of Christendom. What never was successfully hidden are the centuries of rigid, and frequently violent, church control of populations and governments into modern times. Unfortunately, such control is never about the truth of anything, it is purely the exercise of power – that is, politics.

There's no need to rehash that abusive aspect of Christianity. The various denominations of Christians have long used the abuses of other denominations to bolster their own reputations. The result is that the members of many denominations are more ignorant of their own denomination's abuses than they are of all the other denominations'.

This whole history really does nothing to guarantee that any Christian philosophy has its foundation with Jesus and the twelve apostles in Jerusalem. In fact, Jesus left no instructions on how a church would be organized – that obviously fell first to the apostles to decide, but they left no record either. The Catholic church clung to the Jewish discipline of a priesthood intermediary between the individual and God. But it settled firmly on Greek theology, complete with souls, heaven for humans, hell for punishment, and the salvation of condemned humanity.

So what is religious truth? I learned a most accurate definition from a religious scholar: "Religious truth is the consensus of opinion of religious authorities at any given time." In other words, always subject to change. For what it's worth, I believe he was right. It just makes a sandy foundation on which to establish *eternal* truths.

CHAPTER 21

Religion

That wasn't the end of my search. It had intrigued me from my college classes how both the Jews' and Muslims' belief systems intermingled with Christianity, despite their differences. Neither the Jews nor Muslims made any move to proselytize me, but they were always open to discussion about their philosophies. I wasn't entirely unfamiliar with Judaism, having in-law level relationships with both devout Jews and secular Jews. As well, I have a small library of writings on the history of Israel and the Jewish experience. But I wasn't that familiar with Islam, despite the fact that I'd long known and interacted with Muslims. I first knowingly encountered Muslims when I was in elementary school, and frankly I never thought any of them even looked different from the rest of society. As adults Judy and I had socialized with Muslim couples, I'd done private business with Muslims, and my grandchildren visited back and forth with devout Muslim neighbor children. They were all far less conspicuous on the street than were the immigrants from the Indian subcontinent who attended our Truth meetings. Who I'd never mingled with were Muslims torn from their homes and fleeing for safety to places and cultures they'd never planned on living in.

When I asked about visiting a mosque, my friend told me he didn't frequent a mosque, but had prayers with others in someone's home. But he assured me I'd be welcome: "Just go and visit. They will speak English." So I visited the imam in a mosque near where I worked, and he extended the same invitation – prayers any Friday at 1:00 p.m. My schedule allowed me to attend a couple of times a month over the next couple of years.

The first time I attended prayers a man approached me and said the imam had asked him to make me feel welcome. He showed me around the building, where to leave my shoes, where ritual washing was accomplished, etc. He asked me if I knew what *Muslim* meant, and I confessed I didn't. He asked me if I considered myself *submitted to God*, and I said I did. "Then," he replied "you are Muslim too." That surprised me, but I'd already been told that was all that was necessary to be considered a Muslim. On the other hand, I doubt any Muslim would recommend me as an authority on Islam because I've never made a *Shahada*, a recitation of the Muslim Creed, before a congregation.

A *coming of age* ritual is normal and passed on in all societies and religions. For children born into Muslim families, this formality is quite like the way children of the Friends *profess* in gospel meetings. Even the term and practice of *Shahada* is not Muslim in origin, but was adopted by Muhammad from the Sabians,[1] a Middle Eastern religious group that followed the *Zabur*, which many scholars consider to be the *Psalms of David*.[2] They're listed in the *Qur'an* along with Jews and Christians:

> *Surely, the believers (Muslims), the Jews, the Sabians and the Christians – whoever believes in Allah and the Last Day and does righteous deeds – will have nothing to fear or to grieve.*[3,4]

These mosque visits occurred not long after the 9-11 attacks, and I had frank conversations with Fateen, the imam, and others about such matters as terrorism and community relations. I asked him what association his congregation had with Louis Farrahkan of the Nation of Islam. His answer was, "None whatsoever. Their message is black nationalism." (Incidentally, Fateen is African American.) His mosque, *Masjid As-Sabur*, was originally a Nation of Islam congregation, but made the transition to mainstream Islam in 1975[5] and holds to Sunni ideology.

Of course I, like everyone else at the time, had been sufficiently counseled on the wickedness of Muslim doctrine:

If thy brother, the son of thy mother, or thy son, or thy daughter, or the wife of thy bosom, or thy friend, which is as thine own soul, entice thee secretly, saying, Let us go and serve other gods, which thou hast not known, thou, nor thy fathers; ..... Thou shalt not consent unto him, nor hearken unto him; neither shall thine eye pity him, neither shalt thou spare, neither shalt thou conceal him: but thou shalt surely kill him; thine hand shall be first upon him to put him to death, and afterwards the hand of all the people. And thou shalt stone him with stones, that he die; because he hath sought to thrust thee away from the Lord thy God, which brought thee out of the land of Egypt, from the house of bondage. And all Israel shall hear, and fear, and shall do no more any such wickedness as this is among you. If thou shalt hear say in one of thy cities, which the Lord thy God hath given thee to dwell there, saying, Certain men, the children of Belial, are gone out from among you, and have withdrawn the inhabitants of their city, saying, Let us go and serve other gods, which ye have not known; then shalt thou enquire, and make search, and ask diligently; and, behold, if it be truth, and the thing certain, that such abomination is wrought among you; thou shalt surely smite the inhabitants of that city with the edge of the sword, destroying it utterly, and all that is therein, and the cattle thereof, with the edge of the sword.

Ironically, that turns out not to be from the *Qur'an* at all, but from Christian scripture.[6] This is hardly more aggressive than Jesus' statement: *Think not that I am come to send peace on earth: I came not to send peace, but a sword.*[7] Still, in these times of terrorism, it is persistently reported that the *Qur'an* demands *jihad*. There is indeed scripture to that effect: *But those enemies of mine who did not want me to be king over them—bring them here and kill them in front of me.* Ironically, that also is Christian scripture.[8] Mainstream Muslims in the United States have persistently reminded people that the *Qur'an* says that *There is no compulsion in religion.*[9] Other passages reinforce this teaching,[10] among them: *The only duty of the Rasool is to convey **My Message**.*[11] This certainly doesn't mean the *Qur'an* condemns war in all instances – what it primarily stresses is punishment in the afterlife for insubordination to God.

At first I found it difficult to interpret some of the mentions of Christians in sermons – not that I disagreed, because I'd made the same comments myself. It was a startlingly clear insight into the prejudicial way we react to truthful criticism, depending on who delivers it. But comments made in sermons in the mosque were never more critical of Christians than they were of Muslims. Good morals and kindness were the major themes. What surprised me was the frequent mention of Jesus – the most standout mention being: "Muhammad said nothing new. Jesus said it all." The other thing that greatly impressed me was the diversity of the congregation. Racially and ethnically it represented the complete spectrum of the American population, and no ethnicity predominantly. My only apparent characteristic of distinction in that congregation appeared to be that I was Canadian, not that I was Caucasian.

I believe the only appropriate differences of treatment between men and women should be for the reasonable accommodation of biological differences. Yet, I'm unable to comment on how women are treated in Muslim society because there are too many varieties of Muslim societies, and because I see no evidence that American Muslim families behave any differently from the American norm. I'm inclined to believe that Muslim men treat Muslim women much like other men treat women in the societies where they were raised. I don't believe there are more atrocities committed in Muslim families in this country than in Christian families – Christians have their own fair share of diabolical parents under investigation. As for the wearing of head coverings, I believe Muslim immigrant women cannot reasonably be expected to dispose of their *hijab* upon arrival in a Western country, any more than the average American woman could reasonably be expected to go topless in aboriginal lands. One lady I worked with had converted to Islam when she was young, and then left later on in life. She still considered Islam a beautiful religion – her only criticism was the way women were traditionally treated. But she had some very interesting explanations for why Muslim women would accept, if only to tolerate, such traditions as women's coverings. I perceive that many people consider a Muslim woman who does not wear the *hijab* to actually be less devout than the woman who does wear it. That just is not the case. There are plenty of prominent American Muslim women who do not wear a head covering.

Some ex-Friends feel that people born and raised in the Truth really don't know much about other Christian religions. I'm not sure that goes for all of the Friends. I'd been in a number of both Catholic and Protestant churches when I'd lived in Canada. I'd played with both Catholic and Protestant kids, and we discussed our religions with each other. But with a heightened sense of church history and philosophies, I decided to visit some churches as well. I went first to an Episcopal church frequented by one of my professors, and I learned again how small the world can be. Living 3,500 miles from where I'd grown up, I was amazed to learn the man who greeted me at the door had lived and worked in my home town in Canada, knew some of my Anglican relatives there, and maintained a close friendship with one of my fellow teachers there. It occurred to me that, had my grandparents not left the Anglican church, chances are I could already have been attending this Las Vegas church.

At the door I was handed an eight page program, as was everyone else. When the service began, I was called upon to introduce myself to the congregation. I was asked if I was an Episcopalian, and I replied that I wasn't. So a nun approached me and gave me a small cross and a pamphlet. And the service continued.

It was a very elaborate and ritualistic service. The eight-page program included the complete, precisely scripted service from beginning to end, including the congregation's participation. Only the text of the minister's sermon was missing. This contrasted sharply with the routine among the Friends where nothing is ever scripted. I was reminded of my father telling me that, when he was about 10 years old, he was chastised by his brother for not making up his own bedtime prayer – now that they no longer went to church they had to make it up as they went. It was interesting, in a *Protestant* church, to hear mention of it being a *catholic* church.

I also visited a Lutheran church, and I had no interest in going back. It may have been unique to that specific Lutheran church, but it was the deadest exercise I've ever witnessed. On the contrary, I once approached an evangelical Christian church. I was obviously late for the service, because I heard loud preaching and raucous *Amens* from down the street. At the front door of the church I decided I didn't need to witness such confusion. It may offend a lot of people, but I don't consider that kind of chaotic, even consciousness bending, communion to be far removed from that of a drug-incited party. It seems to me that one's eternal future can best be appreciated with a fully sober mind.

Near my house I discovered Lev Hashem, a Messianic synagogue – so I visited there several times. I had a surprising introduction to the synagogue too. When I indicated that I was interested in *Messianic Judaism,* one lady asked me what synagogue I "used to go to." When I told her that I wasn't even Jewish, she said, "But you look like a Jew."

Unlike other Jews, Messianic congregations accept *Yeshua* (Jesus) as the Messiah, but have adopted the Christian definition of the word *messiah.* They don't call themselves Christians. They insist they're Jews, and one person told me, "Jesus came first to the Jews." Not surprisingly, Orthodox Jews condemn their adopted Christian beliefs. Some of the Orthodox criticisms of the Messianics are:

The Messiah doesn't come to start a new religion called Christianity.

Millions of Jews have been murdered because of Christianity. Just look at the six million ... starved, tortured, and gassed to death in the Holocaust .... The Jewish Messiah doesn't come to murder Jewish people: He comes to bring salvation.

Jews don't believe in the Trinity. There is only One God, not three. The first commandment is to worship only One God; therefore, to believe in Yeshua is idol worship.

God doesn't have a son. The virgin birth was a pagan story before the time of Yeshua, and the writers of the New Testament took this story from Greek and Egyptian mythology.

The Messiah isn't divine: he is a just man, and he certainly doesn't die for one's sins. We repent for our sins; a man can't take them away. Only God can take them away.

Jews believe the Messiah will come once, not twice. He doesn't come and then return again.

If Yeshua were the Messiah, then the Jewish People would have recognized him 2000 years ago. Even today, Jewish people do not accept him as Messiah. When the Messiah comes, we will recognize him.

When the Jewish Messiah comes, there will be peace on earth, and the Lion will lie down with the lamb. Today, there are wars going on all around the world. It is clear the Messiah had not yet come.[12]

In the late nineteenth century, some Jewish immigrants to the U.S. were converting to Christianity and worshiping as Methodists. Because they retained elements of their Jewish rites and culture, they were accused of being *Judaizers*. In 1915 an organization of Jews who'd converted to Christianity established the Hebrew Christian Alliance of America, and they *consistently assuaged the fears of fundamentalist Christians by emphasizing that it is not a separate denomination but only an evangelistic arm of the evangelical church*. But in 1975 the Hebrew Christian Alliance of America officially changed its name to Messianic Jewish Alliance of America, and Messianic Judaism was born.[13]

Their services were very ritualistic. I didn't understand a lot of what was happening, but there was singing, dancing, an elaborate bread and salt ritual, reading in Hebrew from a scroll, and the circulation of the *ark of the covenant* to be kissed – not by one's lips, but touched by an object that the person had previously kissed. One service was a ritual celebration of the date of Jesus' birth in the early fall. It lasted three hours, and involved the congregation moving outdoors to the parking lot and, at one point, waving palm leaves in various directions. There was scriptural reference for every aspect of the celebration, but keeping track of it all was quite beyond my ability to remember. As well as English and Hebrew, a few people carried Spanish Bibles.

During another visit I learned what being a member could cost me. The rabbi reminded everyone that they owed ten percent of their salary. And because they had a guest speaker from Los Angeles that day, they also owed the speaker what I calculated to be more than ten percent of my salary that month – not including mileage for his travel. Further, the rabbi told us that if we didn't pay we were "nothing but Pagan Jews".

What seriously concerned me on another visit was a lady from Israel who was soliciting support for *Jewish settlements – in Israel*. As well, she also solicited prayers to have the George W. Bush administration reverse its policy of banning funding for *Jewish settlements*, which bolstered my suspicion. Israel doesn't need money to build Jewish settlements in Israel. The funding was certainly intended for Jewish settlements in the Palestinian West Bank – an ongoing practice that is outlawed by international law, but continues nonetheless as a serious impediment to the Israeli-Palestinian peace process.

Equally interesting was my investigation of Paganism. The first such course I registered for provided another evidence of how small the world is. In the first class meeting the professor introduced herself as a practicing witch, and asked each of us to share our religious background. I explained that I'd left a "fundamentalist Christian group." She asked which one it was, so I explained: "They claim not to have any official name, but they are frequently referred to as Two-by-Twos."

"Oh," she said abruptly. "I know all about them. They're called Workers. My step daughter is one of them." It was probably my most unusual introduction to a new professor.

I expected Paganism would be somewhat exotic, relative to my background. It was, actually, but the most intriguing aspect of Paganism turned out to be its resemblance to Christianity – or more accurately put, Christianity's resemblance to Paganism. There was hardly an aspect of Pagan belief and culture that didn't explain something about Christianity that didn't come from Judaism. The primary difference, of course, was that Pagans are polytheistic. That, incidentally, makes a Pagan a much safer neighbor in a pluralistic society – they have no problem with anyone worshiping a different god.

For probably half a year I frequented the weekly meetups of a local Druid grove. They met in a restaurant over their selections from the menu. The discussions were not unlike those in the Classics class I totally blew off in my college days. I now appreciate what I could have learned if I'd been more diligent in my studies back then.

Paganism is nature based, and their rituals are held outdoors. The Druids I met with are active environmentalists. I attended both Wiccan and Druid outdoor evening rituals. There was always a fire, and they were elaborately ritualistic and followed by a pot-luck. Pot-luck following each ritual appears to have also been a practice among early Christians, until Paul put a stop to it when they abused the practice.[14] A fellow teacher of mine was also a witch, and I accepted an invitation to a Bone Dance at a Pagan temple in the desert at Samhain (Halloween, to Christians). Being close to Las Vegas, they have the benefit of participation by a professional drummer from the entertainment community.

Pagans have no scriptures. They rely on the *Wiccan Rede* as their guide for living. One modern English version of it reads: *"If it harms none, do what you will."* Reward and punishment for compliance or noncompliance to the Rede, they believe, is determined by the *Threefold Law*, or the *Law of Return: "All good that a person does to another returns three fold in this life; harm is also returned three fold."*

I familiarized myself with other religious traditions as well, but the above mentioned are the sampling of the extended Christian family tree. Except for the Pagan relatives, the rest are referred to as Abrahamic religions, comprising a majority of the world's population. At a glance, it looks quite confusing; but as the saying goes: "The more different it becomes, the more alike it remains." It's true – some versions of Christianity are more like some versions of Islam than they are like many other versions of Christianity. Some Pagans have said they feel quite comfortable in a Catholic church. This history belies the likelihood that any one of these religions is *pure* anything, or that any individual's *revelation* is more divinely authentic than another's.

Ironically, the plan for salvation that most resembles that of modern Christian evangelicals is that of Hindus. Hindus have many gods, and salvation for them doesn't actually mean *going to heaven* – but they have *dharma* (the Way) that allows one to break out of the *shackles of existence.* And they have *avatars* (christs) that intercede on their behalf. *The Way* involves adopting a personal god and accepting redeeming grace through an avatar-savior, be it the mercies of Krishna, or some other avatar – in the way modern Protestants find grace through faith in Jesus Christ, and serve him to the saving of their souls.

But knowing these denominational likenesses and differences doesn't help us fully understand religion. The very purpose of religion varies from one religion to another, and similar and borrowed rituals take on different meanings, according to one's theology. Jews, for example, have no need for salvation in an afterlife, except for the reward of an eventual resurrection to physical human life for having lived the life of a righteous Jew. Buddhists are basically atheists, concerned primarily with honoring their ancestors. Many people believe humans return to live physical lives after their present life has passed. But none of this defines religion in all its diverse forms.

One scholar of religion provided what I consider the most workable definition of religion: It is a belief system that has identified an unanswerable question and attempts to provide a solution to that situation. This definition works for virtually all religions. Thus, over time, as questions get answered and new questions arise, religions change. This is how it has always been, and how it undoubtedly always will be. Those religions that don't change decline and usually disappear.

It crosses my mind that this creates a predicament for people who are pursuing universal eternal truth. Who can know what numinous experiences and revelations occurred in times before any of our known civilizations? What *recorded* revelations do we have that can be verified as *indisputable universal truth?* Further, we obviously cannot know such truth. Is the proof in the number of *critical* revelations that have been made in the last 150 years that no prior prophet or thinker has ever received? And still, we have no idea what future generations of mankind will accomplish that could conceivably invalidate any one of our presently valued *truths.* Who, then, has any assurance that such truth is yet available to man? And what compensation does one have for being ignorant of critical revelations that come long after his death?

Religious truth turns out to have a characteristic all it's own – it needs to be inspired. In the real world, a truth doesn't need to be inspired, reason and evidence can constitute the truth of it. However, believing reasonable events described in the Bible is not exactly a virtue. *Whenever a statement in the Bible is unreasonable, and you believe it, you are considered quite a good Christian. If the statement is grossly absurd and infinitely impossible, and you still believe it, you are a saint.*[15] These kinds of beliefs become convictions, rendering them immune to question and reason. Unfortunately, *convictions are more dangerous foes of truth than lies*[16] because lies are open to questioning, but conviction elevates miracles to the status divine truths. Religious truth is, in fact, an unstable commodity – the consensus of religious scholars at any given time.

These are the cultures of modern Western religions. But just as interesting is the study of the relationship of individuals to their respective religions. In many ancient societies the gods had no personal interactions with individuals – they were simply available to dispense favors. Because eternal life in ancient times normally meant living on in one's progeny, only the gods or goddesses of fertility were involved in the matter of eternal life. Otherwise, the only peril to oneself for ignoring the gods was the possible lack of what they could provide for the sustenance of life.

Many organized religions throughout history have been founded by ascetics who maintained as meager an existence as possible in the communities in their day. But as the influence of these individuals grew, their practices were commonly found to be incompatible with life in the society at large. They originate *in theory*, but morph to accommodate people of means quite different from those of the founders, the first accommodation usually being provision for the care and security of families. One of my professors referred to this process as *becoming domesticated.* The Workers fall into this pattern as well. They originated as a homeless preacher group, but for family life that posed problems – it didn't accommodate the commitments of married family life. Curiously, neither did it provide the means of support that the Workers rely on today. The structure of their system soon changed to include both a laity and a clergy, and a version of financial planning.

If a religion is to *prosper*, what follows is organization. The whole purpose of organization is to establish control, and without it all such movements flounder and fragment. This problem was abundantly evident in the years following the deaths of the founders of both Christianity and Islam, and neither movement has been uniform ever since. To establish order among believers, bodies of authority emerged whose purpose it was to define, and dictate, what teachings would be considered orthodox, and what teachings would be heresy. The Roman church, backed by the power of the Roman state, assumed that role for Christianity, and despite all its efforts never succeeded in uniting all believers – or preventing further fragmentation.

The other critical aspect of organization involves the authority to deal with heretics. How the authorities deal with heretics varies, of course, according to how much power they are permitted to assume. The Roman church originally used the power of the state to punish their heretics. When the state collapsed, the church got to prosecute its heretics however it pleased. It was not until states again became powerful enough to exercise control over the church that individuals gained any respite from church punishment. In modern democracies, the power of the church to punish is limited to excommunication. The Truth originated in times of religious liberty, so they have no history of torture and executions. That doesn't mean they haven't ever exceeded their legal authority on occasion. Experience indicates that in any matter of abuse and illegal behavior, policy has never been corrected until some individual has filed a criminal complaint against it.

As I mentioned previously, the Friends and Workers insist they aren't organized – which is really nothing more than a deceptive platitude. They early on had *conventions* to settle on doctrine, and used the power at their disposal to dethrone and alienate the founder for *heresy*. At the arrival of the twenty-first century, organized religions, including the Truth, have been apparently losing ground to the non-religious, non-believers, and the disorganization of the unorganized *spirituals* and *solitaries* – among whom nothing needs to be orthodox. Yet, in this whole gamut of persuasions, the influence of millennia of the powerful domination of Western organized religion reverberates. Even those consummately disinterested in anything resembling religion are still called upon to identify themselves in relation to religion – hence the term *atheist*.

Religious people who subscribe to a denomination consent to the group's dogma, the box that defines the limits of the member's appropriate world view. This is also the case with the Friends and Workers, as it is with any other *unnamed* denomination – except for such religions as Paganism, Unitarian Universalism, and any other religion that holds to no dogma. For organized religions, their dogma and developed doctrines are the basis on which they administer their internal justice, and the more passionately they hold to their fundamental tenets, the more severe the punishments can be for disobeying them. Secular civil law notwithstanding, many seemingly modest and moral fundamentalist denominations are notorious for flaunting their disrespect of civil, and occasionally criminal, law.

Today, many mainline Western denominations will tolerate dissidents, as long as they do not disturb the congregation or openly challenge the authority of the church. This is perfectly legitimate for any private organization, and expulsion is normally the greatest consequence for disobeying the rules. The more common crimes of mainline religious churches are crimes of omission rather than commission – the most notable recent example that of neglecting to report incidents of child sexual abuse. This is also the case with the Friends and Workers.

But dissidents do become problems, for two reasons. In top-down authoritative churches, individuals who challenge directives are a blatant violation of a core tenet of the religion and cannot be ignored. They are prime candidates for shunning and expulsion. This tends to be the case with the Friends and Workers, though the mechanics of such consequences are rarely admitted to be just that simple. Other churches who have a quasi-democratic structure can possibly be more brutal in their expulsion of the non-conformists simply because expulsion procedures may involve whole congregations in confrontational proceedings. This is the aspect of religions that makes them more like party politicians than ministers of peace. But as long as they need to organize, this will be how it works. The organization that cannot define its limits will not survive.

I believe it's safe to say that the majority of Christians have no great concern whether their denomination is perfectly aligned with its professed founding principles, if they even know what they are. What I find more interesting, though, is the great numbers of religious people who are devoted followers, but struggle with problems related to their denomination's doctrine and practices. The numbers of such people are obviously growing in our age, and modern widespread literacy rates, a better educated populace, and modern information technology are undoubtedly the primary culprit.

What is it about *information* that causes one to lose faith? I remember a Worker asking an elderly lady if she had lost her faith after reading a letter revealing the history of the Truth. Her answer was that it didn't shake her faith. But I'd known her well for decades and knew she believed the claim that 2000 years of *apostolic succession* was proof of the Truth's purity. To me, this is like a person buying the brand of medication that has the best promotion and reasonable cost – and then learning that the medication lacks the advertised active ingredients, and contains other ingredients that may be harmful. In the real world that's called fraud and is commonly prosecuted as a crime. Translated into the religious context, such a person not only buys the medication, he also buys into the *truthfulness* of the advertising – because *inspired* beliefs are not to be questioned. The difference between the medication and the religious deception is this: Such medication can kill a person, but in Christian tradition such deception can damn one's soul to hell. I'm more familiar with this type of *derailment* among the Friends and Workers, but I believe this can be found to some degree is most religions. In my experience, as many strangers who have professed in Workers' meetings and remained faithful, as many others have left in disillusionment within a few years.

For many centuries, Christianity was a cerebral experience – reflecting on the teachings of recognized prophets and authorities. However, through the last couple of centuries Christianity has become a more emotional, sensual experience – everything from born again birth pangs, to personal saviors, to spiritual trances. Theologian John W. Nevin denounced revivals as places where *a taste for noise and rant supersedes all desire for solid knowledge* and *no room is found either for instruction or reflection.*[17] The religious critic Harold Bloom commented:

> *... I remain startled by and obsessed with the revivalistic element in our religious experience. Revivalism, in America, tends to be the the perpetual shock of the individual discovering yet again what she or he have known, which is that God loves her and him on an absolutely personal and indeed intimate basis.*[18]

Such denominations now abound in Christendom, but ever-increasing numbers of individuals now also claim not to be religious, but *spiritual*. As an alternative to being religious, I have to confess I don't really understand what they mean – if not religious spirituality, then what kind of spirituality? But it does certainly suggest it has something to do with one's personal sensitivities. Perhaps the noted student of spirituality, Deepak Chopra, has the explanation: *Religion is belief in someone else's experiences, Spirituality is having your own experience.*

These kinds of experiences aren't necessarily incompatible with traditional beliefs of Christians, but technology and education persist in eroding them as they one by one become classified as superstitions, or discarded altogether. An easy example is left-handedness – it was for centuries considered a curse,[19] even among Muslims. I know many people who believed that *religiously*, and others who had their left hands tied in school to correct it. Today such a belief is considered a superstition, and the biblical justification disregarded. I confess to being amused by Paul's admonition against superstition,[20] and his admonition that one's *zeal of God* be *according to knowledge.*[21] This I say because it crosses my mind how horrified Jews must be by the extent of what is now referred to as Greek superstition that's been incorporated into Christian theology, all the while claiming both Paul and the god of Abraham for Christianity. I believe Ashleigh Brilliant was right: *The more sure you are, the more wrong you can be.* I'm far more inclined to be a student of religion than a believer in any brand of religion.

Which really begs the question: Why do people turn to religion anyway? There is a long list of benefits and comforting reasons to *belong* to a religion – all of them temporal, but few of them spiritual. The most straightforward testimony I've ever heard from a religious person as to why he was a Christian came from an Episcopal priest in a panel with other clergymen, including Jews and Muslims. All the others claimed to have *chosen* their faith for some profound and spiritual reason. The priest said he was a Christian because he was raised by Christians in a Christian culture, and no other reason.

For me, the only indispensable reason to be religious is to qualify for a pleasant afterlife. Eternal life is the only benefit that hasn't been promised by any other method. Unfortunately, except for Scientology which was the brainchild of a science fiction writer, everything about modern religious beliefs and teachings have been inherited from prehistorical Pagans and influential thinkers, filtered through decades and centuries of oral tradition and further edited to conform to changing doctrines. In fact, it would not be without reason for a person to conclude that the Christianity of today originated in a prehistorical blood sacrifice Pagan cult.

This is not meant to disrespect in any way either the Bible or thinking minds – it's just that none of them rise above human understanding, and they contradict themselves and each other more than I would expect from a body of eternal truth revelations. Simply put, all anyone has available to commit themselves to is nothing more than what is considered the *truth* in today's culture. I can't imagine that I, considering my status in the eternity of the universe, could be wrong to insist that *I just don't know.*

In this respect, I have a kinship with the anonymous author of the book of *Ecclesiastes*. For someone who believes that life is all about eternal life, a read of this book will help them appreciate their lifetime more fully. He writes all about living life, and the only thing he mentions about after death is that when dead, a man *knows nothing.*[22] This from a man who was considered the teacher, or preacher, of wisdom. But what does wisdom mean? It appears that this wise preacher acquired his wisdom in knowledge gleaned through his senses by observation and experimentation – today called science.

Christianity, on the other hand, has a long history of devaluing the empirical – that is, advocating for obedience ahead of knowledge. *In the Old Testament no one is told to reason with a heretic, and not one word is said about relying upon argument, upon education, nor upon intellectual development – nothing except simple brute force.*[23] This approach does justify the agenda of the world's fundamentalists. In our time, *the impact of fundamentalist religion in driving American anti-intellectualism has been, and continues to be, immense.*[24] The popular televangelist, Joyce Meyer, comments: *"I once asked the Lord why so many people are confused and He said to me, 'Tell them to stop trying to figure everything out, and they will stop being confused,' I have found it to be absolutely true. Reasoning and confusion go together."*[25] I don't believe there's any virtue in ignorance for those intelligent enough to ask the question. I don't believe there can be a truth about any matter that a mature, intelligent person of sound mind cannot handle. There's only one reason why anyone would deny such a person the opportunity to pursue that truth. If indeed there is a Christian-style god, of course, my question is: "Who has ever had a clue what that god is, knows, does, feels, or thinks?" You don't have to be an atheist to say: "I don't know." There's only one reason why I could be confused at this point in my life – that is if I accepted the prevailing Christian insistence that one *must believe* some specific doctrine. Ironically, no one is concerned about why I no longer believe in Santa Claus, and no one asks me to prove there is no Santa Claus. And further, I'm not confused because I don't believe in Santa Claus.

I don't want to believe, I want to know.

~ Carl Sagan

CHAPTER 22

Morality, Honesty, Integrity, and Control

It's fair to say the Friends and Workers live by a high moral standard. I believe it's also fair to say the Friends' neighbors, coworkers, and business associates, in general, also consider them morally upright. I wouldn't be surprised, though, if the majority of the Friends have had neighbors who thought they were weird, but worthy of respect nonetheless. That said, I admit that the Friends and Workers are no more immune to any kind of immorality than any other community. My observation is that the better a community polices its own morality the more effective it is in assuring an *appearance* of morality – but reputations are not built on appearances alone.

But what is morality? The popular concept of morality involves avoiding sexual impropriety, not committing crimes, not defrauding others, and not playing havoc with other people's peace, property, and safety. In elementary school I understood that morality was all about not doing certain things. Among the Friends and Workers morality also involved no jewelry, no make-up, no long hair on men, no short hair on women, no drinking, no smoking, no cussing, no white shoes, no sleeveless dresses, no sandals, no movies, no sports events, no circuses, no television, no radio, no stereo – and whatever else. That made it easy to identify *immoral* people on the street – and to identify wayward coreligionists. But by the time I reached middle school I'd learned that not all of these moral imperatives applied world-wide among the Friends and Workers. And by the time I reached high school I regarded most of those restrictions as Truth tradition ... nothing more.

As an adult, it's always troubled me to hear religious people saying offhandedly that morality is based on the Bible. First of all, I didn't believe everyone who made such statements was all that moral himself. Furthermore, I never thought the Bible was satisfactory guidance in morality, regardless of all the good things it says. I decided in the late 1960's, after witnessing people's responses to the American civil rights struggle of the era, that being a Christian or Friend or Worker is no assurance at all that someone has a moral conscience. I never encountered genuinely unbiased discussion about morality until I happened upon Pagans and atheists. I'd long wondered how it was that non-Christians, who not only lived exemplary moral lives but had a practicable, formulated grasp of the concept of morality, made their moral decisions. I wasn't disappointed – I learned why religious dogma doesn't lend itself to delineated moral principles.

A dictionary will define morality as *beliefs about what is right behavior and what is wrong behavior*. It's a straightforward definition, but it's crass, if not arrogant, to equate it with religious dogma. Carried to its decisive conclusion, morality applies to our treatment of all sentient beings, encompassing all behaviors that can affect the happiness and suffering experiences of such beings. Morality stands apart from religious dogma – believing that Jesus was born of a virgin has nothing to do with moral principle. Morality also stands apart from honesty – otherwise Anne Frank's protector would be considered immoral. It also stands apart from legality – otherwise Harriet Tubman would have done the wrong thing. Ironically, enough of the Bible has been deemed obscene that it has been banned from school libraries.

On the other hand, religion in effect divorces morality from human suffering. Mother Teresa, despite her reputation, was at best an inadvertent promoter of poverty and misery by opposing, in Christopher Hitchins' words, *the empowerment of women and the emancipation of them from a livestock version of compulsory reproduction.*[1] Morality is a two-sided matter, but the measure of its virtue is relative only to its benefit to the recipient of an act. The Bible explicitly justifies deceit in the case of Jacob's sons when they converted their enemies by circumcising them, simply to accommodate their intent to follow up with their slaughter of the whole clan.[2] Such passages permit religious persons (not just Christians) to justify anything for their *own* self serving interests and call it morally acceptable.

To be morally right can be more costly than being religiously justified. The most profound statement I've ever heard regarding morality was by an unnamed young man in search of ultimate truth:

> *"To be truly moral, … I must be willing to do what was right even if it meant that I would suffer the flames of hell for eternity for doing it. Nothing, not even the threat of hell, should deter me from doing what was truly right. That was true morality."*[3]

I have long questioned the morality of *loyalty*, so it's not surprising that I should relate to one of the most common observations of ex members of the Truth – that the Friends are loyal first to the Workers, and other loyalties are negotiable. Indeed, in my case my own faithfulness, honesty, and morality counted for virtually nothing when Harold Hilton asked the Friends to disassociate from me. This practice is widespread among the Friends and Workers, and when it became obvious that we were being squeezed out of fellowship, Bea Rabe's approach to us in sincere consolation was a delightful and precious exception. I've learned through several sources that a number of other Friends at the time agreed with me on what was happening, but none of them made a move to intervene. In this respect, the history of indifference to victims of child sexual abuse is a moral blood stain on the fellowship, and the ministry is directly responsible for promoting it. Members are taught that the value of *fitting in* is a virtue. But in truth, some unnamed wise person has summarized it thus:

> *Some people are not loyal to you… They're loyal to their need of you… Once their needs change, so does their loyalty.*[4]

This explains exactly why, when someone is no longer considered a Friend, his whole circle of friendships is revised. Some find it *inconvenient* to continue their relationship with him, but the ones who empathize will rise to the occasion. Unfortunately for the latter, it could be a dangerous move – they can be branded as *dissidents commiserating with fellow dissidents*. But commiserating with fellows is as moral as saving another's life.

The titular virtue of the Friends and Workers is *truth*, or shall I say *honesty* for purposes of this discussion. Previously I described the unstable nature of religious truth, but an individual's honesty is far less open to negotiation. Morality, by definition, is a principle not subject to the elements of other virtues. However, despite the fact that dishonesty can in the appropriate circumstances be considered moral, dishonesty for profit can never masquerade as a moral act – it's the foundation of fraud.

Honesty is another list of *no's*: no lying, no stealing, no cheating, no hiding the truth about someone or something, no fraud, and no deception. A correspondent of mine eloquently wrote: *Truth should never be afraid of scrutiny. Truth will always withstand any amount of scrutiny or examination. If facts threaten what you think truth is, you better examine what you are calling truth. I welcome facts good or bad. It helps us see more clearly.* This is why Dr. Phil McGraw's mantra is: "Winners deal with the truth.[5] So absent the rare counterclaim of morality, why do people lie, cheat, steal, etc.? Unless one is a pathological liar, they do it to protect some personal interest. I've often enough suggested that we're not always entitled to truthful answers, notably when we aren't minding our own business. But I've previously mentioned the inconsistencies between how the Truth really functions and how it's presented to outsiders. Anyone aware of this situation would undoubtedly conclude that they had something to hide, but the Workers have a more politic defense in this matter – it is that *unsaved people* and *babes in the family* are not yet mature enough for *strong meat.*[6]

Among the Friends and Workers, the temptation to be dishonest in some form is always present. In fact, deception has been somewhat of an institution from the very beginning. The specific intent from the day of the crucial Lurgan meeting (in Clankilvoragh) was to deceive the whole fellowship about their origins. Which explains how a Worker preaching in Italy would sit in someone's living room in the U.S. and make a statement like: "Rome *still* has a Sunday morning meeting like it has since Paul's day!"

Certainly many of the Friends have lied to the Workers to keep themselves out of trouble. I can appreciate that. I once told a Worker that the telephone in our bedroom was broken – I simply didn't want her to find that we also had a radio alarm clock by our bed. Other Workers had seen a radio sitting on our kitchen counter and said nothing, but I happened not to appreciate things this particular Worker had told others about me that she wouldn't say to my face. It's not like I made a practice of lying to the Workers. When asked if I'd been to a movie theater, I said I had – and the interesting response was: "We don't condone that, but you'll never go to hell for it." On the other hand, I've been confronted with accusations that were not at all true, and been treated like a liar when I refused to confess. The lesson is this: What is more important than the truth of a matter is that the Worker emerges from the discussion with his sense of being in control still intact.

Unless anyone doubts that Workers would not be forthright about their dealings, imagine the shock of one of the Friends who discovered that his name appeared on official documents of incorporation filed by the Workers in Sweden – the Friend had never been made aware of the matter. What's really disconcerting is that Workers for the most part have no inhibition when it comes to misleading and deceiving the Friends. The Workers I admire most undoubtedly choose to say nothing rather than be deceptive. But when I discovered Workers being dishonest with the Friends, dishonest about the Friends, and dishonest with each other and about each other, I understood that anyone can be sacrificed for any trumped up reason to protect the reputation of some Worker or the ministry.

There are two times when the *truth* is most important and thus the most costly – truth in advertising, and the *whole truth and nothing but the truth* in judgement.

Which brings me to integrity: *adherence to moral and ethical principles; soundness of moral character; honesty; the state of being whole, entire, or undiminished.* Does this apply to the *little white lie?* That depends on the amount of deception or self interest involved. Religion, however, and especially strict fundamentalism, is as much an enabler of hypocrisy as it is of righteousness. Being a believer is widely touted as the antidote for all ills and deviance – physical, emotional, mental, social, and even intellectual. Unfortunately, this belief seems often to have very little or no regard for personal handicap or genetic disposition. This promotes two problems.

The first one is that persons of taboo personality types, who must play *normal* in order to be *in communion*, must also add to their hypocrisy the perpetual prayer that somehow they can still be saved – all the while enduring and even preaching teachings that condemn them personally. In other words, *don't ask, don't tell*, and all will be okay. Yet, hardly a day goes by that some well respected pious religious person is exposed for a sexual indiscretion. Proportionately, the Friends and Workers don't have any better record than many other religious groups in this respect.

The second problem is that such religious groups are not equipped to handle such matters either before or when they're exposed. They won't accept responsibility for accommodating the hypocrisy, they can't condone the behaviors, and they're ashamed that it tarnishes the reputation of their ministry. This attitude is incompatible with rationally and compassionately understanding genetic predispositions to deviance, or treating any social illness professionally. Because they feel tolerance of any Friends' non-conformity reflects on them personally, their handling of such matters involves defending their own honor more than empathizing with persons who can't be *normal*. A *don't ask don't tell* approach is no solution at all – it only means the group prefers hypocrisy to compassion.

Child sexual abuse is historically one of the worst such problems in many religious groups because it not only involves deception, it involves sheltering criminals from prosecution. What's much easier to camouflage are the non-criminal moral offenses. How many are aware of the gay ex-Worker who went to a respected elder Worker for counseling concerning his sexual orientation, only to be propositioned by the elder Worker? How many people are aware of the elder Worker who invited a young gay hustler to his motel room, only to discover that the hustler was raised in a professing family and knew exactly who the Worker was? On the other hand, persons addicted to tobacco and alcohol can fare much worse – the evidence of their activities can follow them into public, and they can be disfellowshiped.

There's an expression that Christians are fond of using – "standing for truth". It's an honorable adage, but fear of reprisal is far greater than genuine interest in basic moral values, such that the Friends have become, in the words of a friend, a *fellowship of moral cowards*. His statement of wisdom on this matter is this: *Standing for truth isn't a matter of strategy; it is a matter of Christian principle. Let the chips fall where they fall.* Many of the Friends are aware of and concerned about immoral and unethical activity that never gets addressed or corrected, but it's the rare individual who dares to *stand* when a Worker says *sit down.* My own experience has demonstrated what happens when someone stands for a *truth* – an inconvenient truth calls for a prosecution. The *historian* can have a litany of other offenses to make the case against you. My experience has also demonstrated that the true reward for standing for truth is the freedom that comes from not owing your success to complicity with an immorality. It was never a glamorous experience – it was a fearful, one step at a time experience, with nothing but my values to guide and sustain me. I was as shocked as I was disappointed. I was warned, of course, but I had no stomach for the very scope of the craftiness and deception involved in *preserving Truth* in the world. Unfortunately, for a group professing to preserve Truth/truth in the world, sheltering criminals and hiding corruption speaks more loudly of building reputation that it does of integrity.

The logical question is, of course: Why do people tolerate such a state of affairs? There are two apparent answers. One reason is that probably most people either never hear of such fractious events, or don't recognize the hypocrisy of them. The other answer, of a certainty the most prevalent, is that people believe the Truth is indisputably the only possible path to a saved eternity, which makes unquestioning obedience to the Workers compulsory. This conditions people to accept that this is all incidental to their salvation.

The greatest hypocrisy of all is that religious leaders can further demoralize their victims by claiming that they, the victims, are persecuting the church. I recall being told on various occasions that I was "disturbing the church" and "promoting immorality among our young people." I was quite convinced that it was they who were harassing me. What's interesting is that they could get off with it because no one knew about my impeached *dissenting hustle* until the Workers warned people against me. The big disadvantage one has when discretely informing the Workers that there is a problem, is that the one who airs a matter first gets to control the spin – in my case that happened to be the Workers.

But Christianity has long had somewhat of a fetish for persecution, accepting it as a badge of willingness to suffer for Jesus Christ. Their martyrs achieve sainthood, but a claim of persecution can be engineered and used as a source of sympathy. Some Christian martyrs of history simply exposed themselves to danger as recklessly as many modern Islamic terrorists do. But claiming persecution is a much safer strategy. I recall Pope Benedict XVI saying that the child sexual abuse scandal in the Catholic Church was "the greatest persecution of the church."[7] One doesn't persecute people of his own community, they abuse them – and it wasn't the clergy who were being abused, it was the children who were quite without responsibility for the abuse. The clergy can more easily deflect guilt by claiming persecution rather than entertaining the term *abuse*.

It's easy enough to explain why true believers will not leave – they tend to stay until the cost of staying becomes more than they can tolerate. But a common enough claim among exes is that the Truth system brainwashes its membership into obedience. I reject this assessment outright. It's true that professing parents teach their beliefs and values to their children, as do all parents; and they require their children to conform to the lifestyle in their own household as well. Some will claim that this practice by professing parents amounts to brainwashing, but this is not so. Professing parents have no parenting styles that cannot be found in families in the society at large.

Brainwashing involves forcefully converting individuals from their familiar ideology to become obedient to one they consider hostile to their own. Millions have been converted to Christianity in this manner, but to suggest this is a tactic of the Friends and

Workers is preposterous. I do believe, however, that it's common enough for individuals to be *seduced* in some manner to commit to the Truth without any real understanding of what the commitment inevitably involves. In that case it's difficult to know how frequently the result is positive or negative. But then, preaching the gospel does involve persuading people to make such commitments – the converts anticipating *truth in advertising.*

People do, in many religions and in other communities, acquire the ability to just ignore such inconsistencies. This is a syndrome that involves two intellectual conditions. The first one is called *cognitive dissonance,* a psychological conflict resulting from holding inconsistent beliefs and attitudes. My personal example involved the belief that the Truth ministry, despite the personal failings of individual Workers, was collectively above the self serving aspects of raw politics. For decades I was aware of rumblings to the contrary but never investigated. Finally, I came to witness myself what the ministry was willing to do to preserve its own authority and reputation. I could very easily have decided to just let it all be – but it happened to be about *me* too, and I understood unequivocally that I couldn't unreservedly trust the souls of my children to the Workers. The Workers knew perfectly well how I felt about my discoveries, and ironically made no effort at all to convince me of the contrary. The only advice they ever had for dealing with my *discovery* was that I never mention it to anyone, and be patient until people forgot what they'd said about me – just as long as I could pose as a sycophant and presumably discard some of my best *and wayward* friends. Fortunately, by then I'd already learned that *my* peace of mind comes from not *buying into the plan. Don't ask – don't tell* is an unhealthy way to live one's life.

The other condition that keeps the peace is often called *the willing suspension of disbelief.* In other words, a person is willing to suspend his critical faculties and believe the unbelievable – to preserve a comfortable existence. This is what Dale Shultz expected: *Whether the decision is right or wrong, the right thing for all of us is to respect it because of those who have made the judgement. If the decision is wrong, I am sure that the Lord will have ways of correcting that over time.*[8] There is nothing more disrespectful of honest and intelligent people than to expect them to submit to such corruption of integrity.

This handicapping syndrome isn't caused by brainwashing; but neither is it something an intelligent, reasoning individual will succumb to without someone else's influence, called *mind control*. This is no mysterious process that cannot be detected by targeted individuals – it's a process that involves specific identifiable methods and techniques of *thought-stopping*, for the purpose of influencing how a person feels, thinks, and acts.

Such mind control is not in itself either negative or positive – it has positive benefits for individuals suffering from various addictions. But it is still thought-stopping, and practiced in religious groups is destructive because the *locus of control is external to the individual.*[9] In other words, someone other than the individual (normally the group leader) is using it in an effort to change how individuals feel, think, and act – in conformance with the leader's expectations, and whether an individual is healthily self-controlled or not. Saving one's soul is not akin to rescuing someone from an addiction, where one needs to be wrested from whatever is controlling his mind. Saving one's soul through manipulation or control of his mindset is exactly how one becomes a religious addict.

There is, in fact, a professionally developed questionnaire[10] by which one can evaluate the extent of mind control an individual is experiencing. It identifies four areas of influence that, when combined, constitute mind control: behavior, intellect, thoughts, and emotions.

- Some of the listed aspects of behavior control include controls on types of clothing, hairstyles, leisure, and entertainment; the discouragement of individualism; and the expectation of obedience.
- The practice of information control involves withholding or distorting information, or lying; limiting access to media and critical individuals; encouraging reporting on other members; and unethical use of confession.
- Thought control refers to encouraging only good and proper thoughts; stopping critical thoughts and reducing complexities to platitudinous buzz words; and the rejection

of rational analysis, critical thinking, and constructive criticism.

- Finally, emotional control involves narrowing the range of acceptable feelings; shifting blame from the leaders to individuals; and labeling those who leave as *weak, undisciplined, unspiritual, worldly, brainwashed by family or counselor, or seduced by money, sex, or rock and roll.* [11]

This is certainly not the complete list of identifiers, but for anyone troubled by the dynamics of any close relationship, a study of this matter for oneself is a worthwhile pursuit.

According to the professionals who articulated this evaluation process, real mind control will involve aspects of all four categories of control. Individuals who can't counter any one of the four categories of control are vulnerable to cognitive dissonance. I was raised with moral guidance that disapproved of various aspects of all four categories, which probably confirms what I have said many times over the years: "The Truth will never dispense of their seemingly frivolous restrictions because they insist on maintaining measurable evidence of conformity and obedience." So many of the Friends regard such obedience as being *unto God.* I apologize that I cannot remove from my very psyche the sense that such obsessive obedience *doeth loudly smack* of proverbial gratuitous butt kissing.

CHAPTER 23

Politics, Correctness, and Purges

Politics is the exercise of power. Strangely enough, when things go the way one wants, it's called *the right thing to do*, but when things go the way one doesn't want them to go, it's called *politics*. However, it's always politics – even in the most civilized of democracies. Furthermore, politics isn't confined to government – it's how all organizations operate when someone's opinion gets to override another's choices. In French the word *politiques* refers equally to politics and *policies*. It's what keeps any society from descending into anarchy. But among the Friends and Workers politics is reputed not to exist. One Worker explained:

> It is so hard for the religious world to comprehend a relationship like this existing. They cannot begin to produce an association like this, between their ministry and deity. This is a miracle found in God's true way. To us it is an increasing miracle; to those looking on, it is a deep mystery.[1]

> There are groups of people in the religious world and in the business world and the financial world that have a working relationship, but they know nothing about the meaning of the word 'fellowship'. This is the only group of people in the world where the Lord's servants, and the Elders and the Lord's people can work together in such a harmonious way.[2]

Yet I remember a time when I believed it was God who told the Workers when and where to go preaching. And by middle school I'd learned that the provisions for a four day convention for hundreds of people didn't consist of the random donations of the Friends on the day before the convention. And then I learned that Workers couldn't preach just where they wanted – they needed someone's okay.

History, of course, belies the mystery of how the Truth fellowship has developed. Because it's a religious organization, the top-down hierarchical control allows that any policy or decision can be presented as an instruction from God and therefore not to be questioned – a concept well articulated in Dale Shultz' letter in Chapter 16. And not being subject to any freedom of information principle, it's easy enough to preserve this facade, even with the majority of Friends and many Workers. Thus, political maneuvering remains alive and well into the twenty-first century. One ex-Worker acknowledged that *it's not possible to be a hearty 2x2 and understand the 2x2 system.* He referred to that discovery as *the hurtful experience that brought* [him to] *a clear understanding of the system* [that] *rendered it impossible to continue placing any confidence in the system. This makes ... it ... absurd to call for clear statements of doctrine from leaders of the system.*

Excommunication is still a method used to control behaviors and weed out undesirables. The process has been refined to the extent that it can always be turned around to *he-chose-to-leave* – by giving the person a choice that is certain to compromise his conscience. Banishment, if it can be enforced, prevents any turmoil that could arise from any dispute over the appropriateness of the punishment. The bully approach discussed in Chapter 17 is every bit as effective in driving folks away and turning other members against them – and for the most part undetectable by the rest of the congregation.

An interesting explanation presented itself when people began discovering the true history of the Truth ministry through the Internet. A journalist asked Therald Sylvester, former Overseer of Washington state, about the criticisms by ex-members of the cover-up of the history. Therald's response was that "It's been purifying."[3] I perceive that to mean that the truth was fouling up the Truth. It was a perfect deflection from the accusation of deception by the ministry.

Perhaps the most secretive of political maneuvers involve the replacement of Overseers – the process is less transparent than the election of a new pope. I don't believe it's common for any Worker to appoint himself Overseer, but I have it from an insider that Eldon Tenniswood, a long time Overseer in California, did just that, claiming to the other Workers that he'd been told by the previous Overseer that he was the heir – and no one objected. It was common knowledge that Eldon's influence extended much further than California and the states included in that jurisdiction. A Worker from another state told me that it had a lot to do with Eldon's promoting himself. One of the things he did early on was organize elders' and young people's meetings where he basically established his expectations of everyone. His obvious intention was to reach far more people than just those in attendance at the meetings, because he had his sermon and *question and answer* session printed for circulation. I was living in New Brunswick at the time and the transcript was being circulated there. Ironically, our Overseer there told someone that he didn't agree with everything Eldon had said. Interestingly, the lady who recorded one of Eldon's meetings by shorthand told me that her notes were never used – she'd been told the question-and-answer session had already been printed before the meeting!

During the time Eldon was Overseer in California, the influence of Western Canada increased greatly – so much so that a few people in California reportedly felt hurt about what happened when Eldon, and then Dick Middleton had both passed away. Dale Shultz, the Overseer from the little known province of Saskatchewan inherited the California jurisdiction. For a number of years it was rumored that Willis Propp, from Alberta, was in line to assume even greater recognition, but somewhere about the time he involved himself in troubles in Alberta his star dipped, and Dale Shultz became the Overseer for California. Dale's iron-fisted stand for the supremacy of the ministry obviously did nothing to tarnish his reputation. And it's become apparent that California wasn't all he inherited. He has since moved to another state, and he has emerged as *de facto* Overseer of the Worker hierarchy as far away as Vietnam.

In the years following the scandalous picnic I hosted in 2001 and discussed in Chapters 8 and 9, I did become informed about the evil Ingram and Oyler doctrines – *somewhat*. But judging from anything I've learned, I'm far more baffled than ever why the Workers were so terrified about what I was supposed to be up to. If I'd known at the time what they were warning me about I'm sure I'd have had a lot to say about their accusations of me, but I understand that it may not have changed anything anyway.

The *doctrine* mostly affected people in Alaska, Montana, Texas, and Louisiana. *Ingram and Oyler* referred to a Worker named Bob Ingram, who was an Overseer in Alaska, and a Worker named Truitt Oyler, a Worker who was raised and became a Worker in Montana. Two other Workers were also primarily implicated: John Starkweather and Walter Oyler, Truitt's younger brother; both of whom were also raised in Montana and entered the ministry in Montana. At some time in the 1960's Truitt and Walter Oyler and John Starkweather came to hold some beliefs that the other Workers did not accept. In 1967 Truitt and John were sent to Washington and California respectively, and then removed from the ministry, along with Walter, because they continued to teach their doctrine.

A few years later John and Truitt were taken back into the ministry on condition that they sign letters promising not to teach their doctrine. John was sent to Texas and Truitt to Alaska. John became Overseer in Louisiana in 1978, and then Overseer of Texas in 1983. Both were highly respected in their assignments. But by 1985 it was learned that John was again teaching the doctrine and was removed from his oversight – then soon removed from the ministry as well. By 1989 it was determined that Truitt had continued teaching his doctrine in Alaska, and was again admonished and then dismissed from the ministry in 1990 for *justifying both Robert Ingram and himself among the Saints and Workers*. I've never learned how Bob got implicated in the doctrine scandal, other than being accused of permitting Truitt to preach it.

According to the report of one of the Alaska Friends, the elders of meetings in the state received a letter signed by the Overseers of British Columbia, Washington, Oregon, and California explaining that Bob Ingram was removed from the ministry because he had *taken too many liberties* with a number of sister Workers. The Overseers also said that Truitt was being sent to Alberta because he was teaching *divisive* doctrine in the state. The elders took exception to the *spirit of the letter*, and protested that their *input had not been considered*. Meetings were called with prominent senior Workers from Western Canada and the United States, which turned ugly when even well respected Workers would not participate in *honest communication*. Too many of the Friends perceived that the Workers and some of the Friends felt *lives had to be sacrificed* for the preservation of the established authorities. Having failed to resolve the situation, all the Workers in Alaska came under suspicion, and within a year all were sent to other states or provinces, sent home to rest, and/or placed on probation. Some decided not to continue in the ministry. At least ten meetings were removed from homes, and many others lost privileges. Some troublemakers were not excommunicated – their numbers were too great, and many of them were very influential Friends with strong connections in other states. A meeting just for these types of Friends was organized in Anchorage.

During the 1990's older Workers were telling their younger companions what was wrong with the Truitt doctrine, and total meetings were devoted to the matter. Anyone who showed any interest in the doctrine was immediately suspect and in danger of being excommunicated, and Workers who supported Bob and Truitt were excommunicated. John Starkweather's sister, Mary, was dismissed from the ministry in Oregon. Any deviation from the Overseers' beliefs were considered to be *of Satan and unworthy even of consideration.*

Then Everett Swanson became the Overseer of Montana and the purge continued. Everett went from one area to another preaching his *corrected* version of the gospel, explicitly opposing Truitt's *false doctrine.* At the end of an uncertain number of such meetings, Everett would *test* the meeting, asking those who agreed with him to stand. The majority did, and those who didn't were excommunicated. At a convention in Manhattan, Montana, Friends and Workers were asked during one meeting to stand to show which side they were on.

The purge caused grief for many. Families were excommunicated and meetings split apart. Families with adult children living out of the state were separated because those who were out of state were not excommunicated with the rest of their families but thus forbidden to associate with them.

Ironically John Starkweather was not dismissed from the ministry because his salvation was being called into question, but because he was presenting the doctrine in an underhanded way, causing a rift between those Workers who agreed with him and those who didn't. The situation with Truitt in Alaska was somewhat similar, because Bob Ingram permitted Truitt to teach it. But Truitt was banished for his offenses, and John was not – at least while he remained in the Southwest. Whenever John ventured back into Montana he was forbidden from attending meetings.

Bob agreed to *accepting the decisions of the Elders of the Ministry as just and final, and encouraging others to do the same* – so he was allowed to profess and participate in meetings. One former Alaska sister Worker later married Truitt and continued to go to meetings alone, even though Truitt was banished. The Oyler family was banned from the Manhattan convention grounds until 2012, when Truitt's mother and Mary and John Starkweather received an invitation to attend. *However, the workers said that even though they'd allow them to go to convention, they couldn't go back to meeting unless they reprofessed.*

Determining what the offending doctrine was turned out to be much more difficult than predicting the consequences for teaching it. Upon hearing that it had something to do with the divinity of Jesus, the logical conclusion would be that they were involved in the controversy that is as old as Christianity itself – *Was Jesus God or was he a human?* But that was not the case. Truitt's teaching was that Jesus was not God, but he was divine, and he had a human nature that could be tempted but could not sin because he was born of the Holy Spirit and not subject to the curse of original sin. In theology that is called the *Impeccability of Christ*. By comparison, the Workers teaching was summarized in three points: *(1) Christ is totally divine, (2) Jesus is totally human, and (3) Jesus is totally sinless.*[4] The only apparent difference between the two is that the Overseers' version allowed that Jesus could have committed sin, should he have chosen to. Yet, according to Truitt, he had no differences with the Canadian Overseers in this matter. He wrote:

As you may have heard, Willis [Propp] *took me to Vancouver to talk with Ernest* [Nelson] *and Paul* [Sharp]. *We had two days of discussion. There were at least 4 points of doctrine unanimously agreed on that Willis gave me permission to write to some of you.*

1. There were never ungodly lusts, desires or passions in Jesus and never a spirit unacceptable with God. (Jesus was in the likeness of Adam's creation except he was conceived of the Holy Spirit and the Holy Spirit was on him from birth. The power of the Holy Spirit prevented him from becoming a sinner. Jesus was pure in heart and mind always.

2. God is not the author of sin. (Adam was not created a sinner or in sin.)

3. It would have been necessary for Jesus to have lost the Holy Spirit and its power to have sinned. (Had Jesus lost the Holy Spirit, he would have gone the same course as Adam.)

4. Jesus paid the redemption price in full. The death he died was in fulfillment of all the curse that the sinner was under.[5]

Having learned this about the alleged *dangerous* doctrine, I was as bewildered by the uproar over it as I'd been about the accusations that I'd been involved in. It turned out to be something I'd never have had an opinion on one way or the other, but the terrorizing understanding emerged that I could possibly have been required to take a side in the issue, and being neutral was as punishable as being wrong. I cannot imagine a more invasive form of mind control. I obviously was not alone in this opinion. William Lewis, a former Overseer of Texas, said, "I've talked to John and to be honest I guess I don't really know what the fuss is all about."

But some explanations for the whole fiasco have been offered. One of them is that Everett Swanson overdid his emphasis of Jesus' humanity, and clashed with those who thought he was diminishing His divinity. However, longtime Worker teaching has been that if one tries hard enough and prays hard enough, he too can *overcome the flesh just as Jesus did*. One of the presumably dangerous aspects of Truitt's discussing his insight appears to be that it put an unacceptable emphasis on *grace*, which I perceive to be almost a dirty word here on the West Coast.

For decades the teaching has been that *the church in the home and the homeless preacher* is the foundation of Christianity, and theological matters have been neglected. Undoubtedly for many of the Friends, Truitt had introduced an uncomfortably unfamiliar topic, and among the Friends that calls for Overseer scrutiny. The last thing an Overseer wants is a doctrinally confused laity. The Friends have all heard of the sin committed in the Garden of Eden, but they may not have any idea what the doctrine of *Original Sin* refers to. The Friends have all heard of the divinity of Jesus, but most probably have no idea that it is an *orthodox* belief, or even what the word *orthodox* Christianity means. Worst of all was the mention that what they were teaching was in line with Catholic teaching as well – Catholicism has long been considered the arch-enemy of the Truth. But some of the accusations brought against Truitt were patently false – for example, the suggestion that he was being led astray by and involved with the Catholic church.

It's also been suggested that Truitt was targeted because he was *unusually popular* with many of the Friends. I've been quietly told on more than one occasion that Worker popularity is closely watched among the Workers, and actions are taken to keep them at the *lowest common denominator*. Gifted Workers are treated similarly to bad Workers – they get moved around frequently, or dismissed. Some Overseers claimed John Starkweather was wrong *just because he stood up for what he believed*. In any case, the whole episode more resembles political maneuvering than it does a serious doctrinal problem.

Prior to 1999, problems were also developing between the Friends and Workers in the province of Alberta. I'm certainly not privy to all of the obviously problematic situations, but one that ended up drawing a lot of attention was the discovery of a 1995 incorporation of the *Alberta Society of Christian Assemblies,*[6] obviously a project of Willis Propp, the Worker Overseer for Alberta. As mentioned earlier, this is something the Workers prize themselves in avoiding – and naturally this was a troubling matter among the Friends. It turned out that it was as much of a shock to most of the Workers as it was to the Friends. It was reported that one Alberta sister Worker learned of the incorporation when she was in the U.S. Midwest as a visiting convention speaker. One of the Friends there happened to ask her about the incorporation of the Workers in Alberta, and she knew nothing about it.

When confronted about the incorporation, Willis' explanation was that it had been done to facilitate the sponsorship of a missionary to Hungary. However, investigation revealed that the Hungarian government had had no business with the Alberta Society of Christian Assemblies.[7] Another concern of the Friends at the time was the finances of the ministry, or perhaps more specifically of Mr. Propp. Whispers of enormous bank accounts and capitalistic endeavors flew in the face of the Friends who trusted a ministry that professed to go on faith. It reminded me of Shirley Doolittle's shocking claim that God had not instituted a ministry of poverty.[8]

I'm aware of the meeting in Edmonton that was called in 1999, where about sixty of the Friends met with several elders and Worker Overseers from provinces and states as far away as California. It's been described as a group of *honest concerned elders and dear friends pouring out their hearts' concerns* to senior Workers whom they expected could resolve their issues.[9] But they were met with silence by the Workers – nothing was resolved. In fact, hardly a question was answered. One of the Overseers never even looked at them. They probably had learned from the Alaska meeting that it is better to say nothing when you have no defense.

Dick Middleton responded first by reading a letter expressing Californians' confidence in the Alberta ministry, and how providential it was that someone left them their estate when a medical bill had to be paid. Willis Propp asked another Worker to find some documents in a briefcase somewhere, and one of the Friends informed him that they didn't need legal documents. One person asked the Workers three times what they thought about their concerns – no one addressed any of them.

The stonewalling continued with Earnest Nelson, Overseer of British Columbia, remarking that such a large number of Friends as had gathered there was a great tribute to the Workers who pioneered the ministry in Alberta. Eldon Tenniswood concluded that they should all look to Christ to shepherd them.[10] Whereupon all went home, and later learned that it had been decided to leave things just as they were. Coincidentally, that meeting in Edmonton occurred just days before the meeting I described in Chapter 7 where Bill Frost and I met with Dick Middleton and Eldon Tenniswood in the Bay Area – and the results were as unproductive as the meeting in Edmonton. And not unrelated to the Edmonton meeting was the appearance of the open letter edict I shared in Chapter 16, authored by Dale Shultz, then from Saskatchewan.

To deny there were repercussions for the concerns of the Friends in Edmonton would be absurd. A purge, consisting of excommunications and banishments, ensued, with perhaps thirty people being excommunicated in 1999, and meetings being removed from eight homes by June. About fourteen other elders gave up their meetings rather than deal with the trepidation caused by the *inquisition*. Without using actual names, it proceeded in this manner:

- Couple A were advised they could no longer have meeting in their house.
- They disagreed with the decision, and hosted Couples B, C, D, and E and Ms. F in an unsanctioned meeting.
- Days later the Couples C, D, and E were banned from all meetings.
- Next Sunday the Couple B went to meeting at Couple G's home.
- Couple G were subsequently excommunicated.
- Next Sunday the G's went to meeting at Couple H's home.
- Couple H were subsequently excommunicated.
- Couple E went to meeting at the home of Couple J.
- Couple J were excommunicated days later.
- Two weeks later the Couple D went to meeting at Couple K's home.
- Couple K were excommunicated.
- Friend and ex-Worker Miss L attended an unsanctioned meeting of Friends.

- Miss L was excommunicated.
- Couples M and N, visiting from British Columbia, attended meeting at the home of Couple G, as well as two adult children of Couple G and the spouse of one of them. All seven visitors were excommunicated.[11]

The excommunication process turned out to be a brutal affair. One couple, an elder and his wife, tried to discuss some concerns with a sister Worker named Thelma Galbraith. Apparently Thelma lied at the expense of some Friends to hide the Overseer's misdeeds, and the couple disapproved. They informed Thelma that *those who bring lies or false doctrine ... were not welcome* in their home. In the presence of her companion and four other witnesses, Thelma informed them that *lying has nothing to do with doctrine and was, therefore, not any basis to deny the workers the right to come to their home.*[12]

Thelma advised all other Friends to go elsewhere for meetings from that day on, and warned them that if they went there for meeting *even one time, that they would have to suffer the consequences,* and she kept her word. She called an 86-year-old couple in failing health at 10:00 p.m. to inform them that they were no longer allowed to attend meeting anywhere in Alberta. The elderly man once asked Thelma, "So it's your way or the highway?" And her answer was, "That's right."[13] This practice of telephone excommunications became common for almost a year. Interestingly, one couple who had meeting taken from their house but were permitted to go to meetings in other homes, finally decided to disassociate themselves completely after they learned how Willis Propp portrayed their meeting removal during court proceedings in progress that year. Elders, including my own cousin, began turning people away from their homes, on instructions from the Workers and out of fear for their own reputations.

More than one such telephone excommunication got recorded. One in particular was outstanding because it showed that the couple in question had been warned exactly *twenty-four hours earlier* that they had to agree to submit unconditionally to the Workers or they would no longer be part of the fellowship. The hour had come and the couple had not yet gotten back to the Worker with their promise, so they were summarily excommunicated. I was fortunate to have listened to that recording, because it proved most helpful to me when I found myself in a similar position, as I've described in Chapter 10. By chance I got to discuss that very recording with the Overseer in a state in the U.S. Midwest. He told me that his first reaction to what he heard was that it was a fake, that someone had acted it out to scandalize the Workers involved. When he finally realized it was a real and serious event, he said he was disgusted by it.

The Workers involved actually knew what treachery they were up to. A Worker named Jim Knipe visited a couple for the purpose of excommunicating them, and the first two things he wanted to know before he proceeded were: "Is there anyone in the next room?" and "Are you tape recording this?"[14]

When Jim went to visit another elder about his meeting, it was again because he'd let someone who'd been excommunicated come to his meeting. When the elder asked Jim why the visitors might have been put out of meetings, Jim informed him: "That is none of your business." When the elder objected to the stipulation that *the ministry, and only the ministry, had control over who could come into their homes for meetings*, Jim informed the man that he and his wife were *no longer a part of this fellowship*. The man asked if Jim was planning to ask all the elders in Alberta the same question, and Jim Knipe replied that they *had no intention whatsoever to do such a thing*. Later, when Jim spoke to that elder's daughter and her husband about not going to meeting any more at their parents' house, he warned them that if *they (or anyone else) attended the meeting at her folks' place, then they would not be allowed back into a 'regular' meeting* – the euphemism for being excommunicated.[15]

The Workers' claim for all the excommunications is that those excommunicated actually *chose* to leave. It's a deceptive answer, because they were never given a choice, they were given an ultimatum, and everyone knows that. Workers everywhere know a lot more about a lot of things than they let on. And because they do, they're inclined to think that the Friends will know less than they do about what happens in other places. In Chapter 8 I described a discussion I had with a senior Worker from California who attempted to claim ignorance of the Alberta situation, so though it annoyed him seriously, I told him everything he thought I wouldn't know about it.

Another division, or effectual purge, of special interest to me also unfolded recently in Vietnam.[16,17] Recall, I had a forty-year history with my friend Hinh and Phyllis Munn, and had even been tentatively offered a job teaching in Vietnam. In any case, the Vietnam incident did not involve either Hinh or Phyllis, but it was not unrelated to the other two cases I've mentioned.

The first Workers went to Vietnam in the 1950's, and Phyllis and her companion were there in the 1960's, when the fledgling Vietnam church was developing, and the first meeting was established in the home of a man named Bau. Hinh was one of Phyllis' converts at that time. Among those native Vietnamese who eventually became Workers were two men named Châu and Hoa. Then, in the 1970's, all foreign Workers fled the country ahead of the takeover by the Communist government in South Vietnam, and Châu and Hoa were left to *carry the banner* with the other native Workers who remained.

After the country opened up to foreigners again in the 1990's, foreign Workers returned to Vietnam, this time from Western Canada. In the beginning the Vietnamese Friends believed they were coming to help the local Workers, but it soon became apparent they were intent on overthrowing Châu's and Hoa's leadership – younger Workers were told not to listen to Châu. They proceeded to make changes that simulated Western Canadian Truth culture, but not necessarily even universal among the Friends and Workers worldwide. People were no longer to sit while testifying in meetings. They changed the times and procedures for holding Bible studies, the times when fellowship meetings were held, and the local customs for weddings and funerals. The Friends were no longer to eat blood (products), and Workers were no longer permitted to be preachers *at large* – they were assigned to specific areas and expected to confine their influence to those areas.

People were shocked to learn that some Workers didn't speak to each other in their own apartments, and Canadian Workers would belittle native Workers. Many found the Canadian Workers wealthy lifestyle offensive – living in expensive apartments and driving conspicuously expensive motorcycles. They invited people to eat in restaurants, and acknowledged that gifting good restaurant meals with opportunities to practice speaking English was a convenient way to attract people to the Truth. Ironically, they also criticized Châu for helping poor Vietnamese Friends, saying he was using the money to *seduce* them.

The Workers began inviting themselves to the Friends' homes for meals – something North American Workers, if they didn't consider that their due, at least assumed it to be covered by a standing invitation. Châu and Hoa had never done that. For some of the poorer Friends in Vietnam it was a heavy burden to accommodate. One poor lady who had two children lost her welfare allowance when it was learned that she had served a meal to visiting Workers. Darrel Turner, the Canadian Overseer, advised the Friends that if they loaned money to one another it should be considered a gift. He told people that if they wanted to borrow money they should go to a bank, but in Vietnam if someone wants a bank loan they have to mortgage real estate, something some of the Friends don't have.

Among other things that troubled the Friends was that, when they asked why one brother Worker was sent home to Canada, Darrel's answer was that he was "a bull-headed person". People discovered that the Workers would preach things in meeting that could not be found in the Bible, and they would preach principled actions that they would violate themselves. What disturbed the Friends most was to discover that the Workers would lie to them.

When Darrel returned to Canada, Dale Shultz asked his brother Lyle, who had for years been in India, to replace him in Vietnam. Lyle was no more successful in dealing with the Vietnamese than was Darrel. The final straw for a number of Friends came when Lyle refused to allow Hoa to attend the wedding of a young professing couple, and forbade all the relatives of one family from attending. That family no longer let the foreign Workers come to their homes.

Two outstanding events exacerbated the problems between the Friends and Workers, both of them involving the sale and purchase of houses among Friends. The first one was a house in Saigon that was owned by Châu's youngest brother, who lived in the United States.

It was intended as a place for Châu and Hoa, and was registered with the government as the address of the Friends and Workers Fellowship, *Christian Mission in Vietnam*. In 2009 Châu and a number of the Friends worked on the house to prepare it for some professing students to rent.

When the work was done, Darrell announced that the house had to be sold – but Châu refused to allow it to be sold for the obvious reason. Foreigners are not permitted to preach to native Vietnamese, and the house was a required legitimate recognition of a Vietnamese religious community. In fact, Canadian Workers in Vietnam do not even pose as religious preachers – they call themselves teachers to facilitate their interaction with Vietnamese citizens.

To keep the house available to Châu and Hoa, Xuân Hoàn and Minh Thanh, a professing couple agreed to buy the house, and they had apparently made an agreement, through Châu, to purchase the house from his brother. Then Darrel came to the couple and wanted to know how they felt about receiving a *gift from a worker worth $80,000 USD*. They'd never discussed the price with Châu, so they asked Darrel why he would ask such a thing, and he explained that he'd searched on the Internet and found the value of the house to be $80,000 USD. I'm suggesting that Darrel, because he thought Châu owned the house, was anticipating collecting the value of the property from Châu as Châu's *giving to the poor.*

Xuân Hoàn and Minh Thanh's move into the house in Saigon had to be delayed for three years, so it was rented to the students as planned. But it wasn't long before the sister Workers came to the house and ordered the students out, saying that no one could stay there. Châu then received a e-mail from two sister Workers asking him not to sell the house to Xuân Hoàn and Minh Thanh because they couldn't move in for three years – and there was another couple who wanted to buy the house. It happened that the other couple was connected to Minh Thanh's family, so she and Xuân Hoàn accepted that proposal.

But the couple who moved into the house disposed of all of Châu and Hoa's papers and belongings, despite the fact that they'd been warned not to touch them. And they had made no payment. So Xuân Hoàn and Minh Thanh, Châu, and Minh Thanh's relatives met to discuss the problem. Darrell was invited, but did not appear; but the others reached the amicable agreement that Xuân Hoàn and Minh Thanh should buy the house. They moved into the house on September 2, 2009; and with Châu representing his brother, they signed the contract before the appropriate government office three months later on December 3, 2009, with a down payment to the previous owner. On August 28, 2012, the previous owner acknowledged that he had been paid in full.

Then in March, 2010, six months after the house was sold, the Elders from many provinces met with all the Workers in the country, except Châu, along with visiting Workers Dale Shultz, Tsutomu Miyata and Simeon Sarmiento. The three visiting Workers spoke in the meeting, all praising Châu as a humble Worker – and then it was announced that Châu was not in the ministry anymore because he had to leave the ministry to solve the *selling of the house*. Two men stood and attempted to say that the house had already been sold, but Darrel forbade them to speak. Because they were not permitted to speak, many of the Friends and Workers were led to believe the reason given for why Châu was put out of the ministry, and left Xuân Hoàn and Minh Thanh under a cloud of suspicion.

The other problematic sale involved the house in Da Lat that Xuân Hoàn and Minh Thanh had to sell in order to purchase the house in Saigon. None of their friends or relatives wanted to buy it, so they advertised it in the newspaper. But having heard about their problems with the house in Saigon, Mrs. Mai, one of the Friends on Phu Quoc Island, proposed that she buy the house from Xuân Hoàn and Minh Thanh. Her intention was to use the house as a place where Workers could stay. The house was taken off the market, and it was agreed that they would involve no one else in the transaction.

But three foreign Workers came to visit with Jim Girton, the Philippine Overseer who had been in Vietnam when the Workers first went there, and came to see Xuân Hoàn and Minh Thanh. They were accompanied by a native Vietnamese Worker who was very loyal to Darrel and understood English well. Having long had a close relationship with each other, Xuân Hoàn and Minh Thanh confided to Jim what they were doing with their house – Jim had expressed his worries about what would become of Hoa. Obviously word got passed that the house was being sold, and shortly afterwards Mrs. Mai called Minh Thanh to tell her that the sister Workers had gone to her home to ask her if she'd been forced to buy the house in Da Lat, and tried to persuade her not to buy it.

Minh Thanh's daughter confronted by telephone the sister Worker who was supposed to have tried to influence Mrs. Mai – while Minh Thanh and two Workers monitored the conversation. The sister Worker denied having done such a thing, saying her *young Vietnamese companion gave the advice to* [Mrs. Mai] *because she knew the Vietnamese law.* When Minh Thanh's daughter asked to talk to her Vietnamese companion, the Worker claimed the companion was not there. Incidentally, according to Vietnam law it is illegal to interfere with other people's business matters. Although the Workers tried very hard to prevent Hoa from having a convenient place to stay, they were not successful.

Quite aside from any of the problems that developed, Châu was a classic example of a Worker scheduled for *reeducation.* He was given the privilege of a convention visiting tour in the Unites States. He was undoubtedly exposed to the kind of ministry that Darrel wanted him to imitate. Then, after he returned to Vietnam, Châu was removed from the ministry in early 2010 on the false pretense described above. But in July of 2010, Châu was permitted to return to the ministry. Dale Shultz by then had arrived on the scene, and he asked Châu whether he preferred to work in the United States or in Vietnam. Châu volunteered to go wherever Dale wanted him to go. Dale decided he wanted Châu to go to the United States – there are a lot of Vietnamese Friends in the United States, as well as some of Châu's relatives. Darrel shared with the Friends in Vietnam that *"Uncle Châu had to go to USA to learn how to labor in the work!"* But Châu was refused entry to the United States on two occasions, despite the work of a lawyer Dale had hired on his behalf.

Failing to be allowed into the United States, preaching in Vietnam was not really the other option. Dale sent him to Cambodia where he was under the control of a man young enough to be his son, who was in turn under the overseership of Lyle Shultz. Châu could not speak Khmer, so he taught English to children. When Vietnamese Friends went there to visit with Châu, Châu was sent farther away to East

Timor, where they speak a local dialect of Portuguese. After six months in East Timor, Lyle sent him to Australia on a convention tour there. However, he was eventually absent from Vietnam for too long, and the police asked him to return in January, 2014. Lyle Shultz was planning for him to go to Cambodia again, but the Vietnamese government saw differently, and Châu was required to stay in the country.

Hoa, on the other hand, decided to disassociate himself from the Workers following the meeting in 2010 when the announcement was made concerning Châu's suspension from the ministry. When he saw what was happening to Châu, Hoa saw the writing on the wall and determined that his turn would be next, so he left the two-by-two ministry and went on his own preaching the gospel. In the time since then, Hoa has been instrumental in several conversions and baptisms, conventions and gospel meetings, and made arduous journeys to visit Friends in remote areas. Châu and Hoa had been Workers since 1967.

What happened to others in Vietnam at this time is similar to the controlling practices the Workers were accustomed to in North America. Then Bau, who was Minh Thanh's octogenarian father, *offended* policy. A lady named Miss Lan asked Bau to transfer her will to Hoa, whom she wanted to officiate at her funeral. Lyle informed her that, since Hoa was no longer recognized as a Worker, he could not celebrate her funeral; and that she should change the will so Lyle and his staff would celebrate her funeral. So Miss Lan changed her will to say that the Workers *and Bau* would work together to plan her funeral. And the Workers didn't approve of her second will either because Bau's name was included. They told her that she would have to change her will again, and even sent her another will they'd prepared for her. But she refused to sign it, claiming that Bau had been her very close and loving friend for more than fifty years. Recall, California Workers acknowledge accepting people's *estates* to cover medical bills.

Xuân Hoàn and Minh Thanh were on vacation in Australia in 2013, while Châu was still there. While there they wanted to visit Edwin Allen, one of the first Workers to ever be in Vietnam, but they learned at the last minute that their visit would not be allowed. They also attempted to visit Châu, but he told them he was afraid to meet with them because he'd get in trouble for seeing them.

It appears to me that the Canadian Workers underestimated the fortitude of the Vietnamese people in standing for their convictions. One elder, when he had the evidence of why the Workers had put Châu out of the ministry, returned from the elders' meeting in Saigon and shared what he'd learned with his local Friends. They wept, and decided not to welcome the foreign Workers any more because of their deceit.

Morris Grovum, a Canadian Worker, went to visit with Bau and his wife, and he asked them: *"If Mr. Hoa died, who would lead you?"* Bau's answer was that they *are all under the leading of God*, and that they had *gathered with Friends* [for] *years under the leading of God, helping and encouraging each other*. (Long before the Canadian Workers arrived on the scene *to show them how God really intended for them to live and meet*.)

Lyle and his companion came to Bau and wanted to read a letter he had written but not permitted the Friends to see – something that happens quite frequently in the Truth ministry. The letter advised that the Workers deserve one's highest respect, and that Hoa was *"not considered a part of the teacher staff in this country now."* In other words, Bau was being asked to withdraw his respect for Hoa. Bau disagreed: *"That's what YOU say; God never says like that."* Lyle's prompt reply was: *"I can't take care of you any more."* To which Bau replied: *"God will take care of us."* A few days later Lyle went to Xuân Hoàn and Minh Thanh, who refused to let him read the letter because they knew what it said. Lyle's response was: *"If you refuse to obey me, I will not take care of you anymore."*

More than one hundred of the Friends (about half the Friends in the country) have been deemed no longer part of the fellowship in Vietnam. I've been told personally that one of the conditions for continued inclusion in the fellowship there is that a person sign an agreement of submission to the Workers. This reminds me of the first mention I ever heard relating faith to the signing of paper – a Worker in a gospel meeting in Vancouver more than fifty years ago said that in the building of the church down the street, the only person who had any faith was the banker who had signatures on the loan agreement. Unfortunately, I now understand that Workers don't just distrust the Friends, they have on occasion signed treaty style agreements among themselves to define their individual spheres of influence and authority.[17]

This is not gospel – this is all politics, the exercise of power. It has far more to do with control than it has to do with truth. And truth be told, it has just a bit too much to do with money and other people's business. I was very young when I heard it said that people did not need to be put out of fellowship, they all left of their own will when they decided they weren't really part of the group. And for a long time I've been suggesting that some people think God just isn't taking care of His business fast enough!

CHAPTER 24

I Believe

People have asked me what I believe. I know a number of people who consider me faithless and hopeless, but I've never felt more comfortable with my life than I do now. So, I've had to think about this matter. I believe it began in high school with a discussion of the phrase: *Know thyself.* The encyclopedia of Greek knowledge claims that proverb applies to those *whose boasts exceed what they are*, and is a warning to *pay no attention to the opinion of the multitude.*[1] From it I've learned that before I accept anyone's assessment of me, I need to first consider their competence to evaluate me. I've profited many times from believing that maxim.

Another such high school discussion was about the question: *Why do you do that?* I remember someone saying that you can't justify any of your actions if you don't have a valid reason for doing them. Thus the phrase *I don't want to* no longer trumps the phrase *it's the right thing to do*. It confirmed for me that *because a Worker said so* did not necessarily mean *he's speaking with authority*. And occasionally it came to mean that *doing it to please a worker* was not a valid reason. As well, I came to believe that minding one's own business is less damaging and more profitable than assuming to correct another's business. I believe that following another's instructions can be the worst of all excuses for irresponsibility. I believe that opposing change for the purpose of maintaining privilege is, among other indecencies, pure selfishness.

Religious people have an interesting curiosity about the purpose of life – as though we have been intelligently created for a specific purpose. I don't know what that purpose could be, and I don't believe anyone else knows. What is obvious is that every species has a specified purpose in the balance of all life on earth – and man has not proven himself all that competent at contributing to that balance. Science also makes no pretense of knowing how the universe came to be, say nothing about identifying an entity who orchestrated it, or why.

But the Bible's preacher of wisdom concluded that *all is vanity.* I've heard Christians say that an atheist can have no hope, but the preacher of wisdom seems not to agree. He wrote that *the dead know not any thing, neither have they any more a reward...;*[2] and he questioned *who shall bring him to see what shall be after him?*[3] But the preacher had already offered man an apparent unconditional hope – albeit for this lifetime only: *There is nothing better for a man, than that he should eat and drink, and that he should make his soul enjoy good in his labour. This also I saw, that it was from the hand of God.*[4] I believe the responsible man must define his own purpose, and strive to fulfill it.

Now approaching my eighth decade of life, I recall a purpose I bought into early in life. It was that I would live my life to become the kind of old man I'd like to be. If my purpose had been to be wealthy, I'd undoubtedly have chosen a different profession. But I've recently found myself appreciating that I've succeeded in developing a decent measure of altruism, a decent sense of integrity, and the comfort of a family who loves me as much as I love them. Modern Christian doctrine aside, if there's a saved eternity to be had, I can't imagine what more could be required of a human being to obtain it. Within the context of a model Christian lifestyle, I can't imagine how I may have disqualified myself.

And considering the vast and ever evolving theories of gods and what is in their minds, they've all sometimes been sincerely believed to be true, fervently served, and satisfied their believers needs – and also been considered frauds. They probably all have been the justification for a war. I cannot imagine being responsible for determining which celestial theory could be the truly first-and-last – and eternal. I believe as Richard Feynman said: *I would rather have questions that can't be answered than answers that can't be questioned.*

Lacking the ability to *believe in* any religious dogma as absolute truth has two effects. First, it reduces all religions to a single common denominator. And secondly, it bears testimony to the mass confusion of the religious world. This doesn't mean religious people all feel confused – the *heart followers*, the *devoutest of the devout*, are immune to the confusion others experience. They're prone to have only one justification for everything they believe. It is that no one else can grasp what they understand, because they are informed through a different spiritual dimension. Unfortunately, they have a tendency not to recognize abuse and manipulation.

Among Christians, even the Bible has been a centuries long source of controversy. Confusion about what the Bible itself means arises from a number of situations:

- The belief that the Bible is infallible and contains no contradictions.
- The belief that the Bible is a history book.
- A serious lack of knowledge about the origins of Judaism.
- A serious lack of knowledge of Judaism in Old Testament times.
- A lack of understanding non-Biblical history of the same eras.
- A lack of knowledge about the history of Christianity.
- The expectation that science will confirm our understanding of the Bible.

The first problem Christians have with the Bible is that they're indoctrinated with what it *really means* before they ever learn to read. The other problem is that their faith doesn't arise from a holistic reading of the Bible, but from the doctrinal teachings of someone else with an agenda. *Heart followers* are taught that faith trumps everything – even contradictions. They're content to have someone else underwrite their salvation for them. Their loyalty, which I've discussed in Chapter 22, accommodates the problem non-Christians have with Christians: their golden rule is secondary to the loyal defense of their dogma. Friedrich Nietzsche made a couple of astute observations in this respect: *Convictions are more dangerous foes of truth than lies;* and *Faith means not wanting to know what is true.*

Many modern Christians dispute science as much as they dispute each others' theologies. It's a confusion that shouldn't exist, and it can largely be attributed to ignorance of what scientific inquiry is all about. Many find fanciful explanations for biblical contradictions far more acceptable than a resounding scientific proof of factual biblical errors. On the other hand, there's a thriving traffic in pseudo-scientific explanations for many biblical irregularities and omissions. My favorite such explanation was Warren Jeff's claim that dinosaurs never lived on earth – their remains came here in left over dirt that God used from other planets to make the earth.

An equally misleading contributor to the average person's search for all non-theological questions about Christianity and the Bible is where people go to be educated. If one wants an assuredly objective approach to Bible study, *critical* is the crucial word – and specifically *academically critical*, and *non-denominational* is more reliable. Denominational colleges are established to support their denomination's interpretation of the Bible – otherwise there'd be no perceived need for such a school. That normally precludes any *truly* objective consideration of findings from non-theological disciplines. The denominational/theological approach is inherently a closed box, because it cannot run the risk of proving their own doctrine is a fraud. There's a world of truth outside the box if only one cares to know it. That knowledge won't change one as a person as much as it changes one's vision. Bart Ehrman described this best: *any truth I learned was no less true for being unexpected or difficult to fit into the pigeonholes provided by my evangelical background.*[5]

The Bible itself is actually outside the Christian theology box – which allows it to be studied for its true history and for its meaning to the societies in which its writers lived, for information the great majority of Christians have no knowledge of. Yet this must not be interpreted as a recommendation for self-education through the Internet. The Internet is awash with denominational sermonizing and pseudo-science – notorious for its misinformation, but even more notorious for what it ignores of factual history.

Surprisingly, Christians can be equally confused about what's outside their box as by the diversities within it. Good Christians have me pegged as an apostate – that's fair. When I acknowledge that, folks who are seriously concerned for my soul's salvation will sometimes say, "I'm sorry to hear that." But more often they'll assume that to mean I'm an atheist. To suggest that I'm really agnostic is no better, because the ensuing conversation is often more boring or confusing than they can tolerate. And frequently when I've happened to expound to any extent on a non-Christian religion, people have assumed that I'm a Muslim, or a Witch, or a follower of whatever other group I'm discussing. I know why – I'm not supporting their stereotypical beliefs about those people. The really complicated discussion is trying to explain to a Christian that calling a Pagan a Satanist is patently absurd, if you know anything at all about either Pagans or Satanists.

So I've prepared a list of things that I believe that may surprise people. I'll share the part of my list that relates to the Bible:

- I believe the Bible is a very important body of literature.
- I believe the writers of the Old Testament were inconsistent in their stories, and on occasion explicitly contradicted each other.
- I believe a number of the writings in the New Testament were forged.
- I believe Jesus' chapters-long sermon in the gospel of John to be authored by someone other than Jesus, rather than a transcription of an actual sermon.
- I believe the New Testament was compiled to conform with the doctrine adopted by the Roman church.
- I believe there very well could have been a historical Jesus.
- I believe the Biblical authors were faithful to their purpose for writing, but the purpose of much of the writing was neither to inspire nor instruct in salvation.
- I believe their writings were not intended to be cryptic messages that only the ordained can interpret.
- I believe they were not writing about scientific matters that had yet to be discovered.

I have compelling reasons to hold these beliefs. I realize they don't address the questions of what is right and true, or what is wrong and evil. The knee-jerk answer to the search for what is right and true is to consult the Bible, but I've found that the Bible never definitively answers any of these questions. First of all there is theology, but theology isn't really the answer to these questions either. *Theology is not what we know about God, but what we don't know about Nature.*[6] A theology is one's system of beliefs about God's relation to the world, based on one's philosophies concerning nature and the meaning of life. Theologies are developed by men, and reflect the reasoning and viewpoints of the men who develop them, and accommodate the order that such men strive to establish. I personally am not impressed with the virtues of those who came to define modern Christian theology – not least of all for the curses of hell and damnation and Satan that they built into their dogma[7] for the express purpose of scaring people into obedience to the church.

Then there are all the doctrines that are built on the assumptions of the theologists. It's important to remember that in Christianity, most of the theology and doctrines came before the Bible, and far more scripture was discarded than got included in the Bible. It was never a secret that the Roman church selected what it believed would support its theology. Further, the Bible was never even available to non-clerics, and many clerics either, until the Reformation, the printing press, and the ideal of universal literacy became society's guiding philosophy. And Protestants since then have been cherry picking the Roman scriptures for what will enlighten them with respect to their belief system, all the while claiming that the Roman New Testament is the only valid Christian scripture. Ironically, I've had several people tell me when they're confronted with this fact, that "God moved in His mysterious way to preserve the truth for when *we* got to know it" – a classic statement of faith. And yet, Pagan theology by any other name, even when it appears in Christian doctrine, is still Pagan.

But this I do believe:

- I believe in the golden rule, to do to others as you'd have them do to you.
- I believe there's a lot in the Bible that conflicts with the golden rule.
- I believe that sectarian dogma in any religion can inhibit the practice of the golden rule, sometimes shamefully.
- I believe the golden rule is not dogma, but simple logic that is found in virtually all civilizations.

- I believe Jesus received the title *Christ* from his Hellenistic admirers/followers.
- I believe the Christian concept of heaven and hell were constructed for a political reason, that being control.

One thing Westerners tend to display no confusion about is Islam. It wasn't always that way – it used to be largely ignored, or regarded as just strange or exotic. Middle Easterners migrated to the United States as comfortably as any other non-WASP ethnic groups. Unfortunately, Islam today is still basically ignored in favor of concentrating on *Islamic terrorism*. The truth of the matter is, Muslims on average are just like all other ethnic groups on average, including Western Christians. And that isn't because of what they believe – it's because they're equally devoted to their religions.

Every devout Muslim has exactly the same reason for being Muslim as Christians have for being Christian – their respective testimonies to that are remarkably alike, virtually word for word. A Christian spends no time deciding whether to convert to Islam, but neither does the Muslim find Christianity that attractive. Christians criticize Muslims' inability to prove that *Allah is the one, true God*. But then, a Christian has no better proof that his God is the *one, true God*. But there is one category of people who understand Christians and Muslims equally well – non-believers. The non-believer is as baffled by both of them as Christians and Muslims are baffled by each other.

Many American Christians claim that *Allah* and God are not the same being – they don't know that Arab-speaking Christians call their god *Allah*, because that is the Arabic word for *god*. But then, both Christians and Muslims normally do not know that their god has a name – the reason they don't know it is because the Jews, who know His name, refuse to pronounce it for them. Interestingly, I've seen both Muslims and Jews spell *god* thus: *g-d*. The explanation I was given is that they do not want to write such a name in full when spelled backwards it would be *dog*. Come to think of it, I had a teacher in high school who had a loud fit in class because someone had written *Xmas* instead of *Christmas* – "Christ is NOT an unknown quantity!"

When Christians watch the news at night, their listening sharpens at the mention of an Arabic-sounding name – because copy-cat terrorists may be waiting for their children when they go to school. When Muslims watch the news at night, their listening sharpens at the mention of an Arabic name – because Christian crazies are no better than Islamic terrorists, though they frequently mistake a Hindu or a Sikh or a Witch for a Muslim.

But this I believe:

- All religious traditions and beliefs are strange to people of other religions.
- I believe Mohamad left a perfectly acceptable plan for living in a pluralistic society.
- I believe Islam has the best prescription for the use of resources in a society.
- I believe in the Witches' creed.
- I believe Western Pagans (possibly all other Pagans) are most respectful of *the creation.*
- I believe proof is the responsibility of the believer, not the non-believer.

And there is a relief from the confusion of religion that many find in agnosticism or atheism. Whether one accepts that he cannot know about god, or simply believes that there is no god, he doesn't need to accept the burden of compensating for curses religions assign to him. One Christian I know even commented that there comes more *clarity of thought* when one's evaluation of right and wrong doesn't have to be filtered through a religious ideology. In fact, being *a-theist* means they are *a-religious,* which presents a world view that Christians frequently cannot relate to. An atheist correspondent of mine described it thus:

> *I don't need eternal, ever-lasting life. I'm ok with having just one [life] and living it well. I cannot hope and dream for something that, for all intents and purposes, no one has ever seen or experienced. For me, it would be like living my whole life wishing that I lived on another planet. That is my reality.*

Not all religious people confess to questioning some aspect of their faith – thus apparently avoiding any confusion. They're the individuals who, whether using the term or not, hold their faith to be fundamentally inerrant. It will offend fundamentalists to suggest this, but aside from their individual idcologies, all fundamentalists have very similar patterns of behavior, and the majority of American fundamentalists are not aware of the architect who is shaping their ideologies. Nevertheless, they're absolutely certain they're doing the right thing. We know this, because: *You can't convince a believer of anything; for their belief is not based on evidence, it's based on a deep seated need to believe.*[8]

Someone has said that *to be a fundamentalist one must master the art of ignoring the illogical and absurd.* A devout Muslim will believe that Muhammad was transported by night to Jerusalem and heaven, and returned with a message for his followers. Christians will scoff, but it's no more illogical or absurd than believing that a virgin became pregnant. If believers did not consider the story to be factual, someone would surely have invented the explanation of an ancient process of artificial insemination.

One of the dangerous aspects of fundamentalist religion is its tacit approval of major ingredients of individual imagination and hallucination, quite outside the realm of logic and the reality of life. From illogical explanations of physical events to visits from non-terrestrial entities, this is a mind set where reality is not an important parameter in life. Unchecked, this process of *revelation* has often proven deadly, as demonstrated by the Jonestown and other such disasters. The vast majority of fundamentalists never become that extreme, of course, but the thought patterns that lead to such extremes are indeed present in all fundamentalist thinking – Christian or Muslim.

The fact of the matter is that religious ideologists never consider their ideology to be subject to temporal law. For that reason, they operate internally as an autonomous authority – existing in accordance with divine direction. That belief system automatically promotes the notion that when the law of the land interferes with their freedom to do as their ideology instructs, the law of the land is in error. It's in the nature of religions to defend their righteousness from attack by lesser authorities, and Christians have scripture they can use to support that. But the reality of life on earth is that every government is the *de facto* highest court in the land, even in theocracies, and ignorance of the law is never an excuse. If a government is worth anything it will eventually catch up with illegal activities and foil antisocial fundamentalist extremism – Christian or Muslim.

Since the war in Iraq, the world has been treated to a display of consummate fundamentalism in the Islamic State. Without even delving into Middle Eastern politics, this state of affairs is neither surprising nor unusual given the circumstances. It's commonly said that ISIS is the product of Islam – and it is, but in the exact same way that the Inquisition was the product of Christianity. Americans can obsess with the idea that ISIS is conducting a holy war against the West – that's an appropriate assertion, but the destruction of Iraqi society and the enormous loss of civilian Iraqi life was presented as a *crusade* by the American Secretary of Defense.[9] American Christian fundamentalists can be smug and claim that they would never condone ISIS' tactics – that is true, but ISIS is not the Muslim version of their Christian fundamentalism. ISIS is the Muslim version of a powerful American fundamentalist underground movement that has worked anonymously for decades, using mainstream fundamentalists to advance their world view and agenda.

Some such Christian fundamentalists refer to themselves among themselves as *The Family*,[10] and others refer to themselves as *Christian Reconstructionists*[11] – but normally never to the public. And the *only* reason they're not behaving in ISIS fashion is because there's a civil government that can and will hold them accountable for their criminal activities. According to David J. Constable, "Fundamentalism, of any type, due to its prerequisite lack of intelligent thought, could prove to be the worst weapon of mass destruction, of all." The reason ISIS has flourished is because there is no civil government to hold them accountable.

The *Family* began in Seattle in 1935 as an anti-labor alliance.[12] It's a very secretive organization, but at risk to his life a journalist named Jeff Sharlet infiltrated their ranks, and by coincidence identified my local U.S. Congressman, John Ensign, as a member. The long term goal of the Family is to establish a worldwide government under God, *more ambitious than Al Qaeda's dream of a Sunni empire*.[13] In the 1960's the *Christian Reconstructionists* made the call to exercise world *dominion*, *after the mandate given to Adam and Eve in the Garden of Eden*.[14] They believe the world is in need of *a new chosen people*.[15] In the words of David Kuo, deputy director of President George W. Bush's first term White House office of Faith-Based and Community Initiatives, *The Fellowship's* [Family's] *reach into governments around the world is almost impossible to overstate or even grasp*.[16] Their goals are long term and they quietly and patiently manipulate situations to accommodate their own objectives – but it's anyone's guess how they would behave if the federal and state governments were gone. It's their goal to rid us of them both, and they have the resources and mind set to replicate a Christian version of ISIS.

Reconstructionists teach that the purpose of creation is to call *men* [not *women*, incidentally] *to salvation and to dominion, in obedience to biblical law*. And *Christians are to destroy the enemy's city* [civilization], *though normally through voluntary conversions and progressive, long term, cultural displacement*.[17] The Family teaches that *Dominionism* is the *intellectual heart of the Christian Right*, holding that the Bible is a *guide to every decision ...* from whom *God wants you to marry to whether God thinks you should buy a new lawn mower*.[18] Accordingly, their *civil religion* is that the *love of power* can *coexist peacefully with both God and democracy*.[19] They do not submit to state courts: *They must resolve their conflicts within their Kingdom courts ...* [or] *suffer wrong rather than go to ungodly judges*.[20] The purpose of getting involved in politics, as Reconstructionists see it, is to reduce the power of the state.[21]

If anyone wonders where some common present-day misunderstandings of democracy and civil rights has come from, perhaps a check of these folks' teachings will help. According to the Family, democracy is *rebelliousness*,[22] and rights are the *product of an arrogant mind – an infringement of God's sovereignty*.[23] Reconstructionists confirm that: *Rights aren't things that the government is responsible for providing. The government's responsibility is to ensure that somebody else doesn't infringe on **my god-given** rights to life, liberty and property*.[24] Religious freedom refers *not to the freedom of individuals to practice or not practice religion according to the dictates of their consciences, but to the freedom of members of the dominant religion to exercise privileges afforded by its dominant status*.[25] Envy is considered the *feeling* which fills *those* *of lesser wealth, or land, or status*, who *band together to wrest power from above*.[26] The causes of poverty are *attributed entirely to the poor and only those who submit to the covenant are eligible for help*.[27] And, obedience requires that one not question what one is taught – hence the source of reconstructionist history: Americans *learned from the Germans* that history is *a parable, best understood by those who ask no questions*.[28]

Both the Family and Reconstrictionists recognize that mainstream fundamentalists are pursuing more short term goals. They, on the other hand, are more interested in more far reaching and more grandly transforming goals. So they specialize in influence. Reconstructionist ideas have made their way into evangelical and fundamentalist churches through study guides and Christian school (and later home-school) curricula.[29] Reconstructionist R.J. Rushdoony is possibly the greatest champion of Christian and home schooling – though not for anything resembling academic reasons:

> *The purpose of Christian education is not academic it is religious and practical ... the creation mandate, the call to man to know, subdue, and use the earth under God.[30] Efforts at critical thinking and concerns over freedom of inquiry are humanistic – rooted in a false religion. And students are to learn in obedience; teaching the value of questioning, let alone the value of challenging authority, is not part of the curriculum.[31]*

Rushdoony recommended running for public school board for the sole purpose of shutting them down in favor of private education.[32] Most Christian home schooling parents would not identify with Christian Reconstructionism, but they widely accept Rushdoony's views and use home schooling materials that promote his influence.[33] Much of the early Christian school and home school materials were produced by Reconstructionists[34] who publish their own books, sell them through sympathetic networks, and do not share such data outside their group.[35] Increasingly complaints are made that such educators are *enabling child abuse by fighting any legislation that allows social services or law enforcement to effectively investigate accusations*.[36] Rushdoony *embraces the view of biblical law for which Reconstructionists are most often criticized: children who refused to be subject to their parents for training were executed.*[37]

> *"But it is domination that we are after. Not just a voice. It is dominion we are after. Not just influence. It is dominion we are after. Not just equal time. It is dominion we are after. World conquest. That's what Christ has commissioned us to accomplish. We must win the world with the power of the Gospel. And we must never settle for anything less."*[38,39]

The message is clear, and their most important strategy is to *produce generations of Christians who have been imbued with a biblical worldview.*[40] Such fundamentalism is *polite only* in *Washington*; but in the rest of the *world it thrive[s] on violence and raise[s] up those most capable of it.*[41] The models for their *modus operandi* are a recognizable secret: from *fascism, persecution belongs to the powerful ... to dole out,*[42] and from the mob, functioning *invisible like the mafia.*[43] But secrecy is necessary because it *allows scoundrels and despots to turn their talents toward the service of Jesus,* who *prefers power to piety.*[44] And from the Family, as from any terrorist group:

> *One's cell should become "an invisible 'believing group'" out of which "agreements reached in faith and in prayer around the person of Jesus Christ" lead to action that will appear to the world to be unrelated to any centralized organization.*[45]

For those who fear the government's *war on their religion,* I suggest they settle for their hundred billion dollars a year in tax-free offerings and be thankful that a secular government allows them such privilege.

I believe in the democratic principle – which is often mistakenly understood to be the rule of the majority. But *rule of the majority* is not more than a stroke of the pen away from *tyranny of the majority.* Democracy means the rule of the majority **and** rights for minorities. I believe in the fight for democracy, but the fight for democracy is never fought on foreign soil. The fight for freedom may end up being fought on foreign soil, but the fight for democracy is fought at home

– by people who are educated and principled enough to believe in it. The first enemies of democracy are ignorance and greed. And contrary to what many would have us believe, religion is not a proponent of democracy. No religion either encourages or discourages democracy.

> *Religions are in their nature absolutist,* **all** *religions reject the principles of liberalism and popular sovereignty that are at the heart of the democratic ideal. ... Here is the simple, unavoidable truth: there is no such thing as Christianity, Judaism, Islam. There are only Christians, Jews, Muslims. Religion promotes neither love nor hate, neither war nor peace, neither democracy nor fascism. People do those things, and in religion they will find the justification for any and every answer to whatever question they ask.*[46]

The cost of achieving a democracy can and has on occasion been shed blood, but the cost of maintaining a democracy is a proper education in secular government and a tolerance for every taste, belief, and habit of every other law abiding citizen. Rights are not for the benefit of the majority – rights are for the protection of people whose minority status leaves them vulnerable to discrimination and persecution from those who don't approve of them. That is the cost of maintaining a democracy. Further,

> *for human rights to flourish, religious rights have to come second to them. We are all human. We are not all of the same religion, or religious at all. One cannot protect religious rights if they are used as a reason to abuse human rights, human equalities, as so often they are.*[47]

The irony of this whole matter is that the usual proponents of biblical laws would never tolerate them if required to live by them themselves. Of course, the Family and the Christian Reconstructionists anticipate the privilege of administering such law against the *unsubmissive*. But Christians have been warned. The Germans had *Mein Kampf*, and Christians have the *Old Testament*. Yet the Germans democratically opted for *Mein Kampf* – and the slaughter of eleven million undesirables did nothing to solve their problems. American Christians also have the option of ridding themselves of their undesirables, but they need to remember how such a plan backfired on German Christians. Men of character will vote against their own interests when it means benefits for the less fortunate and less privileged.

It is our values that tell us where to go, but it is our character that gets us there.
~Michael Prichard

If God listened to the prayers of men, all men would quickly have perished: for they are forever praying for evil against one another.
~Epicurus (341 - 270 BC, Athens) Greek philosopher.

Reason obeys itself and ignorance submits to whatever is dictated to it.
~Thomas Paine (1737-1809)

Nothing in all the world is more dangerous than sincere ignorance and conscientious stupidity.
~Martin Luther King Jr. (1929 - 1968)

My disdain for any appearance of fundamentalist political ambitions may be interpreted by some as a disdain for freedom of religion. But that is absolutely not the case. Any religious ideology that assumes the right to regulate a democracy is the first affront to what we lovingly refer to as the First Amendment – and the First Amendment is our primary defense against fascism. I realize my disdain for such political ambitions (and I emphasize that it's a disdain for *political ambitions*) brands me a liberal and a humanist, the Christian right's dirty words. Then so be it. But I personally and consciously benefited and valued every day of my life from the guarantees of freedom and protection from the tyranny of a government that is beholden to religion – and Christian religion in particular. I challenge any Christian to demonstrate how I would deny them any freedom necessary to practice their religion.

A lot of people surely wonder how I actually feel about the Truth church that I've left. Truth be told, I believe the style of fellowship of the Friends' meetings is probably the best there is. Minus some rules imposed on them by the hierarchy of the ministry, it can be a model of fellowship – and many such meetings are exactly that. I believe some of the formality can be much overdone – like standing to speak in a meeting with only four people in attendance. I miss looking forward to a comfortable hour with close friends on a regular basis – it was revitalizing and I was appreciated, until someone needed me to be the enemy.

The community of the Friends and Workers is actually a very extensive and closely knit social community. One can travel to virtually any part of the world and be accepted with warmth and friendship by coreligionists. As I have previously mentioned, it isn't at all unusual for one Friend to give another Friend the key to his house – even if he's a total stranger. This isn't because there is any international index of Friends available to them – this is how it is despite the Workers efforts to prevent such a directory from being available to anyone. Most often the fellowship provides parents with a safer pool of friends for their children to associate with. It is an emotional calamity of monstrous proportions to be banished from such a precious, family-like, support system.

I believe the declared plan of the ministry is admirable and honorable, and no offense to Christian scripture. I believe the great majority of Workers are honest and sincere in their purpose and ministry. I remember how I held the system in awe for how it worked so smoothly and perfectly – until I learned about the hierarchy, jurisdiction, governance, and politics that have shaped the present totalitarian organization. I've found it disturbing how many times I've heard older workers describing their training of young workers as *breaking* them – it smacks as loudly of mind control as it does of theological discipline. It's widely recognized that the life of a Worker is abnormal. While normal people are responsible for managing careers, finances, relationships, retirements, free time, and privacy decisions, those responsibilities are primarily not managed by most individual Workers. Their greatest responsibility in life is submission – until rising to a position of authority where he is entitled to expect it.

As far as theology and doctrine are concerned, there's really nothing outlandish about the Friends and Workers'. There certainly isn't anything about them that is unique to them, despite the fact that many have identified what they call serious, even catastrophic errors in their teachings. As far as expecting them to unerringly follow biblical *requirements*, I believe it's folly to expect any religious denomination to ever rise to that level of *perfection* – not because of any human incompetence, but because the Christian scripture doesn't prescribe a clear, complete, and unambiguous plan for such an undertaking. But still, as long as the *declared* doctrine of the Workers is followed, it's quite possible to live what most Christians would regard as an honorable Christian life.

The Truth is not a cult in the newsworthy apocalyptic style. It is minimally cultic in that they maintain a few common Christian cultic rituals and practices. However, the organization is as susceptible as any other denomination to becoming what is commonly regarded as an emotionally abusive and controlling cult. In fairness, no denomination is immune from that possibility, and neither are alternative denominations more susceptible than major mainline religions. The controlling personalities of any denomination are always the ones who manipulate the virtues of their doctrine into mechanisms of control. The congregation that isn't abusive is always a credit to both the congregation and the leaders. Unfortunately, the Friends and Workers have frequently and in many places been subject to such abusive treatment. It's more difficult to rid an organization of such patterns of abuse than it is to drift into their control. Perhaps not surprisingly, there's frequently an effective *prevention* for many such abuses – but it requires a comfortable bank account!

If asked whether I'd ever return to the fellowship, my answer is an unqualified *no*. If I believed there was a hell and a set of requirements guaranteeing its avoidance, I may inquire more into that matter – but I'm quite convinced that hell is more conjecture than possibility. If I believed there was an eternity of pleasure to be had, I may search for the gatekeeper – but that's much more a construction of mythology than any knowable reality. If there were some other benefit to be singularly had through a religious affiliation, I might consider the cost – but I've never identified such a need. If I did return to the fellowship, I would be expected to testify regularly in conformity to their belief system. At this point in my life, I cannot imagine what I could possibly share that would edify their faith.

I'm fortunate to live in a time and circumstances where I have the freedom and the wherewithal to access and know what there is to know. I believe I'm a better friend, family member, and contributor to society because of what I've been able to learn – and that was one of the purposes of my life. But one thing I will *never* do is encourage anyone who is comfortable among the Friends and Workers to leave. First of all, they're comfortable and I don't believe they're deceived into an eternity of damnation. And pragmatically, *you can't convince a believer of anything.*

CHAPTER 25

Leaving

One of the things the Friends and Workers frequently say is that anyone who is not happy with the fellowship is free to leave – and unlike *cults*, no one will prevent them from leaving or pursue them once they're gone. In theory this is true, but it's a naive understanding of the process of leaving a religion, even the Truth.

The majority of individuals who've left the group are undoubtedly the born and raised children of the Friends – children who've either *never* professed, or professed for a brief period of time when young and simply quit attending when they were permitted by their parents, or came of legal age to decide for themselves. It appears most of them just weren't concerned about or interested in spiritual matters. My experience is that very few of these individuals ever return to the fellowship later in life, and most don't join other religions except as a condition for marrying a member of that religion.

The question that rarely gets asked is whether a person can leave the fellowship and move on to another denomination with no adverse consequences. I'm certain some do, but I'm equally certain that these individuals lack something the Workers expect of everyone in the fellowship. That is: a conviction that their ministry is mandatory for salvation, their message is perfect, the Truth has the only truth, their hierarchy is righteous, and their system of fellowship is perfectly scriptural. My grandfather befriended a distant relative in the later years of their lives and maintained a close friendship. I recall my grandfather saying several years after Jim professed that Jim *finally* appeared to have a *full grasp of the truth*. I knew what that meant – Jim had bought into all of the above. Lacking one of those aspects of faith, among the Friends, can *prove fatal* – and make it easier to just walk away.

When *practicing* adults leave, however, it is an event. Unless members are told not to discuss it, such a disappearance can be an emotional topic of conversation – perhaps more so if it's known the individual was excommunicated. This is because the Friends largely learn by example what one can get excommunicated for. Ironically, I've never heard from any Friend or from any Worker that any person has ever had a valid reason for leaving. Sadly the only people who acknowledge any responsibility for someone else's leaving are parents who feel guilty for not instilling enough piety in their children. It's common enough for parents to be criticized for that failing, but my observation has been that greater piety can be every bit as counterproductive as any apparent lack of it.

Most parents are dutifully respectful of their adult children's choice to leave, no matter how badly they feel about it. In fact, many of these children have been known to defend and even recommend the virtues of the Friends and their fellowship even though they don't associate with it themselves. But a small number of parents do persist, even for years, in insinuations and reminders to such children that they're *unsaved* and need to return. These parents visit considerable angst on their children – sometimes intentionally, assuming that it will somehow win them back to the fellowship. On the very rare occasion a parent will simply disassociate themselves from such children. I have one friend whom I've known from childhood whose parents have actually done this, and it has meant decades of serious distress for her. Her parents, on the other hand, are unapologetic for the situation.

I cannot conceive of the notion that a devoutly *practicing* Friend will leave without great difficulty. And leaving voluntarily can be every bit as distressing as being excommunicated. It involves separation, guilt, depression, and a whole range of emotions depending on the circumstances – not the least of which is a sense of betrayal and loss. It's an experience that those left behind simply cannot comprehend, because their whole perspective of the event is more like that of someone watching a ship capsize and the ocean swallowing up any trace or perception that it had ever been there – the fellowship continues undisturbed by the fate of any of them, except perhaps to pray that the same tragedy doesn't befall themselves.

This reaction is understandable, because most of the Friends have no idea how to approach someone who is reputed to have *rejected the truth* as they know it. Their only guidance in this matter is that those who've left have succumbed to a *bad spirit*, which can be contagious and should naturally be avoided. The bad spirit refers to someone taking offense, which one Worker once told me was the most common reason why people *choose* to leave. It's a popular belief among the Friends, and promoted by the Workers, that one owes it to their own soul's salvation to take *no* offense at *any* treatment by others within the group. Sadly, as I explained previously, this ethic can even apply to one's attitude about Workers who are known child sexual predators.

While I was still professing, the 'Keller' family, who attended our meeting, rather unexpectedly left the group. A year later some out of state visitors appeared in our meeting one Sunday, and the lady asked me if that was the meeting the Keller family used to attend, and I assured her it was. She replied, "I heard they were offended about something." I told her I really didn't know why they'd left. But she proceeded anyway to expound on the importance of *never* taking offense because that was an *evil*. It stunned me, really, because I believed that offense was the acceptable response to evil. Interestingly the Fundamentalist Latter Day Saints have a frequently used antidote for this bad spirit – it is to *stay sweet*. I did learn, however, from an intimate relative of the Kellers that they'd decided to leave because of disagreement with Truth doctrine. I also took note that there were far more tears and emotions on the Kellers' side of the separation than there were on the side of those who remained.

I don't know that the Kellers turned to any other group after leaving. But a sizeable number who leave specifically because of disagreements with Truth doctrine do move on to another group, and a great number of those individuals migrate to the more aggressively evangelistic and fundamentalist groups. On rarer occasions I've known of individuals who have turned to more traditional Protestant churches, Catholicism, Buddhism, Hinduism, Islam, and Paganism. On the other hand, many continue to refer to themselves as devout Christians in the now common trend toward independent spirituality.

The most traumatic voluntary leavings are those attributed to abuse, not so much physical, but emotional. Whether they recognize it as abuse or not, the intensity of their confusion and trauma has everything to do with how uninformed they are about emotional abuse and its prevalence, not just among the Friends and Workers, but in the society at large. For them the emotional turmoil begins well before they ever consider leaving, and the very thought of leaving only compounds the difficulty of making that choice. For them the decision develops as a position between *the rock and the hard place* – the choice between submitting to a bad spirit and submitting to chronic depression in the guise of salvation. When my wife and I compared our stories, we surprisingly discovered that each of us had been told by our doctors that they couldn't treat us if we didn't tell them what was *really* going on in our lives. And when we laid it out for them, they each advised the same very simple cure – leave the group. After the accumulating years of disbelief and vilification, the unbiased simplicity of the cause and effect of my condition was both humbling and relieving – and I didn't have to compromise my principles to heal from the ordeal.

Some describe this experience as being *squeezed* out. Somehow they've drawn the ire of someone of rank in the group and become the subject of suspicion and investigation. Possibly they've even reached the point where a Worker gives them the choice between complying with some assigned corrective regimen of behavior, or losing their place in the fellowship. To make such ultimatums effective, Workers are known to impose such restrictions as a twenty-four hour time frame in which such a decision must be made. The terms allowing one to stay in fellowship are never impossible to fulfill, but they can be brutally or unbearably harsh, and are specifically designed to address the individual's error.

I know of one young woman who was given twenty-four hours to end her relationship with her unprofessing boyfriend – the spitefulness of the request being confirmed by the fact that in that jurisdiction one's marriage to an unprofessing person did not interfere with one's permission to have fellowship. What this ultimatum approach does to an individual is reduce him to a virtual slave, his only choice being to obey or suffer spiritual death. To put this in a better perspective, when a person agrees to obey in such circumstances it means that he can be expected to be just as compliant and obedient the next time around. This is an abuse of ministerial authority.

No one voluntarily leaves the fellowship without *counting the cost* – until the cost of staying outweighs the cost of leaving. Everyone knows what others think of those who leave. Everyone knows there can be consequences with family relationships. Everyone knows they'll lose the close network of friendships that the Friends provide. And everyone knows such losses can be for a lifetime. But the negative influences individuals flee can still affect them for years after they've left. This is because of the intimacy of the relationship between the Workers and the Friends. The Workers live in the Friends' homes. They are concerned about what the Friends have in their homes, the habits of the family, and the daily routines of the family members. What is not visible to them is rarely more than a question or a snoop away. That's just how it is in a professing household. Thankfully most Workers have a decent sense of an individual's privacy and respect for their need to organize their own lives, but beware the Worker who *knows what you need better than you know yourself* – if he decides to, he has the wherewithal to strip you of your self-respect and self esteem – or more.

In truth, this approach by Workers is *basically a violation of personal moral values*. One of my correspondents has described it thus:

> *One of the most intimate parts of the human character is the system of personal moral values hidden deepest in our hearts – just as intimate and utterly personal as our sexuality. Normally we keep these intimate aspects of life within ourselves and sharing is only done on a very personal level of closeness and only in a level of complete personal trust, respect, and affection. Violation of intimacy leaves deep and painful scars.*

... [The Workers' concern] demands that we sell this moral intimacy openly and publicly for group approval. In many situations it is done in a underhanded way, as the result of a longer period of grooming. But in the end it always leads to selling personal moral value and the violation that this entails. A doctrine that sticks its fingers into so many aspects of life it has no business to be at all. No wonder that the scars are deep.

Unless anyone doubts that this can happen, I invite my readers to review the accusation I faced and described in Chapter 7. At the very moment I trusted the Worker with a private moral issue that was really none of anyone's business, I earned myself the damnation of being an immoral influence on the fellowship. I will not, however, stoop to commenting on my accuser's moral standard on the same issue.

Then there are the individuals who are excommunicated – that is, they're put out rather than leave voluntarily. In many cases it comes as no surprise to them, but for others it can be a totally unexpected event. My own experience, discussed in Chapter 10, is a good example. The message delivered by that encounter was that I was an intolerable disruption to the church – it was just a coincidence that I wasn't sent packing. But what is more, it was an assault on my moral integrity and my lifetime of devotion to and defense of the Truth. My state of mind in the days that followed was indescribable bewilderment, perplexity, and agitation. Without notice my life had been derailed – irrevocably. There was nothing left that I could dare trust the Workers with.

For people who were raised among the Friends and Workers there is a consideration that is probably not all that common among other groups. Especially third, and possibly fourth generation members have to deal with their family history with the Friends and Workers. They have vivid memories of their grandparents' and great-grandparents' accounts of their conversion to the Truth, and the liberating experience it was for them. Ironically, the churches they left had their own history of liberation from oppressive religions before them – but one's conversion to the Truth is universally touted as being deliverance from *all false religion*. A close friend of mine, an ex-Worker, commented on this bewildering realization.

And now, in my generation, something that had been liberating for my ancestors had become very stifling for me, ... I had considered staying in the fellowship (and earlier remaining in the [ministry]) to be "being true" to God and my ancestors' choices, but the only "faithfulness" can be to God, and to responding to his liberating command, not to what had become to me an oppressive system.

I see the fellowship – then and now – as being so much a part of the larger cultural setting. This does not "excuse" anybody, but for me it means there is no analyzing it without analyzing the larger setting within which it exists.

I have no doubt whatsoever that my parents were satisfied with the fellowship. And I have no doubt whatsoever that my grandparents and great-grandparents converted for the right reasons. Neither would I accuse any of them of anything other than their greatest love and concern for all our family. That said, I cannot explain why the moral standards they taught me came to be so at odds with the practices of the Workers that I have witnessed in the last couple of decades. One thing my father assured me of not long before he died was that I was not wrong in what I disapproved of. Maya Angelou comfortingly said: *You did then what you knew how to do, and when you knew better, you did better.* I understand that even if my parents had been wrong, *You cannot show real respect for your parents by perpetrating their errors.*[1]

But concerning what my ancestors chose, I agree with my good friend that my ancestors did as Maya Angelou suggested – they were doing what they knew to be better, and they had no frame of reference to make any better choices. The difference between their perception of the Truth and mine is this: they believed as they were told that it is the only right way from the beginning of Jesus' ministry, and I understand that it is a modern interpretation that evolved through the various stages of Catholicism and Protestantism to its present form, a thread intricately woven into the fabric of Christendom. This is the reason why, when I realized I would need to live in a new milieu, that I wasn't going anywhere until I understood perfectly well what I had left.

Logic told me that if I were looking for the *truth of the matter* I should examine the foundation of ideologies rather than do taste tests of the most appealing interpretations. I absorbed, as a child, the understanding that something had to be permanently, eternally true, and that interpretations were just interpretations. Hence my thorough investigation of Christianity as a whole, beginning with the very origins of the Bible. Ironically, that aspect of Bible study did not help, primarily because it revealed what should have been the most obvious thing of all – it was written by humans, exactly as the Bible indicates. Further, it was written not by one human, but by many. And from an unbiased perspective it simultaneously offered both justification for and repudiation of every Christian sect I've heard of.

I suspect it would be impossible for any denomination founder to circumvent that dilemma without imagining yet another interpretation of some philosophy. Indeed, I came to realize that everyone's interpretation of the Bible is still an interpretation, and the theology a fabrication to accommodate the interpretation. What astounds me in its profoundly naive arrogance is the often made claim that the Bible simply cannot be understood, except by a select few who are instructed personally by God, *to the exception of all others.*

From this perspective, I fully appreciate why others who have left the fellowship have become agnostics, atheists, or Pagans – groups where there's no dogma to compromise one's sense of morality. I recognize reasons for converting to Buddhism or some other Eastern philosophy – even Judaism, and Islam if one is astute enough to distinguish it from shari'a and Islamic fundamentalism. But it is troubling why *some* of the Friends leave the group intent on endorsing another Christian sect. This I say for two reasons: their misunderstanding of abuse, and how unsubstantial the differences among the sects really are.

Some individuals leave because of distress or abuse and claim to find an astonishing refuge in another Christian denomination – conspicuously those moving from the fundamentalism of the Workers' doctrine to another fundamentalist or evangelical doctrine. Their impulsiveness in making such a move indicates that they believe it is the doctrine of a group that causes the distress and abuse. This is a mistake. Religious doctrines are not abusive of themselves – there are people in all religions who suffer no abuse. In any religion it's people who devise and administer the abuse, invariably in contradiction of their foundational tenets and theology. There is no abiding deliverance from one's vulnerability to trauma and the tactics of abusers until one understands and deals with trauma independently from religious doctrine. Simply moving on to another denomination is not a cure for that – it's an asylum in the company of sympathetic people.

In free societies, abused people have one thing in common – they lack some skill at defining, detecting, and repelling abuse, and have insufficient control in abusive situations. This cannot be blamed on them, but neither is it a religious thing – it's a life skill that needs to be taught. Children don't have the wherewithal to distinguish between a doctrine and how they feel when it's applied to them. I grew up in an environment where I wasn't abused. I had parents who demonstrated how to resist abuse from others, but not all the Friends' children have that privilege. I find that the most traumatized and fragile of ex-Friends usually have stories of emotional abuse within their professing families, or in relationships with other Friends and Workers, involving tactics to force conformity with their legalistic understanding of righteousness. That is first of all abuse, and only secondarily involves religion because that's the tool their abusers use to abuse them. The real danger for these individuals is that they remain susceptible to further exploitation. In today's world religious predators who thrive on the insecurities of such disillusioned souls abound – it's a tax exempt and *filthily lucrative* business that traffics in good feelings and caters to those addicted to religion. The harsh metaphor compares this to jumping from the frying pan into the fire.

This brings me back to my friend's comment about moving on to a more liberating version of Christianity. The curious irony is that all of the most popular liberating conversions are to what are commonly referred to as new religious groups, or NRG's, those of relatively modern origins. And very often they refuse to accept that the Roman Catholic Church, the founding organizer of Christian theology, is even a Christian denomination. It's remarkable how groups can use semantics to disparage their competition.

I'm not naive to the loud and frequent testimonies of individuals having found the *true* way in some NRG. However, like traditional Christians always have, they probably still live between their births in original sin and their demise in hell; and believe they know the only way out of their demise, and everyone they consider to be a *non-believer* is damned – all beliefs inherited from the founding fathers of the Christian church they most abhor. What differences all the various denominations have are just the fine tuning of the same theme, not unlike the fine tuning of constitutions in the democracies of the world. Another correspondent of mine wrote that among many denominations, and particularly among fundamentalists, the predominant doctrine is that *they have the true message from God, and all those that do not accept their "truth" are lost and condemned to eternal punishment for not believing the right things or for not behaving the right way. For someone who has left Christianity altogether, there isn't much difference between the dogma of the 2x2s and the dogma of mainstream Christianity.*[2] And among Protestant fundamentalists, the Roman Catholic church is most often considered the *Whore of Babylon!*

At this point I should address the question of whether I'd ever possessed the conviction the Workers expect in the Friends. I only once in my lifetime heard authoritatively that the Workers believed I possessed that conviction – ironically it happened to be very shortly before I confronted Linda Passage with my concerns. Undoubtedly that favorable evaluation doesn't stand any more. But I challenge anyone to dispute the fact that I was as committed as anyone else to the Truth. I never believed everything everyone told me or expected of me, but as for wavering in my trust in the Workers' mission – I never wavered. In truth, it never crossed my mind to even doubt it's sanctity until I was forced to deal with the corruption of focus in the ministry. I was robbed of my trust more decisively than if I'd been excommunicated – I'd had the trust of a lifetime methodically and utterly taken from me as though it were a surgical excision. In retrospect, I believe it was the most valuable lesson I could have learned about religions and abuse: in the end, abuse always comes from individuals and it is always about power, never integrity. Religions don't speak – abusers interpret them for their personal entitlements.

How I lost my rapport with Christianity is a separate and complex matter. I've never lost what truly moral principles Christianity promotes, but they're basically universal in any case. My loss of faith occurred through an intellectual examination of where the various doctrines of Christianity originated, and discovering that ignorance with respect to religion is the only bliss. Ironically, this all occurred completely within my intended search for truth *within* Christianity. Surprisingly, the result was great relief. Having disposed of the need created by such philosophies, I saw no need to waste my time and devotions on such institutions.

Through my darkest moments there were people who encouraged me. But I can't say that any of the people who *helped* me through my situation relieved me of the aloneness of my experience. To a great degree even my wife and I were in our own separate struggles, because even though we agreed on what was going on, we had our own private decisions to make. The mainstay of my sanity through it all was that I knew that I'd done nothing wrong, had not misrepresented anything, and said nothing about anyone that I did not say to the person himself. The relationships that have survived such struggles are precious and beautiful and true.

I've occasionally been told that someone who has left has claimed they "*wish things could go back to the way they were before.*" Those still inside the group will interpret that to mean they wish they were back *in the fold.* I now can say I also wish it all *could go back to the way it used to be.* But that can't happen. The experience of leaving is like growing up – it's a break with the past that, depending on the individual, can run the gamut of trauma. And however it happens, there's no going back, and it is futile and even unhealthy to try to go back – except in one's fond memories. Those who are prepared for the maturity will thrive on the responsibilities that come with it, and those who are not prepared will unfortunately flounder. Those who embrace the independence of their maturity and its responsibilities are the freest of all people.

What is my view of a higher power? The answer is: I don't have *any* view of a higher power. I've seen images captured in my lifetime of unimaginable events that occurred thousands of years ago in the vastness of the universe – yet I have no capacity whatsoever to explain how any of it happened, and I know of no entity who can speak to me of things I do not, or cannot know. My best answer is that I *just don't know*, and I'm not going to pretend I know *anything* about this. My human best is to apply my mind and intellect to a more pure understanding and practice of all that is moral. I can't believe I'm responsible for anything more. Accepting this humble reality of my human condition is like being born again – a slave to no dogma.

When you have done your duty, then you can rest for all eternity. ~
Nelson Mandela

GLOSSARY

elder = the lay worship leader of a congregation.

emblems = the bread and wine ritual, otherwise known as the Eucharist.

field = the district assigned to one pair of workers; or the jurisdiction of one overseer.

Friend = and lay member of the fellowship.

meeting = a formal gathering for a religious purpose; or a congregation collectively.

overseer = the Worker in charge of a geographical field, usually a state or country.

profess = to give outward expression to one's conversion to the denomination.

professing = (adj.) recognized as a member in good standing in the fellowship.

responsible Worker = the more ranking Worker of a pair assigned to a field.

Special Meetings = a one-day series of regional meetings held once or twice each year.

take part = to participate in testimony and the emblems in a meeting.

test a meeting = to call for converts to make their conversions known in a gospel service.

testimony = to participate verbally in a meeting; or occasionally the fellowship in general.

Truth = the fellowship, or unofficially the denomination.

Two-By-Twos = common unofficial name for the fellowship, due to the two by two ministry.

Union Meetings = Combined meeting of congregations on the first Sunday of each Month.

Worker = a member of the clergy.

Workers List = the annual directory of assignments and addresses of Workers to fields.

BIBLIOGRAPHY

Anderson, Kathie. *Religious Sect Follows Different Path.* The Bellingham Herald, Bellingham, Washington, August 20, 1983

Armstrong, Karen. *A History of God.* Ballantine Books, New York. 1993

Aslan, Reza. *Zealot - The Life and Times of Jesus of Nazareth.* Random House, New York, 2013

Bloom, Harold. *The American Religion.* Chu Hartley Publishers, New York, 1992

Climenhaga, David. *Invisible Sect Has Thousands of Followers.* The Calgary Herald, July 30, 1994

Ehrman, Bart D. *Misquoting Jesus.* San Francisco, HarperCollins, 2005

Ehrman, Bart D. *Did Jesus Exist? The Historical Argument for Jesus of Nazareth.* New York: HarperCollins, New York, 2012

Freeman, Charles. *A. D. 381.* New York, The Overlook Press, 2008

Galloway, Don. *Alberta Excommunications (1999).* http://www.anotherstep.net/summary/summary.2.htm March 17, 2014

Harris, Sam. *Letter to a Christian Nation.* Alfred A. Knopf, New York, 2006

Ingersoll, Robert G. *Some Mistakes of Moses.* The Book Tree, San Diego, CA. 2007

Ingersoll, Julie J. *Building God's Kingdom, Inside the World of Christian Reconstruction.* Oxford University Press, New York, 2015

Jantz, Gregory L. Healing the Scars of Emotional Abuse Fleming H. Revell, Grand Rapids, MI; ISBN 0-8007-5556-1 (1995)

Graves, Kersey. *The World's Sixteen Crucified Saviors, Or Christianity Before Christ.* 6th edition, PDF format. http://www.jrbooksonline. com/PDF_Books/16CrucifiedSaviors.pdf Originally published 1875.

Kropp, Cherie. The Church Without a Name. Telling The Truth, http://www.tellingthetruth.info/home/ June 20, 2015

Kropp, Cherie. *The Life and Ministry of William Irvine.* Telling The Truth. http://www.tellingthetruth.info/founder_book/01wmibook. php July 18, 2015

Parker, Doug and Helen. *The Secret Sect.* Macarthur Press, Sydney, 1982

Prothero, Stephen. *Religious Literacy.* Harper One, New York, 2007

Roberts, Patricia, editor. *Selected Letters Hymns and Poems of Edward Cooney.* William Trimble, Ltd, Enniskillen. 1991

Sharlet, Jeff. *The Family.* Harper Collins, New York. 2008

Simmons, Rabbi Shraga. *Why Jews Don't Believe in Jesus.* http://www. aish.com/jw/s/48892792.html

NOTES

Chapter 2

1. I Corinthians11:16: But if any man seem to be contentious, we have no such custom, neither the churches of God.
2. Jonah 1:17: Now the Lord had prepared a great fish to swallow up Jonah. And Jonah was in the belly of the fish three days and three nights.

Chapter 3

1. I Corinthians 2:2: For I determined not to know any thing among you, save Jesus Christ, and him crucified.
2. I Corinthians 5:1: It is reported commonly that there is fornication among you, and such fornication as is not so much as named among the Gentiles, that one should have his father's wife.

Chapter 5

1. 1 Corinthians 5:1

Chapter 6

1. Verbatim from letter addressed to Norma Frost from Linda Passage.
2. Ibid.

Chapter 10

1. Romans 16:3: KJV - helper in Christ Jesus
2. Galatians 2:16: Knowing that a man is not justified by the works of the law, but by the faith of Jesus Christ, even we have believed in Jesus Christ, that we might be justified by the faith of Christ, and not by the works of the law: for by the works of the law shall no flesh be justified.
3. Ingersoll, Robert G., p.13.

Chapter 11

1. Climenhaga, David. *Invisible Sect Has Thousands of Followers.*
2. Romans 10:14,15: How then shall they call on him in whom they have not believed? and how shall they believe in him of whom they have not heard? and how shall they hear without a preacher? And how shall they preach, except they be sent?
3. Kropp, Cherie. *The Life and Ministry of William Irvine.* Chapter 1.
4. Ibid. Chapter 2.
5. William Irvine in a letter to Dunbars, 1920/10/13
6. Kropp, Cherie. *The Life and Ministry of William Irvine.* Chapter 3.
7. Cooney, Edward. Statement prepared for a Court Case, The Impartial Rporter, Eniskillen, Northern Ireland, July 1, 1913 – http://www.tellingthetruth.info/brg_newspapers/1913.php#1913July17
8. Matthew 10:2-4: Now the names of the twelve apostles are these; The first, Simon, who is called Peter, and Andrew his brother; James the son of Zebedee, and John his brother; Philip, and Bartholomew; Thomas, and Matthew the publican; James the son of Alphaeus, and Lebbaeus, whose surname was Thaddaeus; Simon the Canaanite, and Judas Iscariot, who also betrayed him.
9. Parker, Doug and Helen. *The Secret Sect.* p.5. Matthew 10:8,9.
10. Irvine, William. Letter correspondence. Jerusalem, Dec. 4, 1922. http://professing.proboards.com/thread/22456/newletterirvinestatingstarted Posted Oct. 20, 2014
11. Parker, Doug and Helen. *The Secret Sect.* p.9.
12. Ibid. p.9.
13. Ibid. p.24.
14. *The Pilgrims: Their Beliefs and Practices.* Fermanagh Times. Feb. 21, 1913
15. Kropp, Cherie. *The Church Without a Name*
16. Parker, Doug and Helen. *The Secret Sect.* p.19.
17. Ibid. p.99.
18. Kropp, Cherie. *The Life and Ministry of William Irvine.* Chapter 11.
19. Deuteronomy18: 8-19.
20. Kropp, Cherie. *The Church Without a Name.* Chapter 28. Letter to Laws, December 21, 1927.
21. Ibid. Letter to Mrs. Mattes, May 6, 1928.
22. Ibid. Letter to Helen Kellogg, April 4 1929.

23. Ibid. Letter to Warren Hooper, October 18, 1931.
24. Ibid. Letter to Ritzmans, November 12, 1929.
25. Ibid. Letter to Cummings, December 20, 1929.
26. Ibid. Letter to Edward Cooney, May 5, 1928.
27. Roberts, Patricia, editor. *Selected Letters Hymns and Poems of Edward Cooney.* p.44.
28. Ibid. p.22.
29. Ibid. p.26.
30. Ibid. p.22.
31. Ibid. p.45.
32. Ibid. p.5.
33. Parker, Doug and Helen. *The Secret Sect.* p.76.
34. Roberts, Patricia, editor. *Selected Letters Hymns and Poems of Edward Cooney.* p.5.
35. Ibid. p.6. II Thess.3:6-12
36. Parker, Doug and Helen. *The Secret Sect.* p78.
37. Ibid. p.83
38. Kropp, Cherie. *The Life and Ministry of William Irvine.* Chapter 11; October18, 1937.
39. Ibid. Chapter 11; April 1, 1923 Letter to Wilson? & John?
40. Ibid. Chapter 11
41. Ibid; http://www.tellingthetruth.info/workers_early/walkergeo.php#1988feb16
42. Ibid. Chapter 11
43. Roberts, Patricia, editor. *Selected Letters Hymns and Poems of Edward Cooney.* pp. 43-46.
44. Kropp, Cherie. *The Life and Ministry of William Irvine.* Chapter 11; Willie Edwards Letter to Fountains; http://www.tellingthetruth.info/founder_letters/wmiletbyothers.php#1936October1
45. Anderson, Kathie. *Religious Sect Follows Different Path.*

Chapter 12

1. Chandler, Russell. *Nameless Sect Travels 'Secret' Path.* Los Angeles Times. Sept. 13, 1983
2. Anderson, Kathie. *Religious Sect Follows Different Path.*
3. Woodard, Joe. *Doubts About A Mystery Church, 'Sect or Cult?'* Alberta Report, Sept. 15, 1997

4. Chandler, Russell. *Nameless Sect Travels 'Secret' Path.*

5. Woodard, Joe. *Doubts About A Mystery Church, 'Sect or Cult?'*

6. Magowan, Alfred. *Letter to Wilson McClung, overseer of New Zealand.* Telling the Truth http://www.tellingthetruth.info/workers_early/magowanalfred.php#Wilson Janury 21, 1931

7. Ibid.

8. Ibid.

9. Ibid.

10. Maynard, Steve. *Gospel Tent Meeting Draws 800 Participants.* Walla Walla (WA) Union Bulletin, June 11, 1982

11. I heard Leo Stancliff make this claim several time. Another person shared with me: *One senior worker once said to me that the Bible was written many years ago and the workers have to add teaching and doctrine to ensure it is relevant for today's situation.* ~ Ross Bowden

12. Parker, Doug and Helen. *The Secret Sect.* pp.91,92

13. Magowan, Alfred. *Letter to Wilson McClung, overseer of New Zealand.*

14. This information was shared by an ex-Worker who wished to remain anonymous.

15. Climenhaga, David. *Invisible Sect Has Thousands of Followers.*

16. Zimmerman, Cathy. *Worldwide fellowship needs no building, no budget, no bishops.* The Daily News, Longview, Washington, February 10, 2008

17. Chandler, Russell. *Nameless Sect Travels 'Secret' Path.*

18. Ibid.

19. Zimmerman, Cathy. *Worldwide fellowship needs no building, no budget, no bishops.*

20. Toft, *Church With No Name Packs In Crowds.* Coeur d'Alene Press, June 8, 1984

21. Anderson, Kathie. *Church Without a Name.* The Bellingham Herald, August 20, 1983

22. Parker, Doug and Helen. *The Secret Sect.* pp.42,43.

23. Ibid. p.93

24. Climenhaga, David. *Invisible Sect Has Thousands of Followers.*

25. Parker, Doug and Helen. *The Secret Sect.* p.87.

26. Gardner, David. *Mass Media Cult Scare: How the "Free Press" Targets Spiritual Minorities.* http://consciousreporter.com/cultsandreligiousintolerance/massmediatargetsspiritualminorities/ August 9, 2014

Chapter 13
1. I John 2:20: But ye have an unction from the Holy One, and ye know all things.

Chapter 15
1. Climenhaga, David. *Invisible Sect Has Thousands of Followers.*
2. I Corinthians 6:1-7: Dare any of you, having a matter against another, go to law before the unjust, and not before the saints? Do ye not know that the saints shall judge the world? and if the world shall be judged by you, are ye unworthy to judge the smallest matters? Know ye not that we shall judge angels? how much more things that pertain to this life? If then ye have judgments of things pertaining to this life, set them to judge who are least esteemed in the church. I speak to your shame. Is it so, that there is not a wise man among you? no, not one that shall be able to judge between his brethren? But brother goeth to law with brother, and that before the unbelievers. Now therefore there is utterly a fault among you, because ye go to law one with another. Why do ye not rather take wrong? why do ye not rather suffer yourselves to be defrauded?
3. Excerpts from a letter concerning Worker John Sterling: *John [Sterling] said something I found very strange: "As you know, 'the truth' is not orthodox, and this could destroy 'the truth' as you know it. So we have to be careful that this information does not get into the wrong hands." ..... He also said if some other workers were handling this, that they would immediately kick [Worker's name blanked out] out of 'the truth'--no questions asked. He would be History.*
4. Shultz, Dale. Letter to California workers re R. Mata. Wings for Truth. http://wingsfortruth.info/breakingthesilence2/letterstofriendsandworkers/daleshultzrematajuly2006/ July 6, 2006
5. Ibid.
6. Ibid.

7._____.*Child Sexual Abuse Stories.* The Liberty Connection. http://thelibertyconnection.info/index.php?option=com_content&view=category&id=28&Itemid=38

8. Ibid.

9. Ibid.

10. Ibid.

11. Ibid.

Chapter 17

1. Williston, Bob. *Emotional and Spiritual Abuse.* TheLiberty Connection. http://thelibertyconnection.infoindexphp?option=com_content&view=article&id=377: emotionalandspiritualabuse&catid=13:observations&Itemid= 17 2013.

2. Ibid.

3. Ibid.

4. Jantz, Gregory L. *Healing the Scars of Emotional Abuse.* pp. 44,45,128.

5. Ibid. pp.46,47,128.

6. Ibid. pp.47,48,128.

7. Ibid. pp.20,21,50.

8. Ibid. pp.51,52,128.

9. Ibid. pp.52,128.

10. Ibid. pp.55,56,128.

11. Ibid. pp.55-60,128.

12. Ibid. pp.60,128.

13. Ibid. pp.63,64,128.

14. Ibid. p.64.

15. Ibid. pp.66,67,129.

16. Ibid. p.67.

17. Ibid. pp.68,69,129.

18. Matthew 11:30: For my yoke is easy, and my burden is light.

19. Galloway, Don. *Alberta Excommunications (1999)*

20. Matthew 23:4: For they bind heavy burdens and grievous to be borne, and lay them on men's shoulders; but they themselves will not move them with one of their fingers.

21. Magowan, Alfred. *Letter to Wilson McClung, overseer of New Zealand.* Telling the Truth http://www.tellingthetruth.info/

workers_early/magowanalfred.php#Wilson Janury 21, 1931

22. Matthew 7:6: Give not that which is holy unto the dogs, neither cast ye your pearls before swine, lest they trample them under their feet, and turn again and rend you.

Chapter 18

1. Luke 24:15: And it came to pass, that, while they communed together and reasoned, Jesus himself drew near, and went with them.
2. I John 4:18: There is no fear in love; but perfect love casteth out fear: because fear hath torment. He that feareth is not made perfect in love.
3. I John 4:18.
4. Parker, Doug and Helen. *The Secret Sect.* p.94.
5. Romans 10:2 For I bear them record that they have a zeal of God, but not according to knowledge.

Chapter 19

1. Prothero, Stephen. *Religious Literacy.* p.8
2. Burr, William Henry. *Self-Contradictions of the Bible.* Sacred-texts. com http://www.sacredtexts.com/bib/cv/scb/scb01.htm 1860
3. See Genesis 17.
4. _____. *Tanakh.* Wikipedia. https://en.wikipedia.org/wiki/Tanakh October 19, 2015
5. _____. *Septuagint Version.* Catholic Encyclopedia. http://www. catholic.com/encyclopedia/septuagintversion October 19, 2015
6. _____. *How Do You Know What Belongs in the Bible?* Catholic Answers. http://www.catholic.com/search/content/septuagint%20 canon October 19, 2015
7. Ehrman, Bart D. *Misquoting Jesus.* p.8.
8. Al-Baqarah: 2:[89-90]
9. Freeman, Charles. *A. D. 381.* p.42.
10. Aslan, Reza. *Zealot - The Life and Times of Jesus of Nazareth.*
11. Exodus 29:7; I Kings 1:39; II Kings 9:3.
12. Simmons, Rabbi Shraga. *Why Jews Don't Believe in Jesus.*
13. Ibid. *Jewish Belief is Based Solely on National Revelation.*
14. Deuteronomy 5:3: The Lord made not this covenant with our fathers, but with us, even us, who are all of us here alive this day.

15. John 9:14-16: And it was the sabbath day when Jesus made the clay, and opened his eyes. Then again the Pharisees also asked him how he had received his sight. He said unto them, He put clay upon mine eyes, and I washed, and do see. Therefore said some of the Pharisees, This man is not of God, because he keepeth not the sabbath day. Others said, How can a man that is a sinner do such miracles? And there was a division among them.

16. Deuteronomy 13:1-4: If there arise among you a prophet, or a dreamer of dreams, and giveth thee a sign or a wonder, And the sign or the wonder come to pass, whereof he spake unto thee, saying, Let us go after other gods, which thou hast not known, and let us serve them; Thou shalt not hearken unto the words of that prophet, or that dreamer of dreams: for the Lord your God proveth you, to know whether ye love the Lord your God with all your heart and with all your soul. Ye shall walk after the Lord your God, and fear him, and keep his commandments, and obey his voice, and ye shall serve him, and cleave unto him.

17. Simmons, Rabbi Shraga. *Why Jews Don't Believe in Jesus; Torah Observance.*

18. Prothero, Stephen. *Religious Literacy.* p.38: There are very few passages from the Hebrew Bible that are explicitly rejected in the New Testament, but Leviticus 24:20-21 (which is echoed in Exodus 21:23-25 and Deuteronomy 19:21) is one of them, since in Matthew 5:38-39 Jesus says, "Ye have heard that it hath been said, An eye for an eye, and a tooth for a tooth: but I say unto you, That ye resist not evil: but whosoever shall smite thee on thy right cheek, turn to him the other cheek also."

19. Simmons, Rabbi Shraga. *Why Jews Don't Believe in Jesus; Descendent of David.* See: Genesis 49:10; Isaiah 11:1-9; Jeremiah 23:5-6, 30:7-10, 33:14-17; Ezekiel 34:11-31, 37:21-28; Hosea 3:4-5

20. Ibid.

21. Psalm 44.

22 . Graves, Kersey. *The World's Sixteen Crucified Saviors, Or Christianity Before Christ.*

23. Ehrman, Bart D. *Misquoting Jesus.* p.84.

24. Ibid. p.55.

25. Ibid. p.96.

26. Ibid. p.94: Sometimes .... they thought the text contained a factual error. ...... The problem is that the beginning of the quotation is not from Isaiah at all but represents a combination of a passage from Exod. 23:20 and one from Mal. 3:1. Scribes recognized that this was a difficulty and so changed the text, making it say, "Just as is written *in the prophets...*" Now there is no problem with a misattribution of the quotation. But there can be little doubt concerning what Mark originally wrote: the attribution of Isaiah is found in our earliest and best manuscripts. .... the "error" that a scribe attempted to correct was not factual, but interpretive.

27. Ibid. p.97: Scribes resolved the problem of Luke's shortened version by adding the petitions known from the parallel passage in Matt 6:9-13, so that now, as in Matthew, the prayer reads .... *but deliver us from evil.*

28. Ibid. p.90.

29. Prothero, Stephen. *Religious Literacy.* p.38.

30. Ehrman, Bart D. *Misquoting Jesus.* p.4,10. Mark says that Jesus was crucified the day *after* the Passover meal was eaten (Mark 14:12; 15:25) and John says he died the day *before* it was eaten (John 19:14) – maybe that is a genuine difference. Or when Luke indicates in his account of Jesus's birth that Joseph and Mary returned to Nazareth just over a month after they had come to Bethlehem, (and performed the rites of purification; Luke 2:39), whereas Matthew indicates they fled instead to Egypt (Matt. 2:19-22) – maybe that is a difference. Or when Paul says that after he converted on the way to Damascus he did *not* go to Jerusalem to see those who were apostles before him (Gal. 1:16-17), whereas the book of Acts says that that was the first thing he did after leaving Damascus (Acts 9:26) – maybe that is a difference.

31. Ibid. p. 74.

32. An-Nisâ':4:[153-159]

33. Aslan, Reza. *Zealot - The Life and Times of Jesus of Nazareth.* pp.19,27.

34. Freeman, Charles. *A. D. 381.* p.58.

35. Aslan, Reza. *Zealot - The Life and Times of Jesus of Nazareth.* p.149.

36. Mark 14:12; 15:25.

37. John 19:14.

38. Luke 2:30.
39. Matthew 2:19-22.
40. Galatians 1:16-17.
41. Ehrman, Bart D. *Misquoting Jesus*. p.19. See: Acts 9:26.
42. Acts 4:13.
43. Ehrman, Bart D. *Misquoting Jesus*. p.35.
44. Aslan, Reza. *Zealot - The Life and Times of Jesus of Nazareth*. p.149.
45. Freeman, Charles. *A. D. 381*. p.42.
46. Ehrman, Bart D. *Misquoting Jesus*. pp.74-75.
47. Ibid. pp.153-154.
48. Ibid. p.77.
49. Ibid. p.13.

Chapter 20

1. Acts 11:25,26. Then departed Barnabas to Tarsus, for to seek Saul: And when he had found him, he brought him unto Antioch. And it came to pass, that a whole year they assembled themselves with the church, and taught much people. And the disciples were called Christians first in Antioch.
2. Acts 21:20: And when they heard it, they glorified the Lord, and said unto him, Thou seest, brother, how many thousands of Jews there are which believe; and they are all zealous of the law.
3. Romans 3:20,21
4. Acts 21:21: And they are informed of thee, that thou teachest all the Jews which are among the Gentiles to forsake Moses, saying that they ought not to circumcise their children, neither to walk after the customs.
5. Acts 21:22-24: What is it therefore? the multitude must needs come together: for they will hear that thou art come. Do therefore this that we say to thee: We have four men which have a vow on them; them take, and purify thyself with them, and be at charges with them, that they may shave their heads: and all may know that those things, whereof they were informed concerning thee, are nothing; but that thou thyself also walkest orderly, and keepest the law.
6. Acts 23:27: This man was taken of the Jews, and should have been killed of them: then came I with an army, and rescued him, having understood that he was a Roman.

7. Acts 23:29: Whom I perceived to be accused of questions of their law, but to have nothing laid to his charge worthy of death or of bonds.

8. Acts 24:14: But this I confess unto thee, that after the way which they call heresy, so worship I the God of my fathers, believing all things which are written in the law and in the prophets.

9. Acts 24:24: And after certain days, when Felix came with his wife Drusilla, which was a Jewess, he sent for Paul, and heard him concerning the faith in Christ.

10. Acts 25:19: But had certain questions against him of their own superstition, and of one Jesus, which was dead, whom Paul affirmed to be alive.

11. Acts 25:12,21: Then Festus, when he had conferred with the council, answered, Hast thou appealed unto Caesar? unto Caesar shalt thou go. ..... But when Paul had appealed to be reserved unto the hearing of Augustus, I commanded him to be kept till I might send him to Caesar.

12. II Peter 2:22

13. II Peter 1-22

14. Galatians 2:11-13: But when Peter was come to Antioch, I withstood him to the face, because he was to be blamed. For before that certain came from James, he did eat with the Gentiles: but when they were come, he withdrew and separated himself, fearing them which were of the circumcision. And the other Jews dissembled likewise with him; insomuch that Barnabas also was carried away with their dissimulation.

15. Freeman, Charles. *A. D. 381.* p.53

16. Acts 28:26-29: Saying, Go unto this people, and say, Hearing ye shall hear, and shall not understand; and seeing ye shall see, and not perceive: for the heart of this people is waxed gross, and their ears are dull of hearing, and their eyes have they closed; lest they should see with their eyes, and hear with their ears, and understand with their heart, and should be converted, and I should heal them. Be it known therefore unto you, that the salvation of God is sent unto the Gentiles, and that they will hear it. And when he had said these words, the Jews departed, and had great reasoning among themselves.

17. Aslan, Reza. *Zealot - The Life and Times of Jesus of Nazareth.* p.196

18. Galatians 2:1-5: And I went up by revelation, and communicated unto them that gospel which I preach among the Gentiles, but privately to them which were of reputation, lest by any means I should run, or had run, in vain. But neither Titus, who was with me, being a Greek, was compelled to be circumcised: And that because of false brethren unawares brought in, who came in privily to spy out our liberty which we have in Christ Jesus, that they might bring us into bondage: To whom we gave place by subjection, no, not for an hour; that the truth of the gospel might continue with you.

19. Aslan, Reza. *Zealot - The Life and Times of Jesus of Nazareth.* p.150

20. Ibid. p.70.

21. Ibid. p.151.

22. An-Nisâ': 4:[157]: They say: "We have killed the Messiah, Isa (Jesus), son of Maryam, the Rasool of Allah." Whereas in fact, neither did they kill him nor did they crucify him but they thought they did because the matter was made dubious for them. Those who differ therein are in doubt. They have no real knowledge, they follow nothing but merely a conjecture, certainly, they did not kill him (Jesus).

23. Romans 13:1: Let every soul be subject unto the higher powers. For there is no power but of God: the powers that be are ordained of God. [2] Whosoever therefore resisteth the power, resisteth the ordinance of God: and they that resist shall receive to themselves damnation. [3] For rulers are not a terror to good works, but to the evil. Wilt thou then not be afraid of the power? do that which is good, and thou shalt have praise of the same: [4] For he is the minister of God to thee for good. But if thou do that which is evil, be afraid; for he beareth not the sword in vain: for he is the minister of God, a revenger to execute wrath upon him that doeth evil. [5] Wherefore ye must needs be subject, not only for wrath, but also for conscience sake. [6] For for this cause pay ye tribute also: for they are God's ministers, attending continually upon this very thing. [7] Render therefore to all their dues: tribute to whom tribute is due; custom to whom custom; fear to whom fear; honour to whom honour.

24. Aslan, Reza. *Zealot - The Life and Times of Jesus of Nazareth.* p.190

25. Ibid. p.171

26. Freeman, Charles. *A. D. 381.* p.44

27. Ibid. p.53

28. Aslan, Reza. *Zealot - The Life and Times of Jesus of Nazareth.* p.182

29. Ibid. p.189

30. Ehrman, Bart D. *Misquoting Jesus.* p.72

31. Aslan, Reza. *Zealot - The Life and Times of Jesus of Nazareth.* p.214

32. Ibid. p.171

33. Ehrman, Bart D. *Misquoting Jesus.* pp.153-154

34. Ibid. p.154

35. Aslan, Reza. *Zealot - The Life and Times of Jesus of Nazareth.* p.202

36. Ibid. p.203

37. Ehrman, Bart D. *Did Jesus Exist?* p.214

38. Aslan, Reza. *Zealot - The Life and Times of Jesus of Nazareth.* p.135

39._____. *Mithraism.* Catholic Encyclopedia. http://www.newadvent. org/cathen/10402a.htm   June 24, 201540.   _____. *Jesus and Mithra.*   Freethoughtpedia/wiki.   http://freethoughtpedia.com/ wiki/Jesus_and_Mithra

41._____. *Mithraism.* Catholic Encyclopedia. http://www.newadvent. org/cathen/10402a.htm June 24, 2015

42._____.*Jesus and Mithra.*   Freethoughtpedia/wiki.   http:// freethoughtpedia.com/wiki/Jesus_and_Mithra

43. Barbiero, Flavio. *Mithras and Jesus: Two Sides of the Same Coin.* http://www.viewzone.com/mithras.html October 14, 2015

44. Freeman, Charles. *A. D. 381.* p.59

45. Ibid. p.16,1,162

46. Ibid. p.158

47._____.*Santa Pudenziana.* Wikipedia.   https://en.wikipedia.org/ wiki/Santa_Pudenziana July 16, 2015

48. Freeman, Charles. *A. D. 381.* p.139

49. Notes filed from a Religious Studies class.

50. Freeman, Charles. *A. D. 381.* p.139

51. Harris, Sam. *Letter to a Christian Nation.* p.12

52. Ibid.

53. Matthew 16:19

54. Aslan, Reza. *Zealot - The Life and Times of Jesus of Nazareth.* p.214

55._____. *Sola Scriptura? Not According to the Bible.* Catholics United for the Faith.   www.cfu.org   1988

56. Freeman, Charles. *A. D. 381.* p.132

57. Ibid. p.128

58. _____. *Ancient Christians in India.* Religion and Ethics Newsweekly. http://www.pbs.org/wnet/religionandethics/2009/04/24/april-24-2009-ancient-christians-in-india/2754/ April 24, 2009

59. http://www.jesustheheresy.com/nicene-creed.html

60. Freeman, Charles. *A. D. 381.* p.146

61. Ibid. p.xvi

62. Aslan, Reza. *Zealot - The Life and Times of Jesus of Nazareth.* p.214

Chapter 21

1. http://www.answeringmuslims.com/2012/10/whatisshahada.html

2. https://en.wikipedia.org/wiki/Sabians

3. Al-Mâ'idah: 5:[69]

4. Al-Baqarah: 2:[62]

5. https://en.wikipedia.org/wiki/Masjid_AsSabur

6. Deuteronomy 13:6,8-15 (KJV)

7. Matthew 10:34

8. Luke 19:27 NIV

9. Al-Baqarah: 2:[256]

10. http://en.islamtoday.net/artshow2623441.htm

11. Al-Mâ'idah: 5:[99]

12. Personal letter from: Bibles For Israel | P.O. Box 8900 | Pueblo, CO 81008 January 31, 2016

13. https://en.wikipedia.org/wiki/Messianic_Judaism#The_Messianic_Judaism_movement.2C_1960s_onwards

14. I Corinthians 11:20-22: When ye come together therefore into one place, this is not to eat the Lord's supper. For in eating every one taketh before other his own supper: and one is hungry, and another is drunken. What? have ye not houses to eat and to drink in? or despise ye the church of God, and shame them that have not? what shall I say to you? shall I praise you in this? I praise you not.

15. Ingersoll, Robert G. *Some Mistakes of Moses.* p.216

16. Quote by Friedrich Nietzsche.

17. Prothero, Stephen. *Religious Literacy.* p.117

18. Bloom, Harold. *The American Religion.* p.xiii

19. Ecclesiastes 10:2: A wise man's heart is at his right hand; but a fool's heart at his left.

20. Acts 17:22: Then Paul stood in the midst of Mars' hill, and said, Ye men of Athens, I perceive that in all things ye are too **superstitious**.

21. Romans 10:2: For I bear them record that they have a zeal of God, but not according to knowledge.

22. Ecclesiastes 9:5: For the living know that they will die, but the dead know nothing; they have no further reward, and even their name is forgotten.

23. Ingersoll, Robert G. *Some Mistakes of Moses.* p.260

24. Niose, David. *Anti-intellectualism Is killing America.* Psychology Today, https://www.psychologytoday.com/blog/ourhumanitynaturally/201506/antiintellectualismiskillingamerica June 23, 2015

25. Meyer, Joyce. *Battlefield for the Mind of Teens.* Faith Words, Hachette Book Group, New York, 2006

Chapter 22

1. Harris, Sam. *Letter to a Christian Nation.* P.35

2. Genesis 34:18-29: And their words pleased Hamor, and Shechem Hamor's son. And the young man deferred not to do the thing, because he had delight in Jacob's daughter: and he was more honourable than all the house of his father. And Hamor and Shechem his son came unto the gate of their city, and communed with the men of their city, saying, These men are peaceable with us; therefore let them dwell in the land, and trade therein; for the land, behold, it is large enough for them; let us take their daughters to us for wives, and let us give them our daughters. Only herein will the men consent unto us for to dwell with us, to be one people, if every male among us be circumcised, as they are circumcised. Shall not their cattle and their substance and every beast of their's be our's? only let us consent unto them, and they will dwell with us. And unto Hamor and unto Shechem his son hearkened all that went out of the gate of his city; and every male was circumcised, all that went out of the gate of his city. And it came to pass on the third day, when they were sore, that two of the sons of Jacob, Simeon and Levi, Dinah's brethren, took each man his sword, and came upon

the city boldly, and slew all the males. And they slew Hamor and Shechem his son with the edge of the sword, and took Dinah out of Shechem's house, and went out. The sons of Jacob came upon the slain, and spoiled the city, because they had defiled their sister. They took their sheep, and their oxen, and their asses, and that which was in the city, and that which was in the field, And all their wealth, and all their little ones, and their wives took they captive, and spoiled even all that was in the house.

3. _____. Why I Am No Longer a Christian, Top Documentary Films. http://topdocumentaryfilms.com/whyiamnolongerachristian/ 2009

4. _____. *Quotes*. Gate.com

5. Dr. Phil McGraw. Television show: 2012 01 04

6. Hebrews 5:12-14: For when for the time ye ought to be teachers, you have need that one teach you again which be the first principles of the oracles of God; and are become such as have need of milk, and not of strong meat. For every one that useth milk is unskilful in the word of righteousness: for he is a babe. But strong meat belongeth to them that are of full age, even those who by reason of use have their senses exercised to discern both good and evil.

7. Pope Benedict XVI. *Pope: Sex Scandal Church's 'Greatest Persecution'*. Fox News - World. http://www.foxnews.com/world/2010/05/11/ popesexscandalchurchsgreatestpersecution.html   May 11, 2010

8. Refer to Chapter 16

9. Hassan, Steven. *BITE Model of Cult Mind Control*. Freedom of Mind Resource Center, Newton, MA.   https://www.freedomofmind. com/Info/BITE/bitemodel.php   2014

10. Ibid.

11. Ibid.

Chapter 23

1. Mooney, Howard. *Elders Meeting – Portland Oregon*. Telling The Truth.   http://www.tellingthetruth.info/workers_articles/elders_ mtgs.php   April 5, 1960

2. Elders Meeting, Redmond, Oregon 1985 (Probably By Howard Mooney) http://www.tellingthetruth.info/workers_articles/elders_ mtgs.php

3. Anderson, Kathie. *Religious Sect Follows Different Path.*
4. Letter from Sydney Holt to Washington Worker staff April 6, 1992.
5. Excerpt from undated letter from Truitt Oyler to Don Cruzan.
6. http://workersect.org/2x205rb.html
7. Ibid.
8. Refer to Chapter 3.
9. _____. *Account of Edmonton Meeting.* Another Step. http://www.anotherstep.net/summary/summary.1.htm   March 18, 2014
10. Ibid.
11. Adapted from Galloway, Don. *Alberta Excommunications (1999).*
12. Galloway, Don. *Alberta Excommunications (1999).* http://www.anotherstep.net/summary/summary.2.htm   March 17, 2014
13. Ibid.
14. Ibid.
15. Ibid.
16. _____. *Divisions of the 2x2 Church - Vietnam.* Telling The Truth. info. http://www.tellingthetruth.info/history_divisions/vietnam.php
June 14, 2016
17. http://professing.proboards.com/search/results?captcha_id=captcha_search&where_thread_title=Vietnam&who_only_made
_by=0&display_as=0&search=Search
18. Reference: http://www.2x2vietnam.info/

Chapter 24

1. https://en.wikipedia.org/wiki/Know_thyself
2. Ecclesiastes 9:5: For the living know that they shall die: but the dead know not any thing, neither have they any more a reward; for the memory of them is forgotten.
3. Ecclesiastes. 3:22: Wherefore I perceive that there is nothing better, than that a man should rejoice in his own works; for that is his portion: for who shall bring him to see what shall be after him?
4. Ecclesiastes. 2:24: There is nothing better for a man, than that he should eat and drink, and that he should make his soul enjoy good in his labour. This also I saw, that it was from the hand of God.
5. Ehrman, Bart D. *Misquoting Jesus.* p.8.

6. Ingersoll, Robert G. *Some Mistakes of Moses.* p.53.

7. Armstrong, Karen. *A History of God.* p.284.

8. Dr. Carl Sagan (1934-1996); Dr. Arroway in Carl Sagan's Contact, New York: Pocket Books, 1985

9. https://www.crikey.com.au/2009/05/18/ rumsfeldsiraqcrusaderevealed/

10. Sharlet, Jeff. *The Family.*

11. Ingersoll, Julie J. *Building God's Kingdom, Inside the World of Christian Reconstruction.*

12. Sharlet, Jeff. *The Family.* p. 61

13. Ibid. p.57.

14. Ingersoll, Julie J. *Building God's Kingdom.* p. 5.

15. Sharlet, Jeff. *The Family.* p. 72.

16. Ibid. p. 24.25.

17. Ingersoll, Julie J. *Building God's Kingdom.* p. 47.

18. Sharlet, Jeff. *The Family.* p. 44.

19. Sharlet, Jeff. *The Family.* p. 61.

20. Reconstructionist Rushdoony, Ingersoll, Julie J. *Building God's Kingdom.* p. 160.

21. Ingersoll, Julie J. *Building God's Kingdom.* p. 49.

22. Sharlet, Jeff. *The Family.* p. 40.

23. Ibid. p. 43.

24. Ingersoll, Julie J. *Building God's Kingdom.* p. 112.

25. Ibid. p. 18.

26. Sharlet, Jeff. *The Family.* p. 69.

27. Ingersoll, Julie J. *Building God's Kingdom.* p. 77.

28. Sharlet, Jeff. *The Family.* p. 180.

29. Ingersoll, Julie J. *Building God's Kingdom.* p. 6.

30. Rushdoony. Ingersoll, Julie J. *Building God's Kingdom.* p. 82.

31. Ibid. p. 45.

32. Ingersoll, Julie J. *Building God's Kingdom.* p.71.

33. Ibid. p. 98.

34. Ibid. p. 79.

35. Ibid. p. xii,viii.

36. Ibid. p. 116.

37. Ibid. p. 92.

38. George Grant, author of *The Changing of the Guard*, pastor, author,

and founder of the King's Meadow Study Center.

39. Ingersoll, Julie J. *Building God's Kingdom.* p. 69.
40. Ibid. p. 79.
41. Sharlet, Jeff. *The Family.* p. 157.
42. Ibid. p. 166.
43. Ibid. p. 21.
44. Ibid.
45. Ibid. p. 20.
46. Aslan, Reza. *Zealot - The Life and Times of Jesus of Nazareth.*
47. Orr, Deborah. *The Guardian*

Chapter 25

1. Ingersoll, Robert G. *Some Mistakes of Moses.* p. 38.
2. From my correspondent Nathan Lusher II.

9 781641 514255